To Ted & N...

Thank you for your support. The struggle continues — we will win!!!

Bari-Ellen Roberts
11/10/98

ROBERTS VS. TEXACO

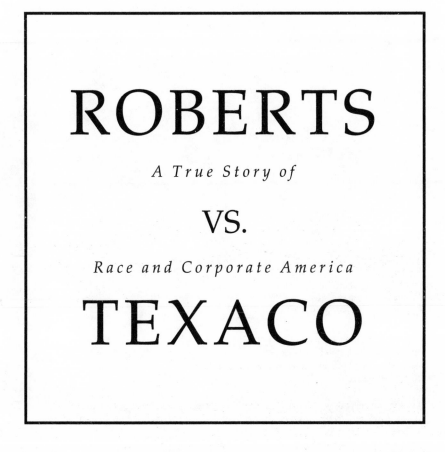

ROBERTS

A True Story of

VS.

Race and Corporate America

TEXACO

BARI-ELLEN ROBERTS

with Jack E. White

AVON BOOKS  NEW YORK

AVON BOOKS
A division of
The Hearst Corporation
1350 Avenue of the Americas
New York, New York 10019

Library of Congress Cataloging in Publication Data:

Roberts, Bari-Ellen.
   Roberts vs. Texaco : a true story of race and corporate America / Bari-Ellen Roberts, with Jack E. White.—1st ed.
      p. cm.
   1. Roberts, Bari-Ellen. 2. Texaco, inc.—Employees—Biography. 3. Afro-American professional employees—Biography. 4. Discrimination in employment—United States. 5. Race discrimination—United States. I. White, Jack E. II. Title.
HD9570.R58A37 1998   97-52303
338.7'6223382'092—dc21   CIP

First Avon Books Printing: April 1998

AVON TRADEMARK REG. U.S. PAT. OFF. AND IN OTHER COUNTRIES, MARCA REGISTRADA, HECHO EN U.S.A.

Printed in the U.S.A.

FIRST EDITION

QPM 10 9 8 7 6 5 4 3 2 1

To Sil Chambers

"If I stand tall, it is because I stand on the shoulders
of others."
—African proverb (adapted)

ACKNOWLEDGMENTS

Sometimes what seem like the simplest tasks involve the most risk. I have searched my heart and head for months, thinking about how to thank all the people who have made this book a reality. I have learned that acknowledgment of others is important to everyday life; none of us does anything without the help or sacrifices of others.

First I want to thank my mother Emma Fraley, my father Herman Roberts, and my stepmother Mary Roberts for giving me the best of everything that they have. To my sisters Fran, Mauvis, Traci, my sister-cousin Vivian, my brothers Herman Jr. and Tim, it is truly an honor to be your sister and to have shared the growing-up experience with you. To Brooke and Staci, I love you, and it is a privilege and a blessing to be your mother. To David and Bria, you are very special to me. To my departed granny Mamie McElhaney and brother-cousin Robert "Sonny" McElhaney, I think of you daily. To Waldo Ford, thank you for getting me up for sunrises to the songs of Bob Marley and for sunsets to the sound of your heartbeat.

In his poem "The Place Where the Rainbow Ends," Paul Laurence Dunbar describes friends as "wealth without measure." I am truly rich because of my friendships with LaVerne Jones, Donnie Tanks-Burkett, William and Melvina Callion, David Addams, Florence and Clarence Prawl, Ona Osirio-Maat, Sandra Thompson, Dorothy Randall Gray, Joy Jones, Deborah Mooreman-Williams, René Redwood, Georgia Archer, Nakia Stovell, Rebecca Lee, Vinnie Hennix, Joe DelliCarpini, Kelvin Sealey, Marcella Maxwell, Cynthia Morrow, Hanne Lore Hahn, Darwin Davis, and the late Frank Mingo. A special thank you to the artist Chris Campbell of Hawaii for your wonderful gift of an oil portrait of me, and we have never met.

A thank you is not big enough for my team of lawyers and specialists who had the skills, dedication, and most important, the vision to believe in the case, and in my fellow-named plaintiffs: Sil Chambers, Marsha Harris, Beatrice Hester, Veronica Shinault, and Janet Williams. To Cyrus Mehri, our guardian, Michael Hausfeld, our avenger, Daniel Berger, Steve Singer, Max Berger, Richard Sampson, Beth Andreozzi, Charles Mann, Jim Outz, and Diane Williams, our sentinels, I now count you among my wealth of treasures where the rainbow ends.

Recognition must be given to Gary Brouse and Tim Smith of the Interfaith Center for Corporate Responsibility for being inspired by faith and committed to action.

Words cannot express the appreciation I have for "Dora." She helped make Roberts vs. Texaco possible.

Sincere gratitude to Jacqueline Goldman and Marlene Ross of Mystic Word "we are transcriptions" for their enduring patience and fast fingers.

Heartfelt thank-yous to my literary agent, Faith Hampton Childs, for taking me under your very expansive and protective wings; to my editor and "classmate," Charlotte Abbott, for believing and then acting upon your belief; and to Jack White, for using your blessed talents and skills to sculpt my words into a work that releases my experiences from the stone.

CONTENTS

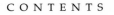

CONTENTS

CONTENTS

ROBERTS VS. TEXACO

"This diversity thing, you know how all the black jelly beans agree."

"That's funny. All the black jelly beans seem to be stuck to the bottom of the bag . . . "

"I'm still having trouble with Hanukkah, and now I have Kwanza . . . It's these niggers, they're shitting all over us with this. . . ."

I listened in mounting disgust as my lawyers read me the transcripts of the secret Texaco tapes that had fallen into our hands. Here were white male managers I had worked with for years, who sat only a few yards from me in Texaco's finance department, talking about me, deciding my fate, tearing me down in words more suited to a Ku Klux Klan rally than the headquarters of one of America's largest and most powerful corporations. Here was incontrovertible proof that behind the big, bright Texaco Star lurked a snakepit of deception and bigotry even uglier than I had imagined. The good news was that, after nearly three frustrating years of legal infighting, stonewalling, and outright deception, Texaco couldn't lie anymore. Victory in our struggle against racial discrimination at the company was surely at hand.

Like thousands of other black professionals who moved into the managerial ranks of Fortune 500 companies during the 1980s and 1990s, I had based my life on a myth. I believed that the American Dream was for everyone, regardless of race, even in corporate America. I believed it when the men of Texaco repeatedly assured me that they really meant what they said in their glossy recruiting brochures: They welcomed diversity; it made good business sense; it was merit, not color, that counted.

I kept my side of the bargain by working as hard and productively as any white man, but the rewards Texaco promised me did not come. Despite consistently high ratings for my performance, I was denied opportunity after opportunity—because of my race. The last straw came when, after a promotion I wanted was given to a white man with lesser qualifications, my bosses actually expected me to train him! "Black jelly beans" like me were stuck on the bottom, all right, because that's where Texaco wanted to keep us.

But this time they had picked the wrong jelly bean. I fought back and I won.

I became lead plaintiff in *Roberts v. Texaco,* a class action suit that not only won the largest financial settlement for racial discrimination in American history—$176 million—but a set of sweeping reforms in Texaco's hiring, evaluation and promotion policies that could make big companies live up to their promises to treat all their employees fairly, regardless of race. If these reforms become widespread, they could change the face of corporate America.

What happened to me is a story that Texaco never wanted you to know. In fact the company did everything it could to try to stop me from telling it, including forcing my resignation. But this story is too important to keep it all to myself; I must share it.

CHAPTER ONE

GREAT EXPECTATIONS

I've never been afraid to compete with white people. I've been doing it since I was a child. I learned from an early age that I'm smart enough to meet any standard they set if the rules are fair and consistent. No brag, just fact.

Given the time and place in which I grew up, I really had no other choice. For African Americans of my generation, excellence meant survival: we had to be better prepared than the whites we competed against to have any chance for success. We imbibed that credo with our mother's milk and staked our lives on it. It's in my blood, as much a part of me as my brown skin and kinky hair.

I was born in Cincinnati, Ohio, to a striving couple whose hopes for a better life remained intact despite all the obstacles that segregation put in the way of blacks right after World War II. Considering where they had started from, my parents had a lot to be proud of. My mother Emma McElhaney had been the pampered favorite daughter of a well-to-do family in

Mississippi until an out-of-wedlock pregnancy at seventeen cut short her dream of finishing college midway through her sophomore year. Her parents agreed to raise her child as their own, and she fled in disgrace to Ohio. When she met my father some years later, she was supporting herself—and a second child born out of wedlock—as a clerk in a dry-cleaning store. Despite the bleakness of her circumstances, my mother never outgrew the aura of privilege she enjoyed in her childhood. She was both beautiful and better educated than most black women of her age—and never let anyone forget it.

My father Herman Roberts, on the other hand, had come up rough and more or less on his own. Orphaned at six, he had been reared in Jim Crow Kentucky by a succession of callous relatives, some of whom forced him to perform heavy manual labor on their farms in exchange for his room and board. Despite that hardscrabble existence he had managed to complete the eleventh grade, a testament both to his great intelligence and willingness to do whatever it took to survive. He was also a spellbinding talker. Within a few months after he began dating her, my mother was expecting again. They married in 1944, moved into an apartment in Cincinnati's downtown ghetto, and began a slow upward climb into black middle class security with Mom's daughter and their infant son. I was born eight years later, on August 21, 1952.

Perhaps because they had overcome so much, my parents always had great expectations for me. Though I more closely resemble my dad, my mother seemed to identify with me more strongly than she did with my sisters and brothers. I was judged by a different and somewhat higher set of standards. Without realizing it, she seemed determined to relive her life through me, as she wished it had been. As a bright and precocious child, I did my best to live up to her dreams, even when doing so seemed unreasonable—or actually put me in harm's way.

It started when I went to kindergarten in 1957. Burdened

4

with caring for my younger sister and brother, my mother couldn't walk me to school from the ramshackle house in the mostly white, lower middle class section of O'Bryonville where we had moved when I was three. So each morning she literally anointed my head with oil, recited the Twenty-third Psalm— "Yea, though I walk through the valley of the shadow of death, I shall fear no evil, for Thou art with me"—and shoved me out the door to get there by myself. On my five-year-old legs, the three-mile walk to Burdett Elementary took an hour and was filled with potential threats, both real and imagined— heavily trafficked streets, strange people, fierce dogs in the yards of the wealthy whites and more affluent blacks I passed along the way. My father had driven me to the school once or twice to show me the way, but I was still not really sure of the route. I had to leave home at 7:30, when it was still dark during the winter. I should have been terrified, but to me the long, lonesome trek seemed like an adventure. I set out, silently repeating the Lord's Prayer to crowd out the fears that might otherwise enter my mind.

Prayer didn't always protect me. One rainy morning when I was in first grade, I was struck by a car as I tried to run across a street without first stopping to look both ways as my mother had ceaselessly commanded. My injuries were not serious at all—just a few bruises—and not nearly as painful as the shame I felt for breaking Mom's rules. I also feared that Mom, who was quick with her switch, would beat me for being careless. As it turned out, this time Mom didn't spank me. She settled for yelling at me about my bad attitude for weeks. I would rather have endured a serious whipping than suffer through her harangues.

That scolding was typical of Mom's "schizy" approach to bringing up children, especially me. On one hand, she ruled with an iron fist, establishing rigid rules to govern every conceivable aspect of my behavior, ruthlessly punishing even the slightest transgression. On the other, she cast me to the wind, plunging me into situations I was not really prepared for with every expectation that I would not only succeed, but perform brilliantly. It was like a commandment. She taught me to read when I was three or four, in part to show off to the neighbors. Her great fear was that I, like she, would become pregnant before I finished college and ruin my life; she wasn't going to let that happen even if it meant whipping me every day of my life. Her tyrannical attitude and heavy-handedness made for an uneasy relationship between us even before I reached puberty. It deepened the isolation I felt because of the age gap between me and my elder siblings, who were already in high school, and between me and my younger sister and brother, who were barely out of diapers. I had two brothers and three sisters but I felt like an only child.

Dad was far more flexible. After years of struggling to earn a living chopping wood, laying bricks, gardening and setting pins in a bowling alley, he had landed a job as a mail sorter in the post office. With his steady income, supplemented by my mother's occasional work as a clerk, they were able to fix up and furnish our house in a modest but comfortable style. Having a family—especially an inquisitive, bright-eyed daughter like me, who absolutely adored him—seemed to quench a deep thirst in my father, who had grown up without one. Unlike my mother, whose wishes for me almost always came out as demands, he was very encouraging. He realized that I would do best if my natural curiosity was given free rein, and he was never too busy to answer my questions. He took me along when he went bowling and spent countless hours telling me about baseball, or explaining the inner workings of mechanical gadgets. He became my closest—and only—friend.

That was in part because there were no other children of my age to play with in our neighborhood. My one attempt as a preschooler to reach out to another youngster led to my first mystifying hint that being "colored" was different. A few times I had played with a blond toddler who lived next door through the chain-link fence. We were happily chattering away one day when a loud voice screamed from her house, "Stop playing with that little nigger!" She retreated into her house and I never saw her again.

I was so baffled by the incident that I ran inside and complained to my mother that my playmate had to go away because there were some kind of bugs, chiggers or niggers or something, in the yard. She sat me down and explained that there were white people and colored people like us and that some of the white people didn't like us because we were colored. It didn't make sense to me.

For one thing, the white people I met when I started school seemed to like me a lot. Though there were few white children at Burdett, the faculty was thoroughly mixed. My kindergarten teacher, Miss Sway, a tiny Jewish woman, quickly discovered that my mother had already taught me to read and allowed me to explore books on my own while the other students were working on coloring books. She made me feel special.

Then there was Charlotte, my classmate and first real friend aside from my dad. She was a red-haired, freckle-faced tomboy who lived in a nice house in Hyde Park, the affluent white district I passed through on my way to school. In the morning, she would wait for me to trudge up the street so we could walk to Burdett together, laughing and singing. I liked her so much that I even dared to break my mother's sacred rule about coming straight home from school so that I could go to Charlotte's house for some juice and cookies. I was amazed by the wall-to-wall carpeting, the first I'd ever seen, the separate dining room, and Charlotte's bedroom, which was all hers, stuffed with dolls and other possessions. I couldn't wait to get home to tell Mom about it.

But when I arrived, my mother had a conniption. She knew precisely how long it took me to walk from school, and I was a half hour late. I had not only been dallying at the home of someone she didn't know, but at the home of a white person she didn't know! She became so enraged that I never tried that again.

My confusion about being colored grew still worse when I reached third grade and got my first Negro teacher: Miss Robinson. Her main contribution to my education was the discovery that, when it comes to race, some black people are even crazier than white folks. Whereas my previous teachers—all of them white—had liked me and treated me as special, this haughty, light-skinned Southerner loathed me because I was dark and had nappy hair. She seemed to identity with the students who sprang from solidly middle-class and professional black families in Walnut Hills, not my seedy O'Bryonville neighborhood. For the first time in my life, someone was treating me like a nigger.

Miss Robinson made a habit of complimenting the other girls on their appearance and hairstyles. The only thing she ever said about my appearance was that my hair was too kinky. Even worse, she kept me from shining, as I was accustomed to. I was among the brightest kids in the class and eager to take part in classroom activities, but she simply would not call on me. In frustration, I would leap up from my desk and shout out the answers to questions she had addressed to another pupil. It didn't help that when I protested to my parents about her, they took Miss Robinson's side. My mother insisted that the problem was all in my head.

One day our increasingly antagonistic battle of wills exploded. As I sat at my desk struggling with a difficult arithmetic problem, Miss Robinson curtly told me I was stupid and nappy headed. That was too much. I burst into tears and angrily snapped, "No, I'm not! You shut up! You're the stupid one!" I was sent to the principal's office.

I knew that my mother would soon arrive at school in a characteristically furious mood, but when Dad also showed up I knew I was really in for it. After listening to the principal and Miss Robinson describe our clash, both of my parents were boiling over. Miss Robinson smirked when my mother jerked me by the arm and threatened to whip me in front of the class. She was actually marching me out the door for that purpose when the principal gently dissuaded her. We went straight home and I received the most memorable beating of my life. Mom and Dad stood on opposite sides of the living room and took turns swatting me like tag team wrestlers until I was covered with bruises. It was the first—and only—time that my father ever laid a hand on me. Being brutalized by the only one in my family I felt close to left me feeling desolate and completely alone. I began to hate school, stopped doing home-work, and became extremely withdrawn.

I threw myself into storybooks that took me to far-off places, like *The Prince and The Pauper.* And I invented an imagi-nary friend called Felicia to exact revenge on the world. She was everything Bari-Ellen was not, a spunky brat with long straight hair, not a bashful loner with wiry braids. Best of all, she was nervy enough to defy my mother's rules and even talk back to her. I spent hours in my room fantasizing cruel pranks I would play on everyone who had wronged me if I were only as brash as Felicia. Miss Robinson and my mom were at the top of my hit list.

If it hadn't been for my grandmother it would have been even worse. In the midst of my funk, she came up from Missis-sippi to care for us for a few months while my mother went back to work. Grannie was unlike any adult I had known. While my mother was often content to let me wallow in the little fantasy world I had constructed, Grannie would not allow it. She'd come up to my room, pry me away from my books, and insist I come downstairs to keep her company. She be-guiled me with tales about her childhood on an Indian reserva-tion or her travels all over the country that were as intriguing as anything I was reading. But the biggest difference between Grannie and Mom was that Grannie didn't have a vindictive bone in her body. She'd spank us if we did something wrong, but that was the end of the punishment. She wouldn't go on and on about the infraction forever as my mother invariably did. Warmed by Grannie's patient love, I slowly began to revive.

That summer both widened my world and made me realize how narrow my place in it was. Somehow or other, my mother had learned about the University of Cincinnati lab school, a free summer enrichment program, and signed me up. It was another example of how she would throw me into something that sounded good although we knew next to nothing about it. This time her impulsiveness paid off. Getting there meant riding three separate buses for nearly two hours, but it was worth every minute. At the lab school, the classroom was exciting again.

I was the only black child among the twenty kids in my class. No one ever mentioned it, but once again, I felt set apart because I was different. Most of the other kids were the sons and daughters of the university's faculty members or public school teachers, and they had been exposed to things I could only imagine. While I had never been out of Cincinnati, they talked casually about ski vacations in Europe and other exotic adventures. And they were smart, smarter even than the bright youngsters in my special classes at Burdett. I was too shy and overawed to make any overtures to them. Instead, I lost myself in the multitude of learning tools the summer lab made available—geography and science books, huge topographic maps, crayons and markers in every conceivable color, all of them brand-spanking new unlike the worn hand-me-downs from previous classes we had to make do with at Burdett.

Perhaps because my nerves were still on edge from my confrontation with Miss Robinson, I was acutely aware that the teachers treated me differently from everyone else, especially the white boys. They received a constant stream of encouragement and commendation from the instructors and were allowed to pursue independent study projects with no supervision. I, on the other hand, was handled like a slow learner; teachers hovered over me to offer assistance with work I knew I could manage all by myself. Once, as an experiment, I deliberately left an assignment unfinished, to see what the reaction would be. When the teacher said, "That's okay, honey, just do the best you can," I was puzzled and a bit upset.

This was an entirely different and unsettling message than the one I had been getting at home and at Burdett, where it was always taken for granted that I would set the standard for whatever class I was in. At the lab school, the assumption seemed to be that I couldn't measure up, so why bother trying to force me? When I compared myself with the other kids, I could see only one difference between us. I could read as well as any of the white kids, and sometimes I knew answers that the other kids didn't. But I was colored. I might get an A for my science project, but it would never be quite as good as the A that a white boy got. I might write a wonderful story, but it wouldn't be quite as wonderful as some white boy's story. No matter how I tried, nothing I did ever won the same praise. At the lab school, white boys were at the top of the pecking order, followed by white girls, and then me. It seemed to be the nature of things, but it didn't feel right. My worries were not pronounced enough to keep me from enjoying the lab school and doing quite well. But they kept dogging me as I tried to make sense of the world.

In my childish way I tried to figure out why being colored seemed to matter so much to people. From conversations with the white children at the lab school, I knew there were places I couldn't go because I was a Negro (as we were starting to call ourselves then), like the swimming pool at Coney Island amusement park or the country club in Hyde Park. Even so, my hometown was a familiar and comfortable place, not terrifying like the television pictures I had seen from the South, where mobs were spitting at little black schoolgirls who looked a lot like me. I had heard my parents talk about the horrible way Negroes were treated "down South" in places like Mississippi, but I was too fearful—and too distrustful of them since the flogging they gave me after the incident with Miss Robinson—to ask many questions. Even thinking about going down there filled me with an increasingly powerful dread.

Those fears escalated the following summer when my family took the first real vacation I had ever experienced, a visit to Grannie's home in Gulfport, Mississippi. I was so apprehensive about the trip that even the prospect of seeing my beloved Grannie again could not assuage me. I was dimly aware from TV that the South had become a racial battleground in which Negro lives were in danger. Only a few months before, the first sit-ins had taken place in Greensboro, North Carolina, and now they were spreading across the south, provoking violent resistance from the Ku Klux Klan. It had all of us in a nervous mood as we prepared to set out on a journey I was sure we wouldn't come back from—except Mom, who blithely babbled on about the big yard and sunshine she remembered from her childhood. Even Dad, who always seemed so brave, was fidgety and morose.

The highest priority was avoiding unnecessary contact with white people. Mom packed big bags of fried chicken and baloney sandwiches, and a jug of Kool Aid, so we wouldn't have to go to the back door of white-only restaurants for a meal. She also brought an old baby bottle that my two-year-old brother Tim could urinate in, to minimize our rest room stops. "Listen to me and listen good," Dad told us over and over. "We're going to travel mostly at night. When I stop for gas nobody can get out of the car. I don't want any trouble with rednecks." I didn't know what rednecks were—maybe some kind of bird—but I knew they were dangerous. If this was what a vacation is like, I thought as we piled into our station wagon and set off just after midnight, I'll never take another one.

I was right to be scared. The trouble started when we stopped in a small town in Kentucky to buy gas. "Don't get out of the car, nigger. Just tell me what you want and I'll get it," the gas station attendant told my father. Dad seemed to shrink. He looked down and replied in a whisper, "Fill it up with high-test and check the oil, please." We pulled away from there so quickly that my little sister Traci slid off the backseat and bumped her head.

When we crossed into Tennessee a few hours later, Dad drove even more cautiously. "There are speed traps all over this state," he explained. "I've heard that they will stop Negroes even if they're doing the limit. Some cops are just looking for a chance to beat up on colored people. I don't want to give them any excuse." But when we weren't looking, Tim threw his "pee bottle" out the widow. In an instant the red lights of a police car were flashing behind us.

"Gimme your license and registration. Where you and your brood heading, Yankee nigger?" demanded the cop who ambled up to the car after we pulled over, in a snarl that still gives me shivers.

"Officer, my family and I are on our way to Mississippi. We're on vacation," my father said quietly.

The policeman snickered.

"Vacation? Whoever heard of niggers takin' a vacation. Must be somethin' that happens up North. It don't happen down here. Anyway, I stopped you because you threw a whiskey bottle out the window about a mile back. We don't allow drinkin' and drivin' in this state and throwin' glass on the highway is stupid."

"It wasn't a whiskey bottle, officer, my baby son—" Dad tried to explain.

Before he could finish, the policeman threw open the door and hurled Dad to the ground.

"I'm gonna take your back-talkin' mister for a little ride," the cop said to my mother. "He be back in a while. Don't you or these children go nowhere." He marched Dad back to his car and they sped off.

Dad was gone for three terrifying hours. When we finally spotted him stumbling up the road in the gathering darkness, my mother let out a soft cry. Dad got behind the wheel and pulled on to the road without saying anything. After a few miles, he started to talk in a voice so low we could barely hear him. "That cop drove me down the road about five miles, took me into the woods, and stole every penny I had on me."

Then he reached under the seat and pulled out something. "But I hid enough money in the car to make it down to Gulfport. We're going on."

After a moment of nervous laughter, we sank into silence for the rest of the trip. We spent a few somber days at Grannie's and returned home without incident.

By the sixth grade, when I was eleven going on twelve, I was given more responsibilities. My sister Traci was now a first-grader and Tim was in kindergarten, but unlike me they were not expected to make it to school by themselves. Traci toddled along with me in the morning, and my mom dropped Tim off for his half-day sessions a few hours later; we all walked home together. I took my assignment as their guardian and protector as seriously as I did my schoolwork, watching over them like a mother hawk to make sure they came to no harm. My three summers at the lab school had gone a long way toward restoring the self-confidence I had lost after the clash with Miss Robinson, and I felt like there was nothing I couldn't handle. White kids like the ones I met at the lab school might have possessions I could only dream about, but they were no smarter than me, and I had proof. I had beaten some of them to win the city's fifth grade spelling bee the previous year. Though my shyness had not faded away entirely, I was starting to make a few friends. I was probably as happy as I'd ever been in my life.

Then I met a hero: Mr. Gaston, my sixth grade teacher. Tall, dark-skinned, and dignifed, he was the most impressive man I'd ever seen, including my dad. He spoke in a baritone so deep it seemed like the voice of God. There's no doubt I had a crush. And he really knew his stuff. His talks about famous black people like Harriet Tubman and Sojourner Truth fit right in with my growing eagerness to learn more about Negro history. The quickening pace of the civil rights movement led by Dr. Martin Luther King Jr. had enthralled me and my classmates, and I wished I were old enough to be part of the struggle. On Saturdays, I occasionally took the bus downtown by myself to attend rallies organized by Rev. Fred Shuttlesworth, an aide to Dr. King who was bringing the movement to Cincinnati. Since I had actually been to Mississippi and experienced segregation firsthand, my schoolmates thought I was an authority on the evils of white folks. It gave me a welcome new cachet beyond my nerdy identity as the smartest kid in the class: I was a pint-sized militant.

At home, the outlook was gloomier; I was sure my mother had lost her mind. She was proud of my achievements at school—after all, I was her daughter—but had become even more tyrannical. As I matured physically, her efforts to control me grew wilder and wilder. She forbade me from riding my bicycle anymore because men could look at my behind. I couldn't go swimming at nearby Owl's Nest park because she didn't want me wearing a swimsuit. She scowled at my dad if he kissed me on the head, or hugged me—he might be my father, but he was a male and not to be trusted or touched. I chafed, but I dared not express my resentments. So I resurrected Felicia, my plucky imaginary companion. Together, we composed vitriolic notes to my mom, which I carefully destroyed before she could see them. I was angry at her, but I was no fool!

Mom's tirades were easier to bear because the future seemed so exciting. My teachers had picked me to start seventh grade at Walnut Hills, Cincinnati's elite public high school, which was more like a private academy. It was for only the best and brightest. You had to pass a test and have a high grade point average to get in. Only a handful of Negroes had ever gone there, and I was determined to join them. Mr. Gaston encouraged my dream and assured me I was a shoo-in if I did my best on the test. I buckled down to my work even more than I had before. I was ecstatic. Everything I had ever wanted finally seemed within reach.

It was too good to last. One day, while my class ate lunch in Burdett's cafeteria, the fire alarm sounded. Mr. Gaston lined us up and calmly led us out to the street through corridors that were already hazy with smoke. Outside, I could see more smoke billowing everywhere and towering flames leaping from the roof. Suddenly it hit me: where are Traci and Tim? I ran to Mr. Gaston and implored him to let me go back to find my little sister and brother, I just had to. Of course, he wouldn't hear of it and made me get back in my place in line, where my anxiety became almost unendurable.

I stood there, wailing, until I saw Traci marching along with the other first-graders. I ignored Mr. Gaston and ran to her, crying with relief. But Tim was still nowhere in sight. It turned out that he had been late getting to school and missed all the excitement.

At home that evening, I watched terrifying pictures of the fire on television. Had it not been for Mr. Gaston getting us out of there, I felt in my heart I might have been killed. The decrepit old building, built before the Civil War, had burned like kindling. It was obvious we could never go back.

But where could we go? A week after the fire the school board came up with an answer. My class would be transferred to Linwood, a white school on the other side of town. We'd get there by bus.

Our first day at Linwood was almost as unnerving as traveling to Mississippi had been three years before. When our bus pulled up, it was surrounded by a mob of jeering white people. "Get those pickaninnies out of here!" "Niggers and flies! niggers and flies! The more I see niggers, the more I like flies!" "Let's lynch them like down South!" Some of my classmates began to whimper and call for their mothers. But Mr. Gaston was as calm and reassuring as he had been during the fire. "Hold your heads up high. Be proud. You're from Burdett," he told us and it settled us down. As we walked past the mob and into the building through a back door, someone shouted from a school window, "Look at them, they look like little black monkeys being led by a big ugly gorilla." Mr. Gaston, smiling and urging us on, acted as if he hadn't heard it. We were scared, but we almost strutted.

The rest of the school year felt like having my nose pressed up against a window pane, looking at something beautiful but not being allowed to touch it. Linwood was a modern, well-equipped school, but we couldn't use its facilities. White kids were taught in sunny classrooms, while we almost suffocated in a gloomy, makeshift classroom up in the attic with no ventilation. The white teachers and students enjoyed a nice cafeteria, but we and Mr. Gaston had to eat our brown bag lunches at our regular desks. All of us, including Mr. Gaston, used the janitor's bathroom. White children frolicked on the swings and ball fields, but we took our recesses inside.

It would have been unbearable without Mr. Gaston. Rather than ignore our bleak circumstances, he used them to teach us lessons and inspire our pride. Overcoming ordeals such as this, he told us, was a part of the civil rights movement. The best way to thwart the bigots who jeered at us every day was to ignore the taunts, keep our dignity, and achieve at the highest level. He persuaded us that the simple act of coming to school was as courageous as facing the police dogs and fire hoses Bull Connor had turned on demonstrators down in Birmingham that spring. Under his patient, nurturing gaze most of us flourished. I made straight As.

A few weeks before graduation, I got word that I had been accepted at Walnut Hills. I already knew who I wanted to be like when I got there, and for the rest of my life.

I wanted to be like Mr. Gaston, who had rescued me from the inferno and transformed a tragic school year into a triumph. He was brave. He was brilliant. He was a fighter.

CHAPTER TWO

COMING OF AGE

Talk about changes. For those who didn't live through them it's almost impossible to understand the tumult of the 1960s and the impact they had on young people like me. When I entered the seventh grade at Walnut Hills in 1964, my hair was pressed into a helmet of tight little curls, I called myself Negro and hid my shyness behind gawky cat's-eye glasses. By the time I graduated in 1970, I was a stone soul Sistah with an Afro so bushy I could barely keep my mortarboard on, and I believed I was black and beautiful. I came into the decade singing "We Shall Overcome" and stormed out of it chanting "Beep! Beep! Bang! Bang! Ungowwa! Black Power!" In a time of colossal upheaval, I had finally found myself.

I threw myself into the exciting cultural and political changes that were sweeping across Black America because I couldn't bear being at home. The angry shouting matches between my mother and father over his philandering had escalated into all-out verbal—and sometimes physical—warfare.

Even worse, both of them had tried to drag me into their conflict. Mom enlisted me as her private eye and Dad used me as a shield.

After months of gathering tension, the whole sorry situation came tumbling down on me one summer Sunday a few weeks before my twelfth birthday, when the only thing I should have had on my mind was getting ready for the challenges at my new school. Our church choir was set to perform at another church in Sabena, a town fifty miles from Cincinnati. Dad and I had made it a habit to go on such trips together, usually by ourselves, and I always looked forward to them. I think we both enjoyed the respite from the squabbling at home, and talked about everything under the sun as we had when I was younger. I always rode in the front seat, like a grown-up, where I could rest my head on his shoulder if I got drowsy— and even if I didn't. Those trips were the only time when I was still his beloved "Cootsie," short for my nickname "Bari-Cuda," and he was still my beloved daddy.

But on this Sunday Dad didn't ask me to come along. Instead he got dressed in his best Sunday suit, straightened his tie in the mirror, and turned to leave when Mom blocked the door.

"Where do you think you're going, Herman?"

"To Sabena to sing with the choir."

"Not without Bari, you aren't."

Dad paced restlessly in the front hall while I rushed upstairs to doll up. A few minutes later we were on our way, with me sitting proudly in my accustomed front seat, chattering away in my polka dot dress and patent leather mini-heels. But instead of his usual talkative self, Dad seemed jittery and distant; I could hardly get a word out of him. When he turned on to a side street and parked outside a house I didn't recognize, instead of following our usual route to the highway, I knew something was wrong.

The woman standing outside waiting for us was no

stranger: it was a beautiful lady who sang in the choir. Even from the car I could see that she had on enough lipstick and eye shadow to make Liz Taylor ashamed, and was gussied up in a tight-fitting dress and three-inch heels. She smiled radiantly and ran up to my dad as he got out of the car to greet her. But her smile quickly faded when she saw me sitting in the front, and I heard her ask Dad, "what's she doing here?"

Then came something I wasn't prepared for at all. "Get in the back, Cootsie," Dad ordered me, as he opened the door for her. I sat there for a moment, paralyzed by surprise, then glumly slid into the backseat. "No, Cootsie," said Dad, gesturing firmly toward the backward-facing bench in the rear of the station wagon, which was usually reserved for my little brother and sister. "All the way in the back."

I was too through. This was the ultimate insult. I climbed over the backseat into the bench, tucked up my knees close to my chin, and fixed my nearsighted gaze out the back window. I don't think I moved for the rest of the trip. My lips were poked out so far I could have tripped over them.

It got worse as the ride continued. Though I tried my best to ignore them, I could hear Dad and the woman laughing and joking in the front seat. Something even more disturbing occurred as we neared the church in Sabena. Instead of pulling directly into the parking lot, Dad stopped a few hundred yards away from the church and let her out. Then he drove into the parking lot and we got out of the car. As we walked into the church he reached out and grabbed my hand like he always did. I ground my teeth as I realized that he didn't want anyone to see him with her but to make everyone think he and I were just out for our usual trip.

After the performance, the movie ran in reverse. Dad made a big show of escorting me out of the church, and then he and I drove a discreet distance away and waited for the woman to swivel up to the car on her wobbly spike heels. As we headed home, I fell asleep at my lonely post in the back of the car until Dad hit a bump. I came up out of my nap, groggy and confused by an unfamiliar sound from the front seat. At first I thought I was still dreaming, but this was a nightmare. As I watched, she scooted all the way over next to Dad, put her arm around his neck, and kissed him right on the mouth.

Once again, I was too through!

I tried to go back to sleep, but I couldn't take my eyes off of them as they cuddled and smooched. I was revolted. It wasn't only that Dad was committing a sin by necking with this woman right in front of me. It suddenly dawned on me why Mom had been so insistent about me accompanying him: to keep him from being alone with another woman. She was going to hector me until I spilled the beans, and then turn it on Dad. For the first time in my life, I felt like I had been used—by both of my parents—and it made me furious. I couldn't think. I couldn't speak. I was paralyzed. My spirit seemed to lift itself out of my body and peer down at the three of us as we sped along the highway.

We were late getting home because Dad stopped at a gas station to tidy up after dropping off our passenger. True to my fears, Mom was sitting on the darkened front porch with a scowl and a thousand questions. Just like she had figured out to the minute how long it would take me to walk to school, she had calculated how long it took to drive from Sabena, and wanted an accounting for the extra time.

"Where have you been? What were you doing? Why is Bari in the backseat? What in the hell is going on?"

"There were too many people for the church bus, so we had to bring some of them back with us and drop them off at the church."

"It only takes an hour to get to Sabena, and if you stopped at the church that takes ten minutes, so you should have been here twenty minutes ago."

"Well, we stopped because Bari was hungry, and I got her something to eat."

"Bari, what did you eat?"

I didn't say anything, just stared at the floor, and wished I could disappear as they continued to bicker. Finally, after what seemed like a lifetime, I got up enough courage to speak: "Mom, I'm tired. I have to go to bed." She waved me away and went back to berating Dad. As I walked up the stairs to my room, he looked dead in my face, lit a cigarette, and gave me a wink. I thought I would throw up. I couldn't have hated him more. Not just because he had cheated on Mom right in front of my face. Or that he thought I was so stupid that I didn't understand what he and that woman were doing. Or because he thought he could manipulate me into keeping his secret. I hated him because he had made me, his beloved Cootsie, his best friend, his most loyal companion, play second-fiddle to that hussy. He had made me get up out of the front seat and climb over that bench so that she could sit in my place. I felt every bit as jilted as my mom would have if she had seen him and his female friend carrying on. For months I refused to be in the same room with him, to eat at the table if he was sitting there, to say anything to him at all. Needless to say, we didn't go on any more road trips together. As for Mom, I could barely look at her. I was not yet twelve years old, but my childhood was over.

As I look back, this was one of the most pivotal experiences of my life. While it hurt me, it left me stronger and more independent. It deepened the alienation between me and both of my parents, not just my mother, and made me more determined to never again let myself be exploited by them or anyone else if I could help it. I had lost all respect for both Mom and Dad and tuned both of them out, whether they praised me or punished me.

Without family and friends to speak of, and Grannie back home in Mississippi, I felt totally on my own. But I wouldn't let myself withdraw as I had after Miss Robinson's taunting. I tried, halfheartedly, to summon my imaginary friend, Felicia, but I had outgrown the psychological comforts she had provided when I was younger. My only hope was to fall back on what I did best, which, of course, was excelling in school. I convinced myself that it didn't matter if my family was coming apart. It didn't matter if my parents had totally lost their minds. It didn't matter if I wasn't pretty. It didn't matter if anyone liked me. What was important was that I could get As, that I could read and understand books, that I could compete with anybody. I might not be able to count on anything else, but I knew I was smart and nobody could take that away.

As the first day of school approached I threw everything I had left into preparing myself. I read through dictionaries to learn new words, burrowed into newspapers to get up to speed on current events, borrowed even more books from the library. As it turned out, I needed that extra edge because everyone at Walnut Hills was a top student who had passed a tough test in order to be admitted. There was no tracking of classes for faster or slower students, and every year as many as twenty percent of the students were transferred to lesser schools because they couldn't handle the work. It was just the right place for a kid like me, a place where I could prove that I belonged because I could compete. Mr. Gaston, my sixth grade teacher, had told me that going to Walnut Hills made you special. Now, for the sake of my self-esteem and maybe even my sanity, I had to believe he was telling the truth.

I'll never forget the awe I felt as my school bus drove up to Walnut Hills on the first day of classes. The school where I would spend the next six years couldn't have been more different from Burdett. Instead of crumbling brickwork and an asphalt playground, it was a huge building sprawling around a high domed central hall, ringed by lush athletic fields. From the brass plaque by the front door to the marble floors of the brightly lit hallways, everything was shining. In the classrooms, there were even more books and maps and educational tools than there had been at the lab school. The surrounding neighborhood, originally Jewish, had been taken over by middle-class blacks who spent their weekends tending beautifully landscaped yards filled with flowers and shrubbery. Had it not been for my summers at the lab school, I would have been in culture shock.

Somehow my mother had found time in between her bouts with my dad to buy me special school clothes, like the tennis sweater, plaid pleated skirt, and penny loafers I had spent days trying on because at Walnut Hills you had to look preppie. It was in many ways more like a private academy than a public high school, and she wasn't going to let any daughter of hers show up there not looking the part.

A handful of Negroes had gone to Walnut Hills over the years, but my seventh grade class was a breakthrough. At an assembly in the auditorium, the principal announced that mine was the first Walnut Hills class to be ten percent Negro, forty out of four hundred students. Three of them—me, my pal Tyra Bennett, and Roger Peek—had been together in Mr. Gaston's heroic sixth grade class. It was the first time that so many black kids from Burdett had made it to Walnut Hills at the same time. You can bet we were proud, and so was our whole neighborhood—even if they were a bit uneasy about what awaited us. A few students from O'Bryonsville had been admitted to Walnut Hills in the past, but most of them had flunked out because they couldn't handle the mandatory Latin class. For me, that was no problem. I could decline Latin verbs like Julius Caesar and had a good grasp of Spanish. My ambition was to be a linguist, maybe a translator like the ones at the United Nations.

Although there was an unprecedented number of Negroes in my class, it soon became clear to me that Walnut Hills was a white school, and that many people wanted to keep it that way. We Negroes were made to feel that we were there on sufferance and had to prove that we belonged. Only two of the real teachers, Mrs. Stanley and Mrs. Dobbins, were black, as was the basketball coach, Mr. Stargell. I later discovered that quite a few of the white teachers were outright racists. Most of them were subtle about their feelings and used code words to express their hatred, but others made no effort at all to hide it. We heard about a science teacher who actually stood up in class and called some black boys "nigger." But such incidents were no more than vague, unsettling rumors to me until my eighth grade English literature class, when I ran into Miss Cahill.

She was an elderly spinster, only a few years from retirement, who looked like a female Ichabod Crane. Although she was very strict and a tough grader, she was a wonderful teacher who really loved classic English literature and wanted her students to love it too; I really enjoyed her class. But one day, as I was talking with Karen Dotson, the only other black student, before we settled into our seats, Miss Cahill walked over and said: "Okay, you darkies, sit down."

I couldn't believe it. I had no idea how to respond. That evening I told my mother about it, but she reacted the same way she had to my complaints about Miss Robinson's taunting. She made all sorts of excuses for Miss Cahill: she's old, she's Southern, she's behind the times, she's your teacher, you must be mistaken.

Nobody took it seriously until a few weeks later when our class clown, a straight-A student named Bob Dworkin, who happened to be Jewish, got everyone giggling by making bird calls during a test. Miss Cahill looked up from her desk and loudly proclaimed, "Bob Dworkin, you make me sick. You're acting just like a nigger." You could have heard a pin drop. Then somebody asked in an incredulous tone, "Miss Cahill, what did you say?" You could see the old lady fumbling to explain away her mistake, more pathetic with every stammering word. "I said, he was acting like a nigger. But I don't mean like a nigger, nigger. I mean like a niggard, you know niggardly. You know, with a d." She was on the verge of tears. Finally, Bob Dworkin burst into laughter: "I got you, Miss Cahill, I got you." She fled from the room to a chorus of derisive laughter from some of the white students. Karen and I just sat there in silence. I think I cried.

After what seemed like a long, long time, an assistant principal came to the room. He sent all the white students away and sat down with Karen and me. "Okay, what happened?" he asked us and we did our best to pull ourselves together and tell him the story. For the rest of the day, I walked from class to class in a daze.

A few days later, my parents and I each got a letter from Miss Cahill saying how sorry she was for the incident. She returned to class after a two-week absence, but something had gone out of her. Her love of books was still evident, but the unique combination of sternness and verve that had made her such a vibrant teacher had disappeared. She called Karen and me to her desk and apologized to us, once again, in front of the whole class. I could feel her sadness.

For the rest of the year, Karen and I, who both had been solid B students, got nothing but As. I felt that it was Miss Cahill's way of making up to us for her errant behavior. But even though I was grateful for the marks, I felt cheated. If I got an A, I wanted to earn it, not simply receive it for being a Negro who happened to be on the receiving end of an insult. In my mind, the high marks I got from Miss Cahill were worth less than a lower mark from a teacher who held up the same standards for everybody, black or white. I didn't need double standards. In a totally unforeseen way, Miss Cahill's attempt to compensate for her outburst had deprived me of something I wanted and desperately needed. It had robbed me of the chance to compete on the same basis as everyone else and prove my mettle. It was the flip side of holding me back because I was a Negro and just as bad. When she retired from teaching at the end of the year, I felt sorry for her but I didn't miss her.

*   *   *

For me, episodes like the one with Miss Cahill brought the rage and chaos that were spreading across the country during my adolescence much closer to home and made them personal. I was only in the sixth grade and still at Burdett when John F. Kennedy was assassinated. I was in the eighth grade at Walnut Hills when Malcolm X was murdered and Watts exploded, in the tenth when Martin Luther King Jr. was shot, and on my way to the eleventh when Robert Kennedy was gunned down. Every one of those losses hit me like a punch in the stomach. With so much uncertainty and fear in the air, I, like many teenagers at the time, became even more skeptical of everyone in authority. There was nothing my parents or "the power structure" could tell me—about myself, our country, white people, love, sex, you name it—that I didn't challenge. I loved every minute of it.

I came to believe that my generation could change the world by standing up against injustice, and the fight could begin right there at Walnut Hills, where I could be part of it.

When I started at Walnut Hills, the civil rights movement was still in an integrationist phase that shaped the way black and white students got along. Unlike their elders on the faculty, many of my white classmates seemed to take pride in having black friends and supporting the movement toward racial equality, and we were eager to reach out to them. The cultural gap between blacks and whites that has become so glaring on colleges campuses these days was submerged in a broader generation gap between teenagers and anyone older than thirty. We hung out together in multiracial groups, went to the same "People Parties," danced the same dances and listened to Motown and rock. A lot of us—especially me—felt a powerful attraction to the civil rights protesters and antiwar activists who were causing so much havoc on television. They were not much older than we were and they seemed so brave.

Being up-to-date with the latest political trend was also

important to me because I no longer stood out so much in the classroom. I did very well in my liberal arts classes like literature, languages and history, but fared poorly in math and sciences, in which I was far less interested. In the ninth grade, I actually managed to flunk geometry, the first F I'd ever received. If that came as a shock to my parents, it was even more of a shock to me: I had never thought I could fail. Although I had to attend summer school to improve that grade I wasn't all that upset because by then I had other things in my life.

For one thing, I had made some friends, including Helen Lightfoot, a very cool girl from O'Bryonsville who was much more in tune with the latest fads than I was. In addition, my growing identification with black militants like Stokely Carmichael and popular black artists like Sonia Sanchez, LeRoi Jones, and the Last Poets helped me to think of myself as more than a bookish wallflower. By now, my indifference to my parents' authority had become almost complete. I did what was expected of me in school—not because they demanded it, but because it made me happy. I didn't flirt too much with the boys who were starting to pay attention to me—not because of my mother's harangues about sex, but because I didn't feel ready. I was polite and did whatever my parents asked me to simply because it was less hassle than being defiant. But beneath the appearance of a dutiful daughter beat the heart of a rebel.

It burst out when I was in the eleventh grade. I had become a staunch member of the black students' union we had started at Walnut Hills when the Black Is Beautiful movement finally reached Cincinnati, a couple of years behind the rest of the country. For Black History Month in February, we planned to throw a big fashion show and bring in Sonia Sanchez to read some of her fiery, revolutionary poems. At the time, I was still wearing a bouffant that seemed out of touch with the times and my changing self-image as we prepared for the black culture festival. How could a proud black woman like me keep pressing her hair to make it resemble white folks'? I needed, really needed, an Afro.

I asked my mother about it, but she put her foot down. So one day after school I marched into Stags Barber Shop, plopped into a chair, and told the barber to cut it all off. When he finished, I looked in a mirror and gasped: a stunning, deep-brown-skinned woman with a cap of short natural kinks was staring back at me. I had mouthed the slogan "Black Is Beautiful," but I wasn't sure it applied to me. Now I knew it did. I was gorgeous.

When I got home, my mother threw a predictable fit. She called me a nappy-headed fool. She even started moaning and groaning. But every sad sound that she made convinced me I had done the right thing. It was my hair after all, and I had paid for the cut with money I had earned myself. I already knew I was my own boss and could make up my mind for myself. Now Mom knew it too, and if she had a problem with that, well, she'd just have to deal with it.

Enter Vence.

I had already had some mild flirtations with boys by the time I finished tenth grade, but nothing remotely serious. That was mainly because Mom wouldn't let me bring anyone to our house. She made such a fuss every time I wanted to go to a school dance or out on a date that I stopped asking her for permission. Instead I went to Dad and he usually said yes, just to be on the opposite side of whatever stance Mom was taking. By then I had figured out how to play them off against each other.

I had earned pocket money by baby-sitting or taking little jobs after school and over the summer for several years. During the break between my tenth and eleventh grade years, I landed the best one yet, as an assistant to the Walnut Hills school secretary. Among other benefits it meant that I could read books in the school library when I wasn't busy.

On one especially sweltering August day, I took a break from my work and wandered out by the football field to drink a Coke and watch the team practice. One of the players in particular caught my eye: a well-built, middle-sized guy who seemed to be making plays all over the field. Something told me to stay where I was when the scrimmage ended and the players walked back to the locker room. Sure enough, the guy I had been watching walked straight toward me and my heart skipped a beat, or maybe two.

I don't know what came over me, but in an instant Bari the Bashful became Bari the Bold. As he walked toward me I extended my Coke and asked in a quasi-coquettish voice: "You want some?" My goodness, he was cute.

He took a sip of the soda and we exchanged a few words about the football team's dreary prospects for the coming season. He seemed to be trying to look at me without actually looking at me, if you know what I mean. He seemed to be as shy as I was. His name was Vence Lewis and he was a rising senior, a year ahead of me. After a few more awkward moments he handed me back the soda and headed for the locker room. I watched him every step of the way.

The next day, I was back in the very same spot, but this time with not only a soda, but a Reese's peanut butter cup. He accepted it with a big smile and again we exchanged a few words before he walked off to the locker room. That weekend, I asked some friends about him and what I heard was not encouraging. He was supposedly smitten with a popular girl named Ann, the first black cheerleader at Walnut Hills and the picture of traditional black beauty, light-skinned and straight-haired. Even worse, he lived in the projects in a rundown ghetto neighborhood. That made no difference to me, but I knew it would make a huge difference to my status-conscious mother.

For the next few days, I did my best to keep running into him, purely by coincidence, of course. We had our first date about a week after that, and I found out more about him. He was the youngest of thirteen kids in an extremely poor family, an honor student, and a standout not only in football but gymnastics. He was awfully ambitious, already thinking about majoring in business in college and making it big somewhere. The more I listened to him talk, the more I felt connected to him. I finally got up the nerve to ask my mom if he could come to the house, and to my surprise, she agreed.

Martha Stewart couldn't have done a better job of straightening up than I did that Saturday. I even picked out my little brother's and sister's clothes to ensure they would make the right impression. At six o'clock Vence arrived in his spectacularly dilapidated car, a clunky 1953 Chevy with doors a different color from the rest of the body and an old-fashioned stick shift. We sat in the living room for a couple of hours, talked and talked, and stared into each other's eyes.

The next week was different. For reasons I still don't know, Vence was standoffish. He even walked the other way when he saw me standing on the edge of the field after football practice. Finally I asked him what was going on.

"Oh, Bari, you know, I'm not ready for a girlfriend yet," he stammered. "I'm what you call a loner."

"Well, Vence, I'm not looking for a boyfriend, either," I lied in as even a voice as I could manage. "It's fine if you don't want a girlfriend. You still don't have to avoid me or not speak to me or whatever."

He gulped out the word "Okay" and stalked away.

Things remained in a holding pattern for the next few weeks after school got started. I'd see Vence in the hall or cafeteria, and we'd chat once in a while, but nuttin' was happpnin'. Then, during the fifth game of the football season, he took a terrible shot from an opposing player while making a tackle and got knocked out of his senses. All I could do was stare helplessly from the stands as the coaches got him back on his feet and took him to the locker room. A while later he came back on the field and played the rest of the game. I thought he was fine.

But the next day someone called me with shocking news: Vence was in the hospital in serious condition with a lacerated kidney. After the game he had driven himself home in his jalopy and then collapsed. All the feelings I had kept stifled because of Vence's indifference to me tumbled out in a flood of tears. I had to see him, to let him know that I cared and wanted to help.

I couldn't get to the hospital until the following Monday. By then, the news that he had been hurt had been in the newspapers and on TV because he was an All-City prospect. I begged my mother to drive me to the hospital to see him, but she put me off. So after school, I got on the bus and went over there by myself. I wasn't prepared for what I encountered. I had never been in a hospital before, and I had idealized them as sparkling places where cheerful and efficient nurses bustled around and every patient recuperated in a sunny private room brimming with potted plants. In contrast, Vence was laid up at the end of a long, gray ward lined with dozens of beds. I tried to keep a smile on my face as I walked past the long row of groaning patients, but it was hard because they looked so pitiful.

When I finally reached his bed, Vence was asleep. I gently rubbed his hand and whispered, "Vence, wake up. Are you okay?" After a minute he woke, smiling shyly and surprised to see me. As we talked his mother arrived. "Oh, so you're the girl Junior's been talking about all these weeks," she told me. "I've heard a lot about you, honey." You know I was shocked.

I went to the hospital almost every day until Vence was released. A few days after he got home he telephoned and asked me to be his girlfriend. Of course I couldn't say no.

*   *   *

My last two years at Walnut Hills brought a whirlwind of changes.

I was starting to think seriously about college. That was what was expected of Walnut Hills students, ninety-nine percent of whom went to top schools like Harvard, MIT, Cornell, Columbia, and Case Western Reserve. My grades, especially in literature and history, were good enough to keep me in the top half of a very competitive class. I had earned advance placement credits in Spanish and English—meaning that I could skip the introductory level courses in those subjects when I got to college and take more advanced classes right off the bat. I was getting recruiting brochures in the mail from colleges that were seeking out black students with high SATs and good grades to integrate their lily-white campuses. I knew—and the school counselors had told me—that I was "college material."

But that didn't mean I was going to go. The biggest obstacle was money. When I brought up the subject, my mom looked me straight in the eye and told me emphatically, "You're on your own. If you want to go to college, you *must* get a scholarship. There's no other way." She and Dad hadn't been able to save enough to pay tuition at the kind of costly private college that most of my white classmates could look forward to. I was still determined to go away to school, to leave Cincinnati, to be off on my own. Increasingly, I filled the void at home by plunging myself into protest.

By my junior year in 1969, Walnut Hills, like much of America, was seething with discontent. Dr. King had been dead for a year and the Black Panther Party and other militants had taken his place as leaders of the civil rights struggle, while many of the white kids had become enthralled by the movement against the draft and the Vietnam war. There had been a number of crazy racial incidents at Walnut Hills that inflamed our passions. One white teacher, for example, had called a number of black students, including Vence, "jungle bunnies" and despite an outcry was still on the faculty. There was still enough solidarity left between black and white students—and enough anger at the school administration—that we planned a joint demonstration to protest all that was wrong in the world. It would take place the first week of June, during exams, to cause maximum disruption. All of us had been paying attention to the tactics that the real protesters like Stokely Carmichael and SDS had been using to dramatize their anger. We were going to bring business as usual at Walnut Hills to a standstill.

As one of the leaders of the Black Student Union, I threw myself into preparing for the big demonstration: a sit-in in the domed central hallway that would start when the first bell sounded, preventing anybody from going to classes. When the big day arrived, I got into my militant uniform—a brightly colored African dashiki—and picked my Afro to its fluffiest height. I was determined to see this through even if I got suspended or thrown into jail.

It went off better than I expected: maybe a third of the whole student body—blacks and whites, hippies and draft-card burners—plunked down in the middle of the atrium, locked arms, and chanted black pride and antiwar slogans in a loud display of defiant solidarity. Nothing like it had ever happened at Walnut Hills. The principal, as we had hoped, went berserk. He stomped out of his office with a bull horn and ordered us to get up and go to class. Nobody moved, just chanted louder. So he threatened to have the teachers come out and identify us so that those who refused to move could be suspended. One of the assistant principals came out with a camera and started snapping our pictures and writing down our names. We still didn't move.

And then came a shock. As I looked around the atrium, I noticed a few students standing by the assistant principal, pointing to students and giving their names.

One of them was none other than Vence.

During the months we had dated I had learned that we didn't see eye to eye on political issues. Perhaps because he came from such a poor family, he was much less inclined than me to take chances with his future by rocking the boat. He was so focused on making it in business that he just didn't get the black culture movement at all. Once I had tried to get him excited about some poems by my heroine, Sonia Sanchez, but he had brushed them off. To him, if a poem didn't rhyme, it wasn't a poem. It was a mystery and a waste of time. That difference in outlook had from time to time caused us to stop seeing each other for a while before we got back together, so I knew we were different.

But I hadn't known he was a snitch.

I was so caught up in the sit-in that I put aside my disgust and locked arms with the people sitting next to me all the tighter. We stayed there until the afternoon when our parents, alerted by the administration, began showing up and hauling us away, one by one.

My mother arrived at about two P.M. with fear and fury written clearly all over her face. I looked at her and for the first time in years I actually begged her to be on my side, to let me stay there with the other kids, to show support—but she didn't listen. She grabbed me by the arm, yanked me to my feet, and pushed me out of the crowd. I was humiliated and angry. She tongue-lashed me all the way to the car and all the way home. "Are you a fool? You can't be doing this kind of stuff. You're supposed to be going to college and this kind of trouble will just mess that all up. Get out of here right now."

She was sure I would be suspended, and so was I. We were both wrong. So many students had taken part in the demonstration that the school board couldn't punish all of us, so they punished none of us. But many parents, especially the white ones, cracked down hard on their children after the protest; a lot of them were no longer allowed to take part in any school activities, and anything that seemed radical was strictly forbidden. It was the last time during my high school years that black and white students joined together for any cause. It left me more militant than ever. Organizing the protest, confronting the power structure, defying the principal and even our parents bonded me to the other leaders of the Black Student Union, most of whom were women. For the first time in my life, I fit in with a large group of people, not just Helen Lightfoot, who not only tolerated me because I was smart but actually thought I was kind of hip. It was an exhilarating feeling. The sisters I was hanging out with became in effect my family. We carried our sense of black unity into my senior year.

The demonstration even led to a major rapprochement with my mother. Not long afterward, a perceptive friend of hers had warned that she was making a big mistake in her handling of me. I was so strong and hardheaded that trying to control me would only make me more rebellious. "She could be off doing other things—drugs like all those white kids, or getting pregnant like all the black girls. Instead she's fighting for ideals. You have to let her be herself or you're going to destroy her." Chastened by that talk, my mom began to back off a bit. She even taught me to drive.

By the time my senior year started, Vence and I had smoothed over our differences and got back together. He had gone off to Dartmouth to play football and major in architecture; his exciting letters about college life made me even more determined that I must go away once I graduated. Despite our family's lack of money, I was confident I could get enough scholarships and other assistance to go wherever I wanted. Since I had taken all the courses required to graduate, I could take pretty much whatever I wanted, so I focused on languages and literature. Which meant that I had a lot of time for my real interest: being black and defiant.

There was plenty to protest about. The racial climate at Walnut Hills had changed for the worse as it had all over

America. The Black Power movement had moved into an even angrier phase; all too often our pride in ourselves was expressed as antiwhite rage. The white kids had changed too. Some of those who had been friendliest to us, especially the Jewish ones, began pulling back because they felt the black movement was becoming anti-Semitic. Others withdrew from radical political causes and became hippies obsessed with drugs and alternative lifestyles. In the aftermath of the big sit-in, the easy camaraderie that had existed between black and white students gave way to smoldering estrangement. The two groups no longer "got down" together at racially mixed "People Parties," listened to the same music, or talked the same slang. In fact, we seemed to be speaking two different languages. If one of us shouted "Say it loud, I'm black and I'm proud," some white kid—even some white kid who had sat in with us—was sure to shout back, "We're white and we're glad."

The ugly rivalry exploded during the spring of my senior year. The Black Student Union, once again, had planned a cultural festival and wanted to invite a fiery militant like LeRoi Jones as a speaker. But after the previous year's conflagration, the administration was in no mood to tolerate any rabble-rousing and turned down the idea. That ticked us off, so we began to march outside the school every day to support our demands.

The picketing went on for a while without much incident beyond angry catcalls between us and some resentful white students, until some black kids from another high school got wind of it and decided to step in. A band of them showed up at Walnut Hills one afternoon and a fight broke out; a white student was badly injured. Even though I had not been involved in the fracas, the administration knew I had been one of the main organizers of the marches. I was suspended and sent home.

*　　*　　*

Mom didn't harangue me. Instead, she seemed resigned to my doing what I thought I needed to and she couldn't stop me. She rather quietly pointed out to me that being suspended wasn't going to help me get into college. I pointed out to her that I had already completed all the classes I needed for graduation and was still being recruited by several schools, so she needn't worry. I returned to classes after a few days, but for me high school was over. I spent the month or so before graduation hanging out with my friends from the Black Student Union.

The reason I could be so blithe about it all was that by then I had already been accepted at Muskingum College, a small Presbyterian school in Ohio, with commitments for enough scholarship aid to make up for my family's penury. I had done so well in my language classes that I won an award that carried a $2,500 grant, a smaller award from our church, and a number of other prizes. My career as a protester had strengthened my commitment to fight injustice wherever I found it. I had been willing, even as a teenager, to take risks when I thought I was right. As it turned out, I had not suffered any serious setbacks because I stood up for what I believed in, but if I had, it wouldn't have stopped me. Like Mr. Gaston, I was a fighter—but with a very much sharper edge.

CHAPTER THREE

THE WORST NIGHTMARE

If I harbored any doubts about wanting to get out of Cincinnati and away from my family, they evaporated on the trip to Muskingum College in New Concord, Ohio. I had never set foot on the campus and didn't really know what to expect, but it had to be better than staying at home. My parents had gotten their act together enough to drive me to New Concord, but their truce broke down as soon as we got a flat tire. We had to sit in the car more than an hour, with Mom fussing at Dad for not carrying a spare, before a state trooper came along to assist us. We arrived at Muskingum too late for dinner and my first person-to-person contact with anyone on the campus was a tut-tutting lecture from the dorm mother about my tardiness. Hardly an auspicious start.

My mother's last words before she and Dad set off were "You have to make this work, you know"—emphasizing "you" to make it unmistakably clear that I was all on my own, financially and otherwise. That was fine with me. It was the first thing she had said all day that I agreed with, and frankly, it was a relief. I was determined to succeed at Muskingum, no matter what it took. I was ready to trade a lack of support from home for an end to meddlesome interference.

I spent a couple of hours alone in my third-floor dorm room unpacking my trunk and repairing my shattered morale before my new roommate returned from dinner. Laura was a fresh-faced farm girl from Pataskala, a little town only a few miles from Muskingum. The college, of course, had warned her during the summer that she was paired with a Negro, perhaps to give her a chance to object. Her reaction was precisely the opposite. She seemed delighted to meet me even though her only contact with black folks had been through seeing a few of them on TV. I knew we were going to be friends.

I got my first real look at the campus the following morning, and it was all I had dreamed of: ivy-covered buildings, stone walkways lined by stately oak trees, students in chinos and pleated skirts with book bags flung over their shoulders, and an occasional professor in tortoiseshell glasses sauntering along, puffing away on a pipe. The only disconcerting part was that there wasn't another black person in sight. Of Muskingum's 1,300 students, only 13 were black. Despite its picture-perfect appearance, aura of Christian tolerance, and self-proclaimed liberalism, the college wasn't ready for us at all.

I don't know what it was about me, but I kept running into white people who had no idea of how to talk to black people without offending them. Maybe my antennae were especially sensitive to racial slights because of all the tension in my last years at Walnut Hills, but I don't think that's the whole explanation. I've had too many conversations with other black folks who arrived at mostly white colleges around the same time I did to believe that what happened to me was rare or even unusual. It's more likely that white institutions, even Christian ones like Muskingum, hadn't really thought about what it meant to let a few blacks in after excluding them for a century. Their assumption seemed to be that black students like me should do all the work of fitting in since they had done us the favor of admitting us. They weren't bigots, just unprepared. It never seemed to occur to them that they, too, had to make adjustments; their good intentions, they thought, should suffice. Like the astronaut John Glenn, Muskingum's most famous graduate, I often felt like I was in outer space.

For example, a few weeks after school started, one of my classmates, Sekani Banda, an astonishingly pretty girl from the African country of Malawi, was invited to an International Day Dinner and asked me to come with her. Like all the other foreign students, Sekani was dressed in her best native cloth-ing—a multicolored African dress, head wrap, and beaded jewelry—while I wore a typically American preppie sweater and skirt. At the dinner, I made it a point to sit with the other American students so that all the foreign students could sit together, showing off their exotic attire. We were having a wonderful time until the dean's wife, who'd been working the room, put on her most ingratiating smile and asked me: "Well, honey, what part of Africa are you from?"

Without a moment's thought or hesitation, I shot back: "Cincinnati, Ohio, Africa."

Her jaw dropped, her face turned red and her hand flew up to her throat. After a few flustered words of apology, she sidled away. Everyone at my table sat silently for an uneasy moment, until I picked up my fork and resumed eating. I was angry, of course, but even more keenly, I felt belittled. Rather than trying to find out anything about me, as an individual, the dean's wife had looked past my carefully chosen all-American clothes and pronounced Ohio accent, seen my dark skin, and classified me as an alien. It was a small, but telling, example of the stereotypical assumptions about blacks that I came to expect from white folks.

But that episode paled beside what happened in my Spanish class. I had done extremely well on my placement exams, receiving nine full credits, which allowed me to take a senior-level Spanish course even though I was a freshman. But the instructor, a dour white man, just couldn't seem to accept the idea that a colored girl from Cincinnati was one of the top students in his class. He graded my written work fairly and I got high marks, but, just like Miss Robinson back in the third grade, he refused to call on me in classroom discussions. I became, quite literally, an invisible woman. When we put on a play in Spanish, I enthusiastically studied the script and volunteered to play many characters. He cast me as "the devil in the corner," which required me to speak my lines from behind the curtain while the other actors, every one of them white, cavorted onstage. I could be heard but not seen.

It was a perfect, though inverted, metaphor for the way black students often felt at Muskingum and places like it during the pioneering days of the early 1970s. Like the silent spook who sat by the door, we could be seen, but not heard.

Don't think I wasn't happy. The small band of black students—seven girls and six boys—was a tightly knit and mutually supportive group whose closeness was strengthened by our minority status on campus. The male upperclassmen all lived together in an off-campus house that became our refuge from on-campus stress and isolation, where we could get together and figuratively let down our Afros, listen to jazz, and be black without inhibition. One of the fellows had a car that we used to visit equally tokenized black students at Oberlin, Dennison, and other predominantly white private colleges in the region. We also studied our tails off because we knew how much was riding on getting our degrees: our futures. After the rigors of Walnut Hills, the classwork at Muskingum was tough, but not overwhelming. I could handle it. I could compete. I could succeed.

On top of that, my relationship with Vence was the best it

had ever been. He was writing and telephoning me regularly and having the time of his life. The Dartmouth football team, on which he played linebacker, was in the midst of an un-beaten 9–0 season that would culminate in the Ivy League championship; he was ecstatic. In October, he asked me to fly up to New Hampshire for Dartmouth's homecoming game against Princeton, and I just had to go.

Out of long-ingrained habit, I asked my mother's permission to accept Vence's offer, and out of equally long-ingrained habit, she refused. That, of course, didn't stop me. I had about $300 left from the money I had earned from my summer jobs and Vence sent me a ticket. It was the first time I had flown. I landed at Boston's Logan Airport, then took a three-hour bus ride to White River Junction where Vence, resplendent in his Dartmouth letter sweater, swept me up in his arms and whirled me around in the air. I giggled like a little girl.

We spent the weekend in his dorm room, and celebrated Dartmouth's 38–0 triumph in a giddy round of impromptu parties. By the time for the trip back to Muskingum arrived, I was in a delirious haze.

By December, I knew I was pregnant.

I phoned Vence to tell him the news. His reaction gave me a shock even greater than the one I received when he snitched on me during the Walnut Hills demonstration.

"Are you sure it's mine?"

I shuddered and broke into tears. It had to be, I assured him. I had never been with anyone else and planned never to be. Didn't he know I loved him? What were we going to do?

He said he would think about it and let me know.

Back in Cincinnati for winter break, I saw very little of Vence. In our only substantive conversation, he talked vaguely about trying to arrange an abortion, but I wouldn't even discuss it. It was not only illegal in those pre-*Roe v. Wade* days, but, for me, just plain wrong. Nor did I consider adoption, because as my grandmother had insisted for as long as I could remember, in my family "we don't give away no babies." But how I would both care for the child and finish school was a mystery. I returned to Muskingum still completely uncertain about our intentions—and about Vence. A few days later he asked me to come up to Boston again so we could make some decisions.

And then he shocked me again. "We're gonna get married."

There had been times when I would have joyously accepted his offer and rushed off to the justice of the peace. But all of a sudden I wasn't so sure. I knew I didn't want a baby at eighteen when my college career was just getting started, and I wasn't convinced that I wanted to marry a man whose first reaction to learning that I was expecting had been to question my faithfulness. For his part, Vence didn't seem any happier about the prospect of having a wife than I was about having a child. Though he said nothing about it, the haggard look on his face and his slumping posture made it clear that he thought his life had been ruined. As I listened to him spell out his half-thought-out plan for our future, I felt that way too.

I returned to school and dug relentlessly into my classwork to keep thoughts of my crisis at bay. I shared my secret with no one except a couple of black classmates. Not even my roommate Laura noticed the growing bulge I concealed beneath oversized sweatshirts and loose-fitting trousers. She must have thought I was just gaining weight. I finished the semester with a solid B average and steeled myself for the trip back home.

Instead of having my parents fetch me, I caught a ride with a classmate to postpone seeing them for as long as I possibly could. Mercifully, when I arrived, they were both at work. I took to my bed, and tearfully prayed myself to sleep, knowing full well what my mother's reaction would be.

I didn't get up until the next morning. Only my dad, with whom I had barely exchanged a word for nearly two years, was home. The moment he perceived my swollen torso and tear-stained face, he gasped in surprise, then quickly recovered. Then came a transformation that still astonishes me and for which I will always be unspeakably grateful. The bitterness and estrangement that had divided us were swept away by a flood of fatherly concern: he was my beloved daddy again. He hugged me, looked deep into my eyes and inquired softly, "Are you okay, Cootsie? Have you seen a doctor?" Then he sat me down at the kitchen table and asked, "Who's the father?" When I told him it was Vence, he sighed and replied, "Well, you know, your mother's going to go crazy." Not just because I was pregnant, but because I was pregnant by Vence. He might be a football star and an honor student at an Ivy League college, but to my mother he was still a boy from the projects. She would never accept him.

Dad had to go to work, so he left me alone to await my mother. By the time she got home late that afternoon, I had retreated to bed. She came into my room, full of cheerful blather about how glad she was that I'd gotten home after doing so well at Muskingum, but I cut her short. I asked her to close the door, clambered out of the bed, and placed my hands on my abdomen. Hoping against hope, I gazed at her, silently imploring her to embrace me as Daddy had done.

A scream of rage burst out of her and she began pelting me with her fists and everything she could get her hands on—books, shoes, anything she could reach. Finally, exhausted, she collapsed on the bed, put her head in her hands, and sobbed.

Then she looked at me and declared in the coldest voice I'd ever heard: "I hope you die. I'd rather see you in your grave than see you with a baby."

Then she silently walked out into the hall with her hands balled into knots and a look of utter defeat etched on her beautiful face. She was no longer young. And neither was I.

Vence's mother's reaction was totally different—practical and to the point. Compared to my mother she was almost serene.

She had as much hope tied up in Vence as my mother had in me, but her method of dealing with trouble was entirely different. She was the soul of mother wit. While my mother saw only abject hopelessness and bottomless shame in my situation, his mother viewed it as an obstacle to be overcome. In short, we needed help, not condemnation. Under no circumstances could it be allowed to destroy Vence's opportunity to finish college and move on to a better life. Since several of her daughters had given birth without being married, and some of them had left the babies for her to bring up, she was thoroughly familiar with the myriad woes that could haunt her new grandchild if he or she were born "without a name"—meaning out of wedlock. She felt from the start that Vence and I must marry to give the baby a name, and both go back to school with as little disruption as possible. She even volunteered to rear the baby for us until we got our degrees. She also immediately started trying to make common cause with my parents.

She half-succeeded. My father, to my constant amazement and comfort, was both uncritical and supportive, and quickly allied himself with Vence's mom. But my mother, still wrapped in inconsolable grief, refused to discuss the matter. Frustrated by her unwillingness, Vence's mother invited herself to our house, set up station in the living room, and confronted my mother:

"Mrs. Roberts, I'm willing to take care of the baby while Vence and Bari finish school. Your husband says he is willing to help out financially and get them a crib. Mrs. Roberts, what are you willing to do?"

"Not a damn thing," my mother replied, in the precise, even voice that signified she was furious. I could see she was gathering steam.

"Not a damn thing. As a matter of fact, I told Bari I hope she dies. As far as I am concerned, she and the baby can both die. That's the way I feel about it and nothing on this earth can change my mind about that."

Vence's mother looked stunned, and my father looked stricken, but my mother went on, her voice rising and quivering, her fingernails clinched into a palm-reddening fist that she shook in Vence's direction.

"Oh yeah, they can get married. That's the least that no-good son of yours can do, give the baby a name. But as far as I am concerned, there's nothing left here but ashes. It's just ashes. In fact, as far as I am concerned, Bari's already dead."

Then she rose from her chair, slowly smoothed her dress, and left the rest of us sitting there, paralyzed by her words.

Thank God I had never spent much time dreaming about how my wedding would be, or I would have been disappointed. My mother refused to sign the papers that would have let us get married in Ohio, and Dad sided with her to avoid an argument. So Vence and I, along with his mom, drove over to Kentucky, where teenagers could marry without parental consent, and unceremoniously tied the knot with a yawning justice of the peace. Both of us saw the marriage mainly as a way out of our dilemma, not a lifelong committment. We'd stay married long enough to give the baby a start, then go our separate ways.

We moved into the projects with Vence's mother to await the birth. It came on July 7, 1971, a beautiful girl with a boisterous cry, who we named Brooke. I had never felt such unadulterated love and commitment for anyone in my life, or such responsibility. Vence and my dad visited us in the hospital, but my mother ignored us. When I called her to tell her that the baby and I were both just fine, she hung up on me.

The next few weeks were totally chaotic. All of us remained with Vence's mom until he returned to Dartmouth for football practice in late August. Our plan, to stay together until we finished school, then divorce, remained in place. Then, at Dad's invitation, I went back home for a few days before leaving for school. He hovered over me and Brooke, playing the proud grandfather, coming home with diapers and formula. My mother acted as though we didn't exist.

The silent treatment continued until, out of the blue, my mother began loudly chastising me.

"Damn it, I was planning to leave your father, and now you're here with this baby and he thinks that's going to make me stay. I had all these plans and you've messed them up. You're going to have to get on up and get out of here, both of you. I don't know what you're going to do, but you can't do it here."

Then an odd look came over her face and she changed tactics.

"I'll make a deal with you. If you leave the baby with Vence's mother and go back to school, I'll help you. I'll pay for it. I will never pay for this baby, but I will pay for school."

I said nothing. What could I say? A year before she had insisted she didn't have a dime to contribute to my education. But now she could come up with the money to persuade me to abandon my child, who was asleep in her cradle only a few feet away. As I stared incredulously at my mother, her fury took over again.

"I know what's going to happen," she ranted. "You're gonna be up there at Muskingum and you're gonna start missing your baby and you're gonna want to come home. You're gonna drop out of school and stay with that good-for-nothing hoodlum and mess up everything. I wish you'd just die."

She flew out of the room. I never heard another word from her about helping to finance my schooling.

I returned to Muskingum for my sophomore year a few days later, leaving Brooke with my mother-in-law. My roommate, Laura, was both astonished and ecstatic when I told her about the dramatic events of the summer; though we had spent months together in a small room, she had never realized I was expecting. The first weekend of the semester, she went home to Pataskala and returned with huge packages filled with pots and pans, as a wedding present. I was floored by her reaction and generosity. To Laura, it made no difference that I was black and she was white; we were simply two young women marking a happy occasion. Her unalloyed joy in my marriage and baby struck me as both naïve and inspiring: they showed that there was real love in the world, even across the color line. I'll never forget her or how happy she made me.

Mom was right about one thing. I tried to concentrate on my studies, but it was a hopeless pursuit: I couldn't keep my mind off Brooke. During lectures, I found myself wondering if she were okay, if she were crying, if she needed a bottle or a diaper. I phoned Vence's mother every day, sometimes several times a day, to check on her.

By the end of the semester, the distance had become unbearable. I had to be with my baby, no matter what. I transferred to Xavier University in Cincinnati, moved in with Vence's mother and got a part-time job as a car hop in a local drive-in restaurant.

Preoccupied with caring for my beautiful infant daughter, I did not put my emphasis on school. I was also in the midst of an exciting discovery: Vence missed the baby as much as I had when I was away at Muskingum. He was calling home all the time to ask about her and to coo to her. His phone bill must have been astronomical. My feelings, too, had evolved in a way that surprised me. Though I had long since grown out of any romanticized expectations about Vence, I had begun to believe that we could turn our tragedy into a triumph and make a good life together, for ourselves and our wonderful child. Our parents had made a disaster of marriage, but we could do better. We were younger, smarter, better educated, and had lived through their mistakes. We weren't in hot love anymore, but we cared deeply about each other and were bound together by our infinite love for the baby. Imperceptibly, with few words spoken but much understood, we abandoned the idea of splitting up and decided to go forward together—

Vence and Brooke and me—to be upward bound as a family. After all, I still believed that my generation was remaking the world into a better, more just place. Compared with that, making a go of marriage seemed easy.

When August came, we packed our few belongings in a U-Haul and set out for Dartmouth, where Vence had arranged to lease an apartment. I would sit out school for a year while Vence got his degree and a job, then finish my degree in whatever city we moved to. Interrupting my education to be a wife and mother at nineteen was the last thing I would have ever imagined for myself. But as I jostled my smiling little girl in my arms, I would not have traded places—or dreams—with anyone in the world.

---□---

CHAPTER FOUR

BIRTH OF A KILLER BEE

Vence's senior year at Dartmouth concluded on a note so high it made us giddy. It was 1973, the year when "Black Capitalism," the government's campaign to expand opportunities for blacks in business, really took off, and big companies were fighting over black recruits with degrees from top colleges. As a rare honors graduate of an Ivy League university, Vence was exactly the sort of prospect they were looking for. Night after night he came home with thrilling accounts of interviews with headhunters who seemed to be offering the world to entice him into signing on with one Fortune 500 company or another. His big problem was not getting a good job, or even a great job. It was which great job to accept.

We spent days debating the pros and cons of each company's offer—fringe benefits, starting salary, location, you name it—before settling on the First National Bank of Chicago. The deciding factor was that the bank had reserved a slot for Vence in its prestigious First Scholars Program, a hot ticket to a high-paying, high-profile executive position in high finance. The bank would start him off at a good salary, expose him to a variety of challenging assignments for two years, pay his way through business school at either Northwestern or the University of Chicago, then give him his pick of positions. No question about it, we were on the fast track to the American Dream and nothing, but nothing, could stop us.

Not even my parents' latest woes could put a dent in my bubble. A few months earlier they had finally separated and now were embroiled in an epically bitter divorce. Mom had taken the position that all of us kids had to choose sides between them; if one of us so much as spoke to Dad she never wanted to see that child again. But my patience with her high-pressure demands had been exhausted. I was my own woman now. And so, when we stopped off in Cincinnati on the way to the Windy City, I visited both of my parents and told them frankly what I thought of the mess they had made.

It was bracing to finally stand up to my mother. I sat through an angry harangue about how crazy my dad was. Then I lit into her, politely but firmly, about how destructive it was to make her children choose between her and Daddy. I didn't raise my voice, and I didn't back down. I made it unmistakably clear that I thought she and Dad should have split up years before, but as usual, their way of doing things had done tremendous harm to my fifteen-year-old sister Traci, who was staying with Mom, and fourteen-year-old Tim, who was staying with Dad. For once in her life, Mom seemed abashed by my assertiveness and confidence, and she took my words almost in silence. But it was still a long time before she reached out to Tim and welcomed him back as a son.

Dad, as always, was more receptive, at least on the surface. I insisted that he and Mom stop quarreling over Traci and Tim's allegiance and start thinking of someone beside themselves. "I'm trying, Cootsie, but your mother has lost her mind," he moaned. "Well, do the best you can," I replied, determined not to take no for an answer. He agreed, though he gave me the clear impression that he didn't think there was much chance that Mom would be reasonable about anything. By the time we left for Chicago, I felt I had done all that I could to bring an end to Traci and Tim's nightmare.

I still get a chuckle when I think about what a couple of yokels Vence and I were when we got to Chicago. We didn't know didley-squat. Take our choice for a first place to live. We found an apartment on the seventeenth floor of a high-rise building on the mostly black South Side. In contrast to the stifling little flat the three of us had lived in for a year at Dartmouth, it had a separate dining area and two whole bedrooms, so that for the first time since we got married we wouldn't have to sleep on a lumpy, secondhand sofa bed in the living room. Though our view was of the traffic jams on the Dan Ryan Expressway, our new home felt like a penthouse. We thought we'd arrived.

What we didn't know was that almost all the other tenants in the building were destitute families who could only afford the rent because they had government subsidies. They resented us because Vence was getting up and going off every day in a suit and tie to a glamorous job in the Loop. Within weeks, the apartment that had seemed so grand began to feel like a besieged outpost in enemy territory. We couldn't miss the sarcastic comments our neighbors made about us as we rode in the elevator or washed clothes in the laundry room. Except for the few months I had spent in the projects with Vence's mother, I had never lived around really poor people before, and I was taken aback by the hopelessness and jealousy of the other tenants. It didn't seem to matter to them that I had never been the sort to put on airs and did my best to be friendly: they thought I was "dicty" (black slang for snooty) simply because I spoke proper English and was somewhat reserved. Our relative affluence soon made us targets. Some of the neighbors warned Vence he'd better watch out for himself. After our car was broken into and stolen, I knew we had to get out of there as soon as we could.

We had arrived in Chicago late in the summer of 1973, too late for me to resume my schooling right away, so I arranged for Brooke to go into day care and took a clerical job at an insurance company. That started new tensions with Vence. Every morning as we set off to work, it was like we were traveling to two different worlds. Vence had leaped right into the heady world of high finance with all its beguiling perks: the big paycheck, the expensive lunches with clients to discuss multimillion-dollar deals, the business trips to faraway cities like San Francisco and New York that I had seen only in books and on televison. I, at least for the moment, was slaving away in a boring job that paid $2 an hour, eating brown bag lunches in a run-down employee cafeteria while my coworkers swapped lurid stories about their boyfriends. I couldn't wait to get back to school, not just for the intellectual stimulation, but also to narrow a disturbing gap that had emerged between Vence's lifestyle and mine.

The sad truth was that Vence's rapid ascent from the projects to the executive suite had gone to his head: though he was still a glorified trainee at the bank, he had begun to think of himself as a big-league financial mover and shaker. He spent a small fortune on a fancy attaché case and a closetful of dark business suits and ties, each of which cost more than the entire outfits I bought on sale from cut-rate stores like Lerner's. Even worse, he started lording it over me, as though the temporary mismatch between his lofty post and my menial job was a permanent condition. His attitude emerged clearly when I asked why he wouldn't take me to business dinners and other events even though other bank employees brought their spouses. "I'm professional, you're clerical, " he replied in a patronizing tone. I felt like a worm.

But not for long. Vence's haughtiness reignited my dormant

competitive spirit and will to succeed. But in my dead-end job at the insurance company my ambition had no ready outlet, which led only to frustration. Ironically, the way out of my funk emerged from a short-term disaster. With no advance notice, the insurance company abolished my entire department and I was out of a job.

As I headed home with what I thought would be my last paycheck for a while, I noticed a neon sign for Prudential Insurance flashing brightly above Michigan Avenue. It lured me like a beacon.

This couldn't be a coincidence. I walked in, found the employment office, and took a test. Moments after I finished, a beaming employment counselor rushed out of her office and announced to me that I'd gotten a perfect score. "I'm sure somebody will want to hire you right away." The next thing I knew, she had arranged for me to meet with supervisors in two departments, group underwriting and group claims.

My conversation with the group claims supervisor was strictly business. The one with the group underwriting supervisor was just the opposite. He looked me up and down as I entered his cubicle, and licked his lips.

"It looks like your future is all behind you. You're sitting on it," he said, as nonchalantly as though he were commenting about the weather.

I was startled. It obviously wasn't the first time I had heard a sexist remark, but I was stunned by the casual way in which he uttered it. I kept control of my tongue, though, because I needed a job too much to protest. *This is one dumb white man,* I thought, and proceeded to find out as much as I could about the job.

After the interviews, the employment counselor called me and said both departments wanted to hire me. The group claims jobs paid a bit more an hour, and that was certainly a consideration. But as we talked, another question sprang into my mind.

"Which one of these managers makes the most?"

"The group underwriting manager," she replied.

"Well, that's the job I want."

In retrospect, the incisiveness of that query still delights me. Though I had next to no firsthand experience in the workforce, I had honed in instinctively on a key piece of information I needed to make my decision. I had not only gone straight to the bottom line but also grasped the long-term implications of my choice. I wanted to work in the department where the boss earned the most even if my own job paid a little less, since it held out the best prospects for my own advancement. The supervisor might be a male chauvinist pig, but once I was secure in my work, I'd squelch him, if necessary. I was totally confident in my ability to handle outrageous white folks. I'd been doing it since I was a child.

As it turned out, I didn't need to. At Prudential's underwriting department, only a handful of workers, black or white, male or female, had been to college, so my lack of a degree was no handicap. In fact, the underwriters who had graduated from college were the objects of ribbing that seemed good-natured but really concealed a fair amount of contempt. The company preferred to make up for its employees' lack of formal education by training them on the job. Within a year, I had taken several courses offered by the company and had been promoted to junior underwriter, which meant that I evaluated the riskiness of insuring various prospective clients and made recommendations on how much Prudential should charge to issue a policy. It was by far the most interesting job I had ever held and it had a good deal of autonomy. I absolutely loved going to work. With my higher salary and Vence's periodic raises, we moved out of our hellhole on the South Side to an apartment in a safer, more upscale neighborhood on the racially mixed North Side.

Best of all, after a year I qualified for Prudential's tuition reimbursement program, which paid the cost of taking job-related classes at local colleges. At last, I would be in a position to resume my college career. In the fall of 1975, I enrolled at Mundelein College, the women's branch of Loyola University, whose campus was not far from my home; the two schools later merged. Prudential wouldn't subsidize language courses for me, so I decided to major in business administration. I wanted to become as expert in business as Vence was, so that if we ever started our own company I could help run it. Besides that, I had fallen in love with the arcane and specialized language of business, the meticulous precision of ledgers, the balance between profit and loss, and the complicated art of the deal. Business was about money, I knew, but it was also about dealing with people, which I had come to enjoy.

Moreover, at Mundelein, a women's college run by nuns, the work of women and minorities was constantly affirmed by the faculty. No students took a backseat because of their race or sex. For the first time since elementary school and Mr. Gaston, I was treated like someone who really belonged there, and I responded with joyful enthusiasm. I worked all day at Prudential and rushed to evening classes. Brooke stayed with a wonderful woman named Judy, who lived in our apartment building with her son, his wife, and her grandchild, until Vence got home and picked her up. On weekends I burrowed into books at the library while Brooke contentedly worked on coloring books at my side. The hard work paid off. I made the dean's list my first semester and stayed on it.

Not everything, however, was going so well. My progress at Prudential and success at school were matched by a downturn in Vence's fortunes. His pride and his grandiose view of himself had suffered some serious jolts. He failed a statistics course at the University of Chicago Business School, and the bank made him take it over at his own expense. Moreover, and far more troubling, his superiors at First National seemed to be developing doubts about him. One manager, in particular, was on his case every day.

Almost every night Vence came home grumbling. To my surprise, he attributed his woes to race. All the years we had been together I had always been far more militant than Vence about racial issues. I had marched while he stood on the sidelines, but now the tables had turned. Based on my experiences at work and at school, I knew that racism was a fact of life, but I had learned that it couldn't be blamed for every setback a black person suffered on his or her job: sometimes it was the black person's own fault. It could be a bad attitude, poor work habits, a lack of qualifications or just a bad fit—it didn't always have to be racism.

At the insurance company, race hadn't seemed to stand in my way at all; indeed it was almost irrelevant. I had moved up the ladder to increasingly challenging assignments while some whites—and some blacks—who started with me were stuck in the same old positions. That was at least in part because I was smarter and worked harder than they did, but it was also because I was an effective student. I tried to treat every assignment as a learning experience, listening carefully to my superiors' suggestions on how to improve and doing my best to implement them. There was no one, in a higher or lower position, that I didn't try to learn from. I believed that if being black hadn't hampered my progress in a relatively powerless position, where I had next to nothing going for me except talent, it couldn't completely explain why Vence was getting hammered in a job where there was so much more opportunity to show off his skills. There had to be something more.

After five years of marriage, I knew that Vence would never admit to any shortcomings. He could be incredibly stubborn and more often than not he rejected advice, especially if it came from his wife. When I suggested to Vence that he should try being more flexible, he wouldn't hear it. Instead, he suggested that I was siding with his enemies. I understood that beneath his bravado lurked a vast store of insecurity that he could never admit to, that his anger was rooted in the fear that his dreams were sliding out of his reach, but I couldn't get through to him. The more I tried to be supportive and offer suggestions, the deeper he dug in his heels. He simply had too much pride to let anyone help him, especially me.

When the end came, it came swiftly. In the winter of 1976, midway through our third year in Chicago, the bank put Vence on probation, citing his supposed "attitude problem." A few weeks later, they let him go. Needless to say, he was crushed. He was only a few months away from completing his MBA at the University of Chicago, so it was logical for him to finish the course and then find a new job. But his morale had been badly damaged and at best he was just going through the motions. I hated to see him like that.

It didn't help matters one bit that I got pregnant again that spring. The prospect of having another mouth to feed seemed to unnerve Vence even more. But I wasn't frightened. I had developed the habit of evaluating the up- and downsides of every situation that faced us, in the same way that I weighed the risks of issuing insurance policies in my job as an underwriter. When I looked at our plight, it didn't seem all that risky. Vence was only a few months away from his MBA, which would make him an attractive prospect for many companies despite his bad experiences at First National. I was doing extremely well in school and had only a few more courses to complete, after which I could move up to a higher-paying position. We could come out of this triumphantly, if only Vence didn't beat himself before he started by giving up hope.

Turned out I was right. In July, right after graduation, IBM came courting. Impressed by his newly minted MBA and experience at First National, the big computer company offered him a job as a salesman at a salary comparable to what he had earned at the bank. His new position required rigorous training, so for the next six months he was on the road to IBM's headquarters in Westchester County, New York, and as far away as San Francisco, leaving me and Brooke alone for weeks at a time. I kept working and going to classes until a few weeks before my second daughter, Staci, was born in February 1977.

During the final weeks of my pregnancy when I was neither working nor going to class, I finally had time to think of the future. With two children to care for, it would be extremely taxing to be a parent, full-time worker, and full-time student. One role had to go. I decided to quit Prudential when my maternity leave was over and get my degree as fast as I could. Sure, it would pinch our budget to pay my tuition, but the scholarship I had earned from the State of Illinois because of my grades would cover some of the cost. I felt that I had postponed completing my education long enough already; if I waited longer, I might never finish. So when Staci was four months old, I entrusted both her and Brooke to Judy during the day, and I returned to Mundelein even more committed than I'd been before. I crammed three semesters' work into two by taking courses all week long and on weekends and still made the dean's list.

In June 1978, I graduated with honors in business management; next to the days when Brooke and Staci were born, it was the happiest day of my life. I felt exultant, vindicated, restored, reborn, and ready for anything. I had known since I was a toddler that I would get a college degree from a fine school and be a success. That faith had sustained me through all the reverses and setbacks I'd suffered, at school and at home. From this point on, my mother's moaning and sighing about finishing school had no meaning. (In fact, she even showed up with her new husband, glowing so brightly you would have thought it was her graduation, not mine.) Vence's patronizing comments about being professional while I was clerical had no meaning. I had proven myself against all the odds when everyone else doubted me—and no one could take that away.

On top of everything, I had an exciting job. In the weeks before graduation, recruiters had swarmed over the Mundelein campus in much the same way they had descended on Dartmouth when Vence graduated. As a top business student, I had several big companies looking at me. I chose the offer from Chicago's Harris Bank, which was starting a management training program similar to the one Vence had been in. It was perfect. The salary, $12,000, wasn't bad for a brand-new graduate back then. It was located in Chicago. It would also give me sophisticated practical training in business and finance to complement the academic instruction I'd received at Mundelein. I could become a real pro.

At Harris, our group of twenty-five management trainees was bursting with energy and enthusiasm. They called us the "killer bees." Five were black, several were Jewish or Asian, and ten or so were female. It was the most diverse group of peers I had ever belonged to, and we quickly developed an esprit de corps that superseded our ethnic divisions. Whenever we'd zip past each other in the halls—we were always hustling—we'd greet each other with the "killer bee" high sign and keep on stepping. Everybody who worked there knew who we were and seemed to regard us with special fondness: we were the upcoming stars.

We'd meet two to three times a week for classes and spend the other days working in different departments. I was assigned first to the training and human resources department, and told to prepare a manual for training tellers. It was an invaluable experience. I didn't know the first thing about the job, so I had to learn everything there was to know about it before I could write the manual. Among other things, I spent hours picking the brains of veteran tellers, some of whom were a bit reluctant to share their secrets with an untested newcomer. Securing their cooperation, through a combination of cajolery and plain old careful listening, sharpened my people skills. After that, I was sent to Harris's Executive Professional Banking Service, a special floor for high rollers who kept accounts of more than $100,000 and couldn't be expected to stand in line to cash their checks with the great unwashed public. I'd had enough training by now to offer investment suggestions to the wealthy physicians and small business owners. As a kid, I had always wondered what my dad had meant when he said that it takes money to make money, but now I was seeing his principle in action. And playing a part in it.

After a few months, I got an assignment that would change my life. I was sent to a new area of the corporate trust division called the master trust department. A bit of explanation is in order: at the time, mid-1979, many large corporations maintained dozens of pension plans for their employees in different divisions or different locations. As often as not, the funds they were required to invest in these pension plans were placed in a wide variety of money market accounts, bonds, insurance contracts, blue chip stocks, and real estate with little coordination among them. By placing all of the money into one "master trust" account, they could better manage it, ensure bigger returns and smaller tax liabilities, and pay fewer management fees. One of Harris's competitors, Northern Trust, had pioneered the area and was making a killing. Now Harris wanted to follow suit, and I wanted to get in on it.

As I saw it, master trusts could be an explosive growth industry. Banks were taking a bath on loans and investments in real estate, but the pension business was thriving. And after my first six weeks in the department, I was hooked. There were only two people working there besides me—a fellow who had defected from Northern Trust and knew the most about how master trusts really worked, and the boss, David Sturdy. Dave was the most supportive executive I'd ever met. He was about thirty-five years old, a Vietnam vet, and a bit of a nerd. He was just as excited about master trusts as I was, and wanted to share everything he had learned with me—or anybody else who would take the time to listen to him. Dave had tremendous faith in me, despite my greenness. If a client was coming in, he trusted me to give investment advice on his IRA or Keogh plan. "You've had the training, Bari. You can help him. You don't need me," he'd say.

He was my first real mentor since Mr. Gaston. His confidence in me bolstered my confidence in myself and made me believe that my race wasn't important. He proved that not all white men were bad.

I wish I could say the same for the senior executive who temporarily put a crimp in my dreams.

It happened when I applied for a newly established permanent job as a trust administrator in the master trust department. Dave had strongly recommended me for the job to the senior vice president in charge of the corporate trust division, who would make the hire. With Dave's backing and my exemplary performance, I just knew I'd get the job.

My meeting with the senior V.P. got off to a good enough start. He sat behind his desk, leafing through a folder with my work record, and making quiet comments.

"Um, I see you've been working with Dave Sturdy and he has a lot of good things to say about you," he said, slightly smiling.

"He's been a good teacher." I smiled back.

"And I see you took the master trust assignment because none of the other killer bees wanted it."

"That's not quite true. I took it because I really wanted it. I think it's a very exciting area."

The mood suddenly changed. The senior vice president closed the folder and looked levelly at me.

"Young lady, I want to be honest with you," he said. "You

can't have the job. Our customers will not accept a black woman as a trust administrator."

I was dumbstruck for a moment. I couldn't believe it. I had been meeting, on my own, with customers large and small, offering advice, taking care of their needs, satisfying them in every way, and not one had ever complained. In fact, some had praised me.

"I can't believe that," I retorted, struggling to remain poised. "You know, it seems to me that a customer will accept whoever the bank chooses to represent it. That's been my experience so far."

He cut me off. "No, no, no, young lady. It's not us. It's our customers."

"I think you're wrong," I said, and got up.

In my business courses and previous jobs, I had learned that it was important for a woman never to cry in the workplace. So I stifled my tears of frustration and rage until I could escape from the building. I walked blindly down LaSalle Street until I came to the Chicago Board of Trade, found the lady's room, and locked myself in a stall. For the next half-hour I wept uncontrollably out of disappointment and anger. I felt like I'd been shot. I had worked so hard and come so far and had been so happy. I knew I could make a huge contribution and was being denied simply because of my race. *This kind of racist crap is supposed to be over! I am not going to take it this time!* I thought.

I eventually calmed down enough to return to the bank and confront Diedre, one of the killer bees' supervisors. I wanted some answers.

"I heard you got turned down for the master trust job," she said, looking serious and sympathetic. "Why do you think he did that?"

"Because I'm black and a woman."

"Oh, Bari. Don't say *that!*"

"That's what *he* said."

"But that's not what he *wrote*. He wrote he rejected you because you didn't have enough experience."

"Diedre, let me tell you something," I replied evenly. The protester in me had taken over. "Nobody at this bank has any experience in master trust unless they walked across the street from Northern Trust. He told me he didn't think the bank's customers would accept me because I'm a black woman. I heard him with my own ears. I'm not deaf. That's what he said."

"Oh, Bari, I don't believe that."

At that point, I was ready to start throwing things. Here I had been undeniably insulted and denied a promotion to which I was clearly entitled because of my race and sex, and this white woman was grinning in my face and writing me off. She was giving a bigot the benefit of the doubt when there was absolutely no reason for doubt at all. It was all I could do to maintain my composure, but I managed to sit there a bit longer without cursing her, then went back to my office.

Dave Sturdy understood what had happened as soon as I told him. He clenched his fist and pounded his desk: he was as upset as I was. "That bigoted son of a bitch," he stuttered. "Bari, I've worked with you. I know how capable you are. But some people, some people, haven't learned to judge people fairly. It's gonna take a long time. I'm so sorry." He couldn't do anything about the situation, but at least he sided with me, and that was something.

My trip home on the elevated train that evening took only twenty minutes, but it felt like an eternity. My mind was racing with a jumble of thoughts, all of them negative. I felt that any hopes I had for moving up the ladder at Harris had been dashed. No matter how bright I was, how hard I worked, how much I contributed, there was a lid on my aspirations. Harris didn't want me—or any other black woman—in the executive suite. Harris wanted me—and all other black women—in a teller cage or hiding in the back room, not heard, not seen, not respected.

Vence was not supportive at all. In fact, when he heard my story he was almost gleeful. "See, when I told you what was happening to me at First National, you didn't believe it," he gloated. "You were *so* high and mighty and now you've been put in your place. I told you so, didn't I?"

It was probably the first time I really thought of divorce.

By the next morning, I had resolved to make the best of a bad situation. I met with Diedre again to see what other jobs might exist. Perhaps a bit chastened by our previous conversation, she tried hard to find an alternative that I would enjoy. The best she could come up with was a position in the personal trust division, which handled the banking affairs of super-wealthy clients. From there, I might be able to work myself back into the corporate trust division. I took the job.

It turned out to be an education in the ways of wealthy white people, or at least some of them. Part of my job involved playing hostess to multimillionaire clients, bringing them tea and cookies, laughing at their jokes, smiling in their faces. I quickly learned that despite their riches many of these folks were truly dysfunctional, just like the characters on the *Dallas* TV show. I couldn't help overhearing chit-chat about alcoholism, drug abuse, incest, wife swapping, and family feuds. Some client or other was always rewriting his or her will to cut out some relative they were angry with. Despite all their money, they weren't enviable in the slightest. It was eye-opening.

It was also heartbreaking.

One of our clients was a rotund, very dark-skinned, middle-aged black woman from Gary, Indiana, who had received a huge settlement from a steel company after her husband was killed on the job. She had the habit of coming down to the personal trust department with her eight rowdy children in tow every time she wanted to withdraw a few bucks. She wallowed in the individualized service the personal trust department offered, but her very presence seemed to make the other white clients squirm. I took a look at her account information and calculated that at the rate she was withdrawing the money, she would soon exhaust it. She clearly needed advice.

On her next visit, I invited her into the conference room for a chat. She was carrying a baby in her arms. I started by gently pointing out to her that the money she had received from the steel company had to be used to bring up that child and his brothers and sisters. If she kept squandering it, it would all be gone.

Big mistake.

The woman carefully laid the baby on the conference table and slammed her palm on the table.

"Why you in here talkin' to me?" she shouted. "Ain't my money good enough to get me a white banker?"

I was transported to the Twilight Zone.

Still in a haze, I left the room and told the supervisor that he would have to deal with that client personally.

Then I walked out of Harris Bank onto the street, and never looked back.

CHAPTER FIVE

THE BIG TIME

If there is any one thing that distinguishes me from my mother, it's our way of coping with setbacks. Where she sees only ashes, I see embers that can start a new flame. So it was with my ordeal at Harris Bank. Instead of destroying me, it ground away all my naïveté, and left me stronger and more determined. Once again, I had learned, through upsetting and unmistakable experience, that prejudice against ambitious black women was rampant and hardly confined to white males. Yet it was also not universal. For every narrow-minded white sexist like the senior vice president who had turned me down for a job I deserved simply because I was a black woman, there was an ignorant, self-hating Negro like the woman who had spurned me for the very same reason. But—and this is what heartened me—there was also an open-minded and supportive colleague like Dave Sturdy who would look beyond my color and sex to appreciate what I could do. To people like Dave, performance wasn't everything. It was the only thing. It was the bottom line.

The trick was to find more people like Dave to work with.

Fortunately, I discovered a trove of them at my next job at Continental Bank, where diversity and mutual respect in the workplace were part of the corporate environment. As Chicago's largest bank, Continental was a whole new, and much better, world than Harris. It was not only financially muscular enough to take risks that smaller banks couldn't afford, but it seemed to move to a different, more freewheeling beat. It gave blacks and women the space to strut their stuff just like the white boys, as long as their endeavors paid off.

It was just what I needed.

I was assigned to a small group in the corporate trust department that was pioneering a lucrative new market—helping small and medium-size companies insure themselves against product liability, medical, and similar claims. There was huge potential for growth because at the time, major insurance companies were targeting huge corporations, leaving smaller firms to fend for themselves. There were only five people in our department—the boss Henry Tucker, a vice president on the fast track to becoming a senior vice president; his deputy, Jill Gardener; Dan Kitokowski, a young MBA; the secretary; and me—and we ran it like an independent operation. Henry, a thirtysomething lawyer who had reached the rank of captain during his navy service in Vietnam, had a swashbuckling entrepreneurial spirit and complete faith in his team. Under his leadership, our department was one of the fastest-growing divisions at Continental. He treated us more like peers than subordinates, and we worshiped him in return. All of us called on potential clients, brainstormed about ways to improve our products and service, and spent countless hours after the normal workday figuring out ways to beat our toughest competitors and make our department expand.

Did I mention that Henry was black?

He was the first black professional supervisor I'd ever had and he took a shine to me—not only because he liked me, but because it was in his self-interest. Because of his wartime service, when his very life had depended on subordinates of all different colors, he knew he could only accomplish his mission if everyone on his little team was a strong performer; he couldn't afford any weak links. And so, with no special urging at all from me, he set out to complete my education in the world of finance.

Unlike Harris, which put brakes on my dreams because it believed white customers would reject me, Continental had utter confidence in my ability to deal with any client of any race. Yet within the bank itself, there were inflexible bureaucratic barriers between differing ranks of employees, which severely limited my exposure. Vice presidents, for example, did not normally meet with lower-ranking bank administrators like me unless they directly supervised them. Henry tore down those walls. He took me along with him to meetings with senior management where an employee of my relatively low level normally would not have been welcome, with the instruction to keep my mouth shut and just sit there and absorb everything. As it turned out, although they must have been surprised when I showed up at the meetings, no one ever objected to my staying there; Henry was just too well regarded. For the first time in my career, I was exposed to the machinery of corporate decision making, to the ways in which ranking executives set goals and determined strategies, and I soaked it all up. I sat in at meetings between clients and the bank's investment counselors at which we worked out sophisticated techniques for growing their money, at sales meetings where we concocted new marketing campaigns—the whole nine yards. It was almost like being back in class, but this time it was for real.

Henry's top aide, Jill Gardener, was another stirring role model. Unlike most of the female executives I had dealt with before, who tried to act just like men, she managed to be both tough and feminine. She wore beautiful dresses to work, not the standard drab business suits most women executives favored, and obviously spent time on her hair and makeup. Like Henry, she took me under her wing. She helped to rebuild my shaken self-confidence by prodding me to be more daring, to go outside the box, and bend the rules without breaking them. "Sometimes you're so cautious you miss opportunities," she'd tell me. "You're being too rigid because you're so afraid of making a mistake. That's a mistake. Try to be more flexible and creative. Try to see what a customer needs, not just what we have to offer. It might lead to new ideas."

Henry and Jill went a long way toward restoring my faith in the path I had chosen. If they could make it, I knew I could. Though my previous job had been sheer torture, their success demonstrated that not all workplaces were the same when it came to women and minorities. Just as blacks didn't have to settle for second-rate citizenship, I didn't have to settle for a second-rate career just because I was a black woman. I could go as far as my abilities warranted, as long as the game was fair.

While I was still at Harris, I had heard of the National Trust School at Northwestern University, a summer institute for training financial trust administrators, and I had badly wanted to attend. It was the best training program of its kind in the country, a rigorous summer course in every aspect of handling trusts and estates from investments and wills to intricate banking regulations and arcane tax implications. When you finished it, you really knew your stuff. But Dave Sturdy's bosses at Harris had rebuffed my entreaties because they thought it would be a waste of money to invest in the skills of a bank officer their clients wouldn't accept.

Henry not only wanted me to go, he made sure it happened. After his boss, a senior vice president, turned down his first request to approve my attendance on the reasonable ground that I had only been at Continental for a year, Henry refused to take no for an answer. He appealed the rejection and his passionate advocacy won over the senior vice president. Henry was the kind of mentor I needed, the kind who fought for me.

I was determined to be the kind of apprentice a mentor like that deserved, one who would return his investment in me with a high rate of interest. I promised him that he wouldn't be sorry, that I would finish in the top ten percent of the more than three hundred students from leading banks all over the country who were taking the course. When summer came, I threw myself into the subject matter with unbridled energy, moving into a Northwestern dormitory during the week and returning to our condo to be with my family only on weekends, which I spent getting reacquainted with the girls. True to my pledge, I finished not just in the top ten percent of the class, but in the top five percent, and won a certificate for special merit.

A few weeks later I was promoted to senior trust administrator, with a big raise and enhanced responsibility.

It was the fall of 1980 and I was on the way up.

Sadly, Vence was on the way down. In only a couple of years on the job, he had become the complete IBM man, with the dark suits, white button-down shirts, and drab wingtip shoes the computer company's employees wore almost like a uniform. But he was a disaster as a salesman of mainframe computers for some of the same reasons that his career at First National Bank had foundered. His stubbornness and unwillingness to bend the rules—to go outside the box, as Jill Gardener had urged me to—had alienated some of IBM's best customers. On top of that, he lacked the gregariousness it takes to be a deal maker. Not long after my promotion, he came home in a huff because two of his clients had called his supervisor and demanded that he be taken off their accounts. That was a major crisis that could cost him his job.

Once again, Vence insisted that his troubles were all because of his race.

I knew that wasn't true. I wasn't silly enough to maintain that racism wasn't a huge obstacle to black people's aspirations; I knew that it could be from my own experience at Harris. But I also thought it was all too easy to blame bigotry for everything; many blacks used it as an easy cop-out to excuse their personal failures. I had to consider that Vence was at IBM, which had a reputation as one of the best places for blacks to work; I even knew some of them personally and they were doing well. Vence's troubles weren't because he was black. They were because he was not a good salesman. But when I tried to tell him there were things he could do to improve his performance, as usual it fell on deaf ears.

In an attempt to save Vence's career, IBM offered him a fresh start with a different assignment and a transfer. Since he didn't seem well-suited for dealing directly with customers, they'd use his analytical skills as an MBA to help manage their in-house real estate and construction division in White Plains, New York. If he took it, we'd have to move.

I strongly considered letting him move and staying behind in Chicago. I had big reasons to do so. I had just been promoted. I was in love with my work. With Judy's help I could manage to care for Brooke and Staci. My future seemed brighter than ever.

But in the end, my desire to keep our family together proved stronger than my career aspirations and misgivings about my marriage. For all our differences, there were many things about Vence I admired and even loved. He and the girls worshiped each other, and I was reluctant to take any step that would threaten their bond. In December, I resigned from the best job I had ever had, and packed up and moved to Stamford, Connecticut, a twenty-minute drive from Vence's job in suburban Westchester County.

* * *

As part of Vence's relocation package, IBM offered to help me find a new job. It didn't take long. Vence's boss referred me to Chase Manhattan Bank, a giant institution whose resources and reach dwarfed even those of Continental. Because of my training at the National Trust School and prior banking experience, I was quickly offered a position in the master trust department that Chase had recently started, for twenty-five percent more money than I had earned at Continental. I took it enthusiastically. At last I would get a chance to work on master trusts as I had long hoped to.

The speed with which I found a new job wasn't my only reason for thinking the move wouldn't be so bad. Stamford was astonishingly beautiful, an almost magical small city on the northern coast of the Long Island Sound where magnificent wild swans and squawking Canada geese flocked along the shore. We found a spacious townhouse right across the street from a highly regarded school where Brooke could attend fourth grade. After school, she could easily walk to the nearby house where Angie, a gregarious Italian woman, ran a small day care center where I left Staci when I caught the train to New York. Everything seemed set.

Little did I know. Within months after we enrolled Brooke in school, she ran into a problem that reminded me of the worst of my childhood experiences. She was one of only three black kids in her class and her teacher was picking on her. Like her father and me, Brooke spoke perfect standard English with a clear and completely understandable accent, but her teacher falsely accused her of slurring her words and was constantly correcting her pronunciation. Even worse, the teacher had begun to deliver some not so subtle racist messages that were undermining Brooke's self-esteem—that white was the color of happiness and black was the color of doom. I realized that something was terribly wrong when Brooke no longer wanted to play with her black dolls and begged me to buy her some white ones.

Unlike my mother, I did not take the teacher's side. I never once doubted the accuracy of what my daughter told me about her destructive classroom experiences and did not hestitate to protect her. I met several times with the teacher and principal, politely but insistently making my point—and, to their credit, the educators not only listened but heeded my complaint. Within weeks, the teacher's attitude improved remarkably and Brooke began to really enjoy going to school.

Then there was Jack, my first supervisor in Chase's master trust department, who turned a job I really liked into an ordeal. He was, not to put too fine a point on it, a control freak whose inflated ego seemed to depend on heaping abuse on his subordinates. His main target was Christina, a Panamanian woman who worked as a trust administrator, one level below me. She couldn't go to the bathroom or take a phone call without Jack criticizing her. However, she lacked the self-confidence to fight back even when she was on solid ground and he was being totally unreasonable. It was pitiful. He eventually fired her.

After her departure he tried to pull the same stuff on me. If I took two minutes more for lunch than the allotted forty-five minutes, he'd browbeat me when I returned to my desk. If I went to the rest room, he practically lurked outside the door to see when I emerged. If I got a personal phone call, he'd loudly demand to know who I was talking to. I bore these insults silently because, apart from his obnoxious behavior, I found my work challenging and invigorating. It finally got to be too much after I'd been on the job for about six months.

One of my duties was to execute the complicated financial transactions our clients had instructed us to perform. Since the master trust department handled the pension plans of many Fortune 500 companies with billions at their disposal, each day we were moving tens of millions of dollars in and out of their accounts. Given the complexities and magnitude of our trading, small discrepancies were fairly common—so common in fact that Chase's policy was to write off mistakes of less than

$1,000 on such trades because they could be easily corrected on the next business day.

One morning, Jack started off the workday by loudly berating me in the office, in front of dozens of people, because an overdraft had appeared on my tally sheet. "Why didn't you handle this overdraft when it came in yesterday?" he shouted, standing over me and shaking some paperwork in my face.

At first, I thought I had made an error exceeding the $1,000 limit, but a quick check of my records showed that the overdraft was only a dime. All this ranting and raving over ten lousy cents on a transaction worth millions of dollars! I couldn't believe it. I was furious, but I remained cool.

I had learned a thing or two about handling issues like this under Henry and Jill's tutelage. So instead of exploding right then and there, I calmly called Jack into a conference room for what diplomats call a free and frank exchange of views.

"I'm not working for you anymore," I told him.

"Good, you're quitting your job," he replied gleefully.

"No, you misunderstood me," I replied. "I'm not resigning from Chase. I like my job and I'm good at it. I'm going to keep working here, just not for you. When we walk out of the room, Jack, I'm not reporting to you anymore."

He literally ran out of the conference room, shaking with frustrated rage. Minutes later, I was called into the office of Jack's boss, a stuffy senior vice president who I'm sure didn't want to deal with this kind of hassle.

"Jack tells me you're quitting your job," the senior vice president began.

"That's not correct," I replied calmly, though I was shaking inside. "I'm just not going to work for him anymore."

"Would you mind telling me why?"

If I had been more hotheaded, I probably would have called Jack a racist, which I'm sure that he was. But that was not my style. I knew that bringing up the race issue with this powerful white man could be counterproductive. Everyone in the department knew that Jack was his protégé and he would be sure to defend him. Calling him prejudiced would shift the discussion away from Jack's abusive and unprofessional behavior to whether or not he was a bigot. Either way, it had nothing to do with the fact that he was a jerk and had badly mistreated me. I wanted a conversation about an employee-supervisor issue, not a discussion of race relations. So I stuck to the issue of Jack's behavior—and to my guns.

"Jack's treating me like I'm in kindergarten, not in the workplace," I said. "His harassment is preventing me from doing my work as well as I can and hurting the department's performance." Then I outlined my specific complaints.

You could have heard a quark drop.

The senior veep came from behind his desk and sat down in the chair next to me. "Young lady, I think Jack is the finest trust officer at Chase. He's worked really hard to build up the master trust department and brought in a slew of new clients. He has my confidence."

"Well, that's what I thought you would say since you're the one who promoted him," I replied sharply. "But let me point out that I'm not criticizing his performance as a trust officer. I'm saying that he and I don't have the right chemistry and I could perform better with a different supervisor."

The senior veep sighed heavily. "I've got some thinking to do," he said gravely. "I'll get back to you."

After lunch, the senior veep called me back into his office. There was a calculating smirk on his face.

"I've got a proposition for you," he said, with more than a trace of mirth in his voice. "We have seventy small accounts in this department that Jack and the other top guys don't have time for because they're too busy with our bigger customers. We've been trying to figure out what we're going to do with them. How would you like to take them on? You manage them for a year, and if you do well, I'll promote you to trust officer, the same level as Jack."

Wow! I exulted. My own accounts! The chance for a huge promotion and a big, big raise! I gratefully accepted and got up to leave, thinking that I'd been wrong about this white man and his malign intentions. Instead of punishing me, he was giving me the biggest opportunity in my career! He was surely one of the good guys, the sort who would give people a chance to prove themselves regardless of what color they were or whether they wore a skirt! My ship had come in!

"Oh, one other thing, Bari," the senior veep added as I wafted toward his door. "You won't have anyone to help you with these accounts. You'll have to deal with them all on your own."

His smirk had widened into an impish leer.

By sticking me with an impossible task, the senior veep thought he was setting me up to fail. He wanted me to mishandle those accounts so he'd have an excuse to fire me.

The joke was on him.

One of the peculiarities of New York banking is the ethnic split between the front room where the high-ranking bank officers strut their glamorous stuff and the back room where lower-paid clerical workers actually perform the essential nuts-and-bolts labor of executing and recording financial trades. For some reason, ninety-nine percent of the front-room types at Chase were white males, including large numbers of Italian Americans like my nemesis, Jack. The backroom workers, on the other hand, were disproportionately black and female and many of them hailed from the Caribbean. Reflecting long-standing tensions between black immigrants and native-born black Americans, this mixed crew of Jamaicans, Barbadians, Trinidadians, and Panamanians had regarded me with suspicion from the moment I arrived at the bank. But after I stood up to Jack, whom they hated for abusing Christina, who as a Panamanian was one of their own, they suddenly saw me as a heroine.

They wouldn't allow me to fail. For them, it was payback time.

The senior veep had, indeed, stuck me with a Herculean task. Handling all the paperwork for seventy accounts, and double-checking to make sure that each complicated investment instruction was propery executed, was a full-time job in itself. Then I would have to do "retentive marketing," calling on clients to keep them happy so they would not defect to another bank, another full-time assignment that would leave me no time to drum up new business. Every other trust officer had a staff of assistants to help them deal with clients. I didn't see how I could manage it all without any help. I needed allies.

That's where the back room came in.

Over the next few days, I talked with literally every one of the dozens of backroom workers. I told them what had happened between Jack and me and about the arduous assignment I had been given. I told them that I knew how important they were, and how much the bank depended on their savvy and sophisticated knowledge of how financial trades were actually made. I also implored them to give me whatever help they could so that I could succeed at the white boys' Mission Impossible. I was almost begging.

Their response was astonishing. With their years of experience, they knew all the time-saving shortcuts that would help me oversee my accounts without assistance. For example, while every other administrator in the department had to fill out long, complex forms for each transaction, the backroom operators devised simplified forms I could complete in a matter of minutes. Since I had no assistant to remind me when important trading deadlines were impending, they took that duty upon themselves, assuring that nothing fell through the cracks. In effect they became my assistants, and even more important, they became vested in my success.

And we became friends. Each morning I stopped in their work room on the way to my desk, with a box of donuts and coffee. Unlike the other front-room types, I took time to chat and exchange little jokes. Eventually we became so close they started calling themselves "Bari's Army."

With their help it soon got to the point where I could not only handle my list of existing clients, but could actually go looking for new business. Over the course of a year I obtained five new accounts while retaining all those I began with. With the help of the backroom gang, I was an enormous success. I had beaten the odds.

When the senior veep called me into his office at the end of the year, he tried to act as if he had known all along that I'd meet his challenge. The impish leer had been replaced by a genuine smile. True to his promise, he promoted me to trust officer, with a staff of administrators and a handsome increase in salary. I was the first black woman to become a trust officer in the department, a real racial breakthrough.

That weekend, I threw a big party for the backroom gang, and we celebrated long into the night, to the rhythms of calypso and reggae.

I'd never eaten so much jerked pork or drunk so much ginger beer in my life.

Meanwhile, Vence's nosedive had accelerated. He'd been given a small staff in his job in IBM's purchasing department and was proving to be as problematic a supervisor as he had been a salesman. Once again, his flaw was rigidity. During the horrendous winter of 1982, an awesome blizzard struck, closing schools and government offices, and stranding hundreds of workers. But Vence was not the kind to let adverse weather affect his actions. He somehow got to the office and discovered that one of his men, whose home was located on a slippery hillside in Peekskill, New York, had called in and said he couldn't make it.

Instead of accepting the excuse, Vence telephoned him and belligerently ordered him to "get your butt into the office."

The worker declined. The next day when he did come in, Vence bawled him out and tried to dock his pay.

That was a blunder.

The employee went straight to Vence's boss, with whom he had been friendly for two decades. Once he opened the door, many other members of Vence's team were emboldened enough to voice similar grievances against him. His boss reinstated the worker's pay and dressed Vence down for his heavyhandedness.

Once again, when Vence told me about it, he blamed the incident on the employees' bigoted attitudes. "They just don't want to work for a black," he said.

The idea of divorce was becoming more attractive. I didn't need Vence anymore. I had outgrown him. We had been married for twelve years.

The next eight years would prove to be the most exhilarating and rewarding part of my career, as Chase's master trust department grew exponentially and moved onto a worldwide stage. The department had started out with a couple of billion dollars under its care and was now managing hundreds of billions. As a rising tide lifts all boats, I, too, was on a rising tide.

After my promotion to trust officer, I finally was given an administrator to assist me: Joe Marcello, an Italian American from Bay Ridge, New York, a neighborhood not known for its hospitality to black Americans. At our first meeting, he was clearly not happy about working for any black, let alone a black female; he felt like he'd lose the respect of his homeboys. But next to winning over the backroom crowd, making him an ally was a piece of cake. Like Henry Tucker, I believed that my job would be easier if my team were outstanding, so I made Joe an offer he couldn't refuse. I took him to lunch and promised him that I would teach him everything I knew. "When I'm not here, you'll really shine with what I teach you,"

I told him. "You'll be the best damn administrator in the group if you'll listen to my advice."

He was smart and teachable and I mentored the hell out of him. I introduced him to all my backroom buddies and encouraged them to help him out just as they had helped me. I took Joe on client calls so he could learn firsthand about marketing. To broaden his perspective and deepen his knowledge, I got him in on meetings administrators usually didn't go to, as Henry had done for me.

The next thing I knew Joe was calling me "goombah," the slang term he reserved for his closest Italian friends. With his enthusiastic help and burgeoning skills, I was able to go out and recruit even more clients.

When one of the other trust officers left Chase, I moved into the big time. The small accounts I had fostered were given to somebody else and I was assigned to a new client list of enormous Fortune 500 companies, the kind of firms that only an experienced and highly trusted bank officer is ever allowed to work with: General Foods, Hoffman LaRoche, United Technologies, Colgate Palmolive, and fatefully, Texaco, Inc., the fourth largest oil company in the United States. Each one of these companies had entrusted between $300 million and $1 billion to the master trust department, a staggering sum that almost equalled the total of all the small accounts I had managed before. To cope with the load, I was given a second administrator to help me—another Italian American named Vito Milillo. I treated him just as I had treated Joe, and in the wink of an eye, he too was calling me "goombah."

Even my old tormentor Jack had changed his attitude toward me because I had proven myself. Some of the customers I was taking over had been his clients for years. In what amounted to a display of respect and confidence in me, he escorted me to their offices and introduced me personally to their treasurers and chief executive officers. As Joe and Vito's skills improved, I was able to rely on them to get the routine paperwork done and could concentrate more on growing the business. I eventually turned over all the administration to my two "goombahs" and devoted myself to the pursuit of new customers.

This was what I had always dreamed of and I was a natural at it. By now, I had redone my "look" to reflect my executive status. I favored the female equivalent of nonthreatening bankers' clothes—tailored business suits in dark colors and next to no jewelry—and my hair was styled into a curly permanent, a far cry from the bushy Afro of my days as a militant student. I looked so much the part that Chase included a picture of me in a brochure it put out to tout the master trust department. I was the human equivalent of 1010 WINS Radio, a New York station whose slogan is "All News, All the Time." I was all business, all the time, 24-7-365.

My biggest challenge was balancing my job and being a mother. I had to be in the office at 8 A.M., so I left home at 6:45 for the one-hour commuter train ride to the city. Most weekdays, Vence, who worked much closer to home, would pick up the girls from Angie's day care center around the corner and spend an hour or so playing with them and helping Brooke with her homework in the early evening. I'd get off the commuter train at 7 P.M., and rush home to make dinner and get the girls in bed at a reasonable hour. Then I'd go over any paperwork I had brought home for an hour or two before collapsing. I was often exhausted.

I tried to recoup the lost time on the weekends. Every Friday night Vence, Brooke, and Staci would pick me up at the train station and we'd go out to dinner at a restaurant the girls had chosen—I ate a lot of meals at McDonald's. On Saturdays, we often ventured into New York to visit a museum or see a Broadway show like *The Wiz* or the *Tap Dance Kid.* Anyone looking at us would have assumed the four of us were a stable and happy family. They would have been wrong.

That was because Vence had never been sadder. Between my salary and annual bonuses, I was now earning as much as he was, and he felt threatened by the closing gap. Sometimes, he'd sit down with a pencil and paper and calculate how much each of us was actually bringing home, allowing for withholding tax and other deductions. By his calculations, he was still making a larger financial contribution even though our salaries were nearly equal. By his lights, that made him the boss of our family. I could feel that the end of our marriage was near.

Of course, I still got a reminder from time to time that prejudice was still very much a force, even in sophisticated corporate circles. For example, after I was assigned to take over one company that had been doing business with Chase for years, I paid a call on a senior financial analyst there to discuss ways to expand our relationship. I thought the meeting went very well. But when I got back to Chase I heard some alarming news from my boss. Only moments after I'd left her office, this woman, who had seemed so cordial during our meeting, had told the company's treasurer she wanted me taken off the account.

I asked why.

"Well, she said you didn't seem to understand what they wanted and she doesn't have any confidence in you."

I was, to say the least, extremely surprised. If there was anything I was sure of it was that I knew master trust inside out and had done a good job of presenting our proposal.

That afternoon I telephoned her to see if I could straighten out what I was sure was a misunderstanding, but she never gave me a chance. She just starting yelling into the phone and abruptly hung up.

Something clicked. My instinct told me that I had run into another white person who had trouble accepting a black woman as a peer. And I wouldn't take it. But again, I decided to focus on the issue of her unprofessional conduct and leave the race card alone.

I wrote a long, detailed letter outlining my understanding of how the company wanted its master trust to work—where the funds would come from, how they wanted them invested, when benefits should be paid out, and so on. I took it in to the senior vice president and asked him to review it.

"This looks like what they want," he said, after reviewing it. "Don't worry. You're staying on the account if I have anything to do with it."

As I sat in his office, he placed a call to the financial analyst who had complained about me and invited her to the bank for a face-to-face conversation.

When she got there, he told her that he had complete confidence in me. That Chase was not in the habit of undermining its employees for no good reason. That he was not taking me off the account. And that if she couldn't accept that, he'd take it up with her boss, who, he was sure, would be surprised by her attitude.

Not surprisingly, she backed down.

The moral of the story was that Chase—or at least some of its leaders—was willing to back me against a racist. Despite his initial attempts to sandbag me, my boss had come to respect and value me because of my top-notch performance; I had turned a powerful potential enemy into a fan. Chase had given me all I ever wanted, a chance to compete on the same basis as everyone else. No special favors. No special treatment. Just let me play on the same field and by the same rules as the white boys and I'd do just fine. I had proved it, time and again.

Sadly it was different with my next boss, Art, who took over the master trust department when the senior veep who had promoted and supported me left Chase's employ. Art was a smart enough guy, a lawyer from a top school, but he knew next to nothing about pension management and master trusts.

So I taught him as I had taught Joe and Vito, in effect becoming his mentor even though he was technically my superior. Whenever a potential customer asked for a proposal from us, Art relied on me to produce it. His total dependence on me, on the other hand, gave me a good deal of leverage. For the first time I began to venture outside of our usual territory in search of new business. I went out to San Francisco, for example, to try to land Levi Strauss, a really big fish with millions to manage. Art was thrilled with my work.

But Art did not always come through when I needed him. In fact he was spineless. I learned that I couldn't rely on him to watch my back after another unsettling tête-à-tête with a client.

When United Technologies, the big Connecticut defense contractor, appointed a new assistant treasurer I saw a chance to lure more of their $3 billion in pension funds away from our rival, Citibank. I called him and made an appointment for late afternoon the next day.

I arrived a few minutes early, but the man's secretary was not at her desk. So I sat down and took a last look at the proposal I had prepared to make sure I was ready.

A few moments later, a tall white man stuck his head out of an office and glanced in my direction. Evidently not seeing whomever he was expecting, he went back into his room. A few minutes later, he repeated the performance. Another few minutes later, he went through it again.

I decided to speak up.

I rose to my feet, put on my most businesslike expression, called him by name and introduced myself.

His face went stony, but he asked me into his office. After a few moments of awkward silence, he finally spoke.

"Let me be honest with you," he intoned in a syrupy Southern drawl, and I braced myself for what I knew was coming. "Well, first of all, I'm used to my bankers looking like me. And if they don't, they look like Farah Fawcett, and you don't look like either one."

Whoa, I said to myself. Our meeting abruptly broke up.

Since UTC was in Connecticut and it was late, I went straight home and phoned Art. Our conversation was a textbook example of cowardice masquerading as liberal tolerance.

"He actually said something like that to you in this day and age," Art said in an incredulous tone.

"Yeah, he did," I said.

"Well, should we send someone else?" asked Art, proving, to my dismay, that he was incapable of comprehending the magnitude of the incident. "Well, you know, we really need the business, Bari," he went on, now shifting to an almost whiny, imploring voice.

My God, he just doesn't get it, I thought. "I don't think we should send anyone else," I replied. "What we ought to do is complain to his superiors about his racist attitude and make them do something about it."

"Oh, Bari," said Art. "That's a big step."

I hung up.

He never made a complaint and we did not get the business.

But his weakness in the face of this affront left a vacuum that I knew I could—and must—fill. I began going after new clients wherever they were located without asking his permission, though I kept him informed about what I was doing. Art made no objection or effort to rein me in. I signed up Georgia Pacific down in Atlanta and doubled our business with General Foods to half a billion dollars. I was also handed one of Chase's largest master trust accounts, AT&T, and got my first chance to go international, since they did business all over the world.

In 1984, I was promoted to second vice president, a major step upward. My protégés, Joe and Vito, had also been promoted, a sign that my mentoring had paid dividends.

Two years later, the master trust department was reorganized and I got another big promotion. I was elevated to vice president and given responsibility for overseeing all of the department's business in the Eastern United States, where almost all our big clients were located. I had a staff of more than twenty people, including two junior vice presidents, and a gaggle of trust administrators, secretaries, and assistants. All told, my team was managing accounts worth more than $11 billion for some of the world's biggest companies. I was making $65,000 a year, sweetened by a lavish annual bonus.

Not long after I became a vice president, I invited my mom and her new husband to come visit us and took them to lunch at Chase's executive dining room. As we ate, one of my white male colleagues came to our table and introduced himself.

"Well, you know my daughter here is *the* vice president of Chase Manhattan," said Mom, puffing up to her full magnificence.

"Yeah, I know," my coworker replied, going along with the joke. "We all work for her."

Mom beamed even more radiantly. I couldn't bring myself to tell her that Chase had scores of vice presidents. It was just too much fun watching her bask in my reflected glory.

By 1989, my marriage had collapsed. Vence's difficulties with his staff at IBM's purchasing department had led to another transfer to an even more mundane job, this time in contract administration. He had not received a raise in more than two years while my salary and bonuses were steadily rising. Each upward tick in my income seemed to contribute to his frustration.

The bottom finally fell out at what had begun as a rare social outing for us. Along with a girlfriend of mine and her husband, we went to see Billie Jean King, the great tennis champion, play in a Virginia Slims tournament at Madison Square Garden; she had always been a special favorite of mine because she had so much pluck. After the match, the four of us retired to a nearby restaurant to have drinks. My girlfriend rose to go to the ladies room and I got up to go with her.

"What are you two, a couple of dykes?" growled Vence.

My girlfriend's husband naturally was furious. He and Vence had a shouting match in the restaurant that nearly came to blows. I was mortified.

That evening, as Vence and I drove home to Stamford, I reached a decision. I knew our marriage was over—indeed if I hadn't been so fearful of breaking up my family, I would already have been long gone. I still saw many good things about Vence, especially his devotion to Brooke and Staci; he was a loving and attentive father. I wondered how much the girls would suffer if their parents split up, and if I would be able to handle them without Vence's help. But by the time we got home, I realized that I could never be happy with Vence again, and that growing up in an unhappy, strife-filled home like ours posed an even greater threat to the girls. A few months later I moved out and filed papers for a divorce.

The failure of my marriage inevitably damaged my work and my health. Brooke was now a nearly grown woman of eighteen and she blamed me for the breakup. Our relationship became very tense and argumentative. Staci was just twelve, an age when children are especially vulnerable to divorce, and she needed a lot of attention. I could no longer travel at the drop of a hat to pursue a hot lead or work long into the night on some project or other—Staci needed me at home. Something had to give. It turned out to be me.

I became very sick with a debilitating and mysterious ailment that totally sapped my energy. For the first time in my life, I began to miss days at work because I was too sick to come into the office. My performance began to slip. I went to several doctors but none of them could diagnose my symptoms or come up with effective treatment.

Finally, in desperation and deep depression, I took a leave of absence that stretched into a year while I sought a cure for my still undiagnosed illness. Finally, the fourth doctor I consulted came up with the right diagnosis: I had a tear in my small intestine that was poisoning me and could eventually kill me. I had to undergo four operations before it was patched, and in fact I nearly died.

By the time I felt strong enough to think about returning to work, Chase's master trust department had gone through another reorganization and moved its headquarters from Rockefeller Center in Manhattan to the new Metrotech Plaza in Brooklyn. That meant my commuting time would shoot up from an hour each way to more than ninety minutes each way, which would be intolerable. I couldn't afford to waste that much time traveling back and forth from work, leaving Staci alone.

I had to find a job closer to my home with hours I could handle. I had no doubt that someone with my experience, contacts, and demonstrated financial skills could easily find an attractive position.

And that's when I heard from a friend that Texaco was in the market for people like me.

CHAPTER SIX

"TEXACO'S CHANGING"

Until my dear friend Susan Philbrick, whose husband, Peter Wissel, was a high-ranking Texaco executive, brought up the idea during the summer of 1990, the idea of going to work for that particular company never would have entered my mind. Shoot, I didn't even buy Texaco gas. I had formed a distinct and decidedly unfavorable opinion of the people who ran Texaco over nearly a decade when I helped to manage Texaco's master trust account at Chase, first as a low-level trust officer and finally as the vice president and team leader with overall responsibility for the business. I had seen how ineptly they coped with one of the worst disasters to ever befall a Fortune 500 corporation. The way I looked at it, most of Texaco's misfortunes had been caused by its own high-handedness, and it hadn't learned much from adversity. In my mind, Texaco was a textbook case of corporate pride run amok.

To make a long and sensational story short, Texaco's troubles started in 1984 when it acquired the Getty Oil Company

in one of the largest mergers in American business history—
in the process brushing aside a deal that Getty's largest stockholder had already made to sell a big chunk of the company
to Pennzoil. Since Getty's largest stockholder was Gordon
Getty, the eccentric son of the legendary billionaire, J. Paul
Getty, the case became a cause célèbre on both the business
and social pages. Pennzoil filed a huge lawsuit against Texaco
in the Texas state courts asking for $10 billion in damages for
disrupting its pact with Getty. The subsequent trial garnered
worldwide press coverage for months. It ended in an ignomini-
ous defeat for Texaco, which was ordered to pay Pennzoil an
astounding $10.9 billion in damages and punitive awards. Tex-
aco appealed the ruling over and over again. It even tried to
haul a couple of jurors in front of a judge to prove they were
biased. But none of these desperate maneuvers worked. In
1987, Texaco filed for bankruptcy to protect its assets while it
continued to fight the judgment in the courts. It wound up
losing $4.4 billion that year and its stock price fell through
the floor.

That, in turn, prompted Carl Icahn, a flamboyant master of
the so-called art of greenmail that was epidemic during the
high-rolling 1980s, to start buying up Texaco shares at bargain
prices. His goal was to acquire enough shares to make Texaco
either do his bidding or get rid of him by buying him out at
a handsome profit. He then started leaning on Texaco, pressuring it to stop wasting shareholders' money on futile legal battles and settle the case with Pennzoil. Under Icahn's sway,
Texaco finally agreed to pay Pennzoil $3.3 billion and drop its
legal appeals. But Icahn was just getting started. In 1988, he
mounted an epic proxy battle to unseat Texaco's board of directors and replace it with one of his own choosing. He lost
the proxy fight by a narrow margin, but Texaco agreed to buy
out his holdings. He walked away with I don't know how
many gazillions of dollars in profits.

I had followed all this not only in the papers but in firsthand reports from members of my team at Chase who worked directly with Texaco's pension account. We all thought Texaco deserved to lose the Pennzoil case because its top management had disrupted Getty's handshake deal with Pennzoil without so much as a by-your-leave. Such hubris on a corporate scale was consistent with my evaluations of individual Texaco executives I had come to know over the years: almost to a man—though Susan's husband Pete was a rare and welcome exception—they were smug, standoffish, and utterly inflexible when it came to pension fund strategy. They didn't want to hear ideas from anyone else, even when it could help them a lot. Like Captain Queeg in the *Caine Mutiny,* they personified the inflexible attitude that there is a right way, a wrong way, and a Texaco way to do things, and, come hell or high water, they would do things the Texaco way.

During the 1980s, for example, Chase had developed a number of innovative programs that could greatly benefit pension managers by increasing the return on their money by investing in overseas equities and short-term stock-lending plans. Firms as established and conservatively managed as AT&T, General Dynamics, Hoffmann La Roche, Avon Products, Boeing, IBM, and Colgate-Palmolive had quickly grasped the advantages these programs offered and incorporated them into their pension fund strategy. But Texaco wouldn't touch most of them. They tried the short-term stock-lending program for a while, then abandoned it as supposedly too risky. Even though they were doing business in more than one hundred foreign countries, they rejected investing in foreign securities on the grounds that Texaco was an American company that would keep its money in America. Over the years that jingoistic approach probably cost Texaco's pension fund millions of dollars it could have earned with a more daring approach.

At our biannual conferences with major clients, the Texaco representatives invariably had the least to contribute. They listened politely as experts from other big companies discussed new ways of managing their multibillion-dollar pension accounts more effectively, but offered few new ideas of their own. Their account had grown tremendously, from a few hundred million dollars in the early 1980s to half a billion after the Getty merger, to a billion or so by the time I left Chase, but their attitude about managing it had not evolved very much. If Chase had been Baskin-Robbins with its thirty-one flavors of ice cream, they'd have settled for plain vanilla every time— and forget the sprinkles.

That haughty attitude softened a bit toward the end of my tenure with Chase, as Texaco struggled to emerge from the bankruptcy. The need to reorganize had, at least temporarily, knocked the men of Texaco off their high horse. Executives who had been snooty to the point of obnoxiousness suddenly became polite, solicitous, even wheedling—because they needed something from us. The government was all over them. Month after month, they'd practically beg us to deliver complex financial reports weeks ahead of schedule to satisfy the government agencies that were demanding the information. It taxed my staff to the limit to meet these requests, but we satisfied them without complaint. The Texaco guys expressed gratitude, but once they got through their difficulties I fully expected them to revert to their arrogant norm.

If I had been at my best, I would have laughed off the idea of working for Texaco as a rather sick joke. But when Susan broached the idea, I was far from at my best. I was still weak from my third operation for the intestinal lesion and facing the prospect of a fourth round of surgery to complete the repair. I was heartsick about leaving Chase for the simple reason that I couldn't handle the commute from Stamford to our new headquarters in Brooklyn. Both of the girls were having a hard time with our family's breakup, and I was deeply worried about them. In short, I was in some ways at my lowest point in years and just plain vulnerable when Susan mentioned that Texaco was looking for people like me.

She was a hell of a salesman.

I had first met Susan when she was manager of General Foods' pension plan, which had a master trust account with Chase, but our relationship quickly bloomed into an abiding friendship. As part of my recuperation, I had begun to take long daily walks in one of Stamford's beautiful shoreline parks, often in Susan's company; she was thoroughly familiar with the dilemmas I was wrestling with. On one such walk Susan suggested that Texaco just might be the solution to some of my problems. Its corporate headquarters were in Harrison, New York, she pointed out, a mere twenty-minute drive from my home in Connecticut. It was an enormous company with excellent benefits and competitive salaries. It was a sprawling multinational that did business all over the world, so there was a possibility for the kind of international assignments she knew I was hungering for. I was acquainted with a lot of people there, which would ease the transition to a new position. And they could use my skills.

Susan painted such an attractive picture that my skepticism gave way to curiosity. The clincher was her belief that Texaco had learned a lesson in humility from its recent travails with Pennzoil and Icahn. The company had taken a long hard look at itself and knew that it needed to change. It was looking for new people. It wanted diversity. The interesting thing is that Susan stressed that Texaco was looking for female executives. It wasn't until our third or fourth conversation that she added that they were also looking for blacks.

Texaco's changing, Susan told me.

Over the next few months I heard that line over and over again.

Texaco's changing.

Texaco's changing.

It was almost a mantra. I could almost hear it in my sleep.

*   *   *

The more I thought about it, the more sense it made to at least explore the possibilities. For one thing, I knew I had talents that Texaco needed. I could help them improve the management of their pension accounts. I could manage people. I could also learn from them, especially about investment strategy. It could be a win-win situation of exactly the kind I had always aimed for since my business classes in college. So why not give it a try?

At first I considered approaching Susan's husband Pete, who had recently been promoted to Texaco's assistant treasurer, but I was uncomfortable with exploiting a personal relationship with the husband of a very dear friend. So instead I wrote a formal letter to Shelby Faber, the general manager of Texaco's pension fund, one of the few people at the oil company that my team at Chase had good things to say about. He replied almost instantly, inviting me to come in right away for a preliminary interview.

We met a few days later, under circumstances that struck me as puzzling and almost bizarre. But as I learned over the next few months, these oddities were simply a part of the Texaco way. To start with, when I arrived, Shelby didn't invite me to his office, or even back to the finance department where I had assumed we would meet. Instead, with the furtive air of a college student sneaking his girlfriend into a dorm room, he briskly escorted me to a small conference room in a completely different part of the building, looking nervously over his shoulder from time to time as we walked along. When I asked where we were going, he fidgeted and replied that since a lot of people at Texaco knew me he thought we should meet more discreetly—for my protection.

Since I didn't need protection from anything, I thought his explanation was rather strange. There was really no reason at all why he should be concerned about being seen with me. But I made no comment.

It got even creepier during the interview. I had sent Shelby a copy of my résumé along with the letter and he knew about my achievements at Chase.

"Texaco's changing," Shelby told me eagerly. "We need new ideas. We need new strategies. We need new people."

But when he handed me what looked like a job description, I was astonished and disappointed. The tasks it described were far beneath my level of experience, as someone who had been a vice president at one of the world's biggest banks, managing billions of dollars. They could have been handled by a talented clerk.

I took a look at the paper and composed myself, stifling an insulted feeling. "If this is what you have in mind, there are some people who worked for me at Chase that I could recommend," I said. "It's much too junior for me."

My directness seemed to startle him. He squirmed around in his chair and finally said, "well, we don't have a job for you right now. I'll have to get back to you." The meeting was over.

Just before I left, however, we had a visitor. David Keough, Texaco's senior assistant treasurer, stuck his head in the door, acted like he was surprised to see me there, and greeted me enthusiastically. His arrival, I realized, was no accident. The only way he could have known that I was meeting Shelby in this far-off part of the building was that Shelby had told him about it. His feigned surprise at seeing me was part of some kind of strategy. But try as I could, I couldn't imagine why Keough and Shelby were acting this way. Keough and I were not friends, but we were well acquainted. There was no reason in the world for him and Shelby to go through with this silly charade.

As I drove home I mulled over the likelihood that Shelby had been testing the waters. He had offered me a job he knew I wouldn't accept to see how I would react. The cynicism of his approach left me confused and somewhat disheartened. Why not just offer me a position suitable for someone with my credentials and salary level, instead of all this time-wasting rigmarole? If I were a white male with identical credentials there was no way in the world they would have insulted me by offering me a job like that! What the heck was wrong with these people?

For the next few weeks I put all thoughts of going to work for Texaco completely out of my mind and pursued other job opportunities. I was on the verge of accepting an offer from a major insurance company when Shelby called me again.

"We've been working on the job description to see if we can come up with something that's right. What do you think about these tasks?" he said, then proceeded to tick off a list of mundane duties that to my mind was still far beneath someone with my capabilities.

I was offended by the offer, of course, but I didn't say so. That was partly because I liked Shelby, and partly because I was in a polite frame of mind.

So I said, "You know, Shelby, I would not be interested in that job at all; it's way too junior. But at least you're making some progress." Once again, I offered to refer him to some people who worked for me at Chase.

Not long after that conversation, I became sick again. From Labor Day until mid-September, I was hospitalized for another major operation—the fourth in only a year. I didn't hear from Texaco until the end of the month when I had started feeling better. Shelby telephoned me and invited me to lunch.

Our second face-to-face encounter was even spookier than the first one. Shelby met me in the reception area, grinning nervously and glancing around, then hustled me down a back stairway to a small, secluded dining room that seemed to have been set up for a clandestine rendezvous.

When I asked him about it, Shelby replied in conspiratorial tones, "We don't want anybody to see you. We think that's best."

Still baffled by all the precautions I tried to probe a bit deeper. "Why shouldn't anyone see me? Do you think somebody's going to tell Chase I'm talking to you about a job or something?"

"Oh, yeah, that sounds good," he replied in a surprised tone that suggested to me that he had never thought about it at all. "Yeah, doing it this way will protect you from Chase."

I was still mystified, but I decided to let it go.

At least the substance of this conversation was a big improvement. I knew that the ground had shifted when Shelby asked me, "What kind of responsibility do you want if you come here to work?" I read a lot of significance into his choice of words. In both our previous conversations, he had described my potential duties as "tasks"—a word that comes to mind when I think about junior level employees. For the kind of job I was after, I think of responsibility and accountability, two words he was using now. At long last, it seemed, Texaco was finally getting down to business, figuring out how I might fit into the real scheme of things. They were speaking my language.

I told Shelby that, among other things, I wanted to manage people and help Texaco improve the performance of its pension accounts. Beyond that I wanted to learn. I was especially interested in working with actuaries, who forecast the company's needs long into the future, because at Chase I had never done that kind of exotic technical work. I also told him I wanted to know more about planning investment strategies because at Chase we had usually been carrying out someone else's investment decisions, not making the decisions ourselves.

Near the end of our conversation, Shelby's demeanor changed and he became almost reflective. He began to talk, quietly but with genuine feeling, about the hard times Texaco had endured. The Pennzoil trial had been an ordeal, but the bankruptcy and battle with Icahn had been even more debilitating. Texaco had come out of it all with a new sense of purpose. Top management realized that the company needed to change. They needed new approaches. They needed new attitudes. They needed new people. He used that phrase again:

Texaco's changing.

As I left, the slogan was ringing in my ears. I drove home believing that at last Texaco and I might be coming to terms.

Little did I know. Shelby had promised to get back to me in a few days with a formal offer, but I didn't hear from him. When I called to ask him about it, he told me that since it was close to the end of the year, all the paperwork with the human resources and payroll departments was taking longer than he had expected. Having worked in a sprawling corporate environment for years, I knew that could happen, so I bought his explanation. But a part of me was already persuaded that Texaco was just playing games.

My instincts were right. Within days of our phone conversation, a letter from Texaco came in the mail. I opened it eagerly. But as I read, my optimism quickly gave way to a new burst of frustrated anger. The letter offered me a job as a "financial analyst" in the finance department, a position at least one level below the kind of job I thought we had been discussing. Even worse, the proposed salary was $50,000 a year, $15,000 less than my straight pay at Chase, not to mention the $15,000 in annual bonuses and awards I had been earning at the bank. This was an insult.

In mounting fury, I telephoned Shelby. He was all verbal smiles as he answered the call.

"Did you get the letter, did you get the letter?" he demanded, in excited tones. "What do you think? When can you start?"

"Yes, I got the letter," I snapped back. "And frankly, it's hard for me to believe that after all that talking we did you would send me a letter like this. It's too junior a job. The salary is way too low. You know I can't accept an offer like this, Shelby. It's not even close."

The line went silent.

"I'll get back to you," he finally said.

It took weeks. At the end of October, Shelby reached me again.

"Dave Keough wants to talk to you," he said.

Shelby, the underling, hadn't been able to close the deal and bring me on board. So now Texaco was calling in the first string.

David Keough had style. Unlike most of the Texaco types I had dealt with, he was a true gentleman, whose perfect manners and genuine modesty posed a stark contrast to the swaggering pretensions of the people around him. Dressed in an impeccable dark gray business suit and quiet tie, he walked from behind his huge desk and greeted me warmly when Shelby ushered me into his office. This time around, there had been no elaborate maneuvers to conceal my presence at Texaco. I was taken straight to the finance department in full view of anyone who happened to be there. I had come out of the shadows. From that openness alone, I felt we could at last make a deal.

After an exchange of pleasantries, Keough seated me in a comfortable chair and sat down on the couch.

"We made you an offer, what don't you like about it?"

I told him what I had told Shelby. He listened intently.

"I don't think you guys are really looking for *me*. You've offered me two positions that weren't suitable for someone with my credentials, " I concluded. "I understand that Texaco's changing, but it doesn't seem to be changing very quickly."

"But we are," Keough insisted. "We have a big quality initiative on. We want to win the Malcolm Baldridge Award," he said, referring to a highly coveted prize given by the U.S.

Commerce Department each year for innovative corporate management. "We're going to prove we're back on track and better than ever."

Then Keough started in about the "Quality Initiative" that had become the raison d'être for everything at Texaco as it emerged from the bankruptcy and the traumatic struggle with Carl Icahn. A big part of it, he insisted, was that Texaco wanted to bring in new people from the outside, to embrace different points of view and benefit from different experiences.

Another part of it—a big, big part of it, he strongly implied—was that Texaco was changing the way it rated and rewarded its employees. The company had created a new evaluation system—called "PMP" for Performance Management Program—that he said was much more objective than the system it was replacing.

People who did well on their PMP could expect steady promotion. "You come here for a couple of years, get a couple of strong reviews, and you could move on up."

"It's even possible that someday you could be sitting where I'm sitting, as an assistant treasurer of this company."

I sat there and listened as he went on.

"We're working on creating a job that's just right for you because you are the kind of person we need here. It takes time. I'm sure you can appreciate that."

How much time, I asked, thinking of the insurance company that had offered me a job and a tantalizing feeler I had just gotten from Citibank.

"Not long, I promise you," said Keough. "And now, there's someone else I would like for you to talk to."

He took me to the office of his boss, David Crikelair, Texaco's treasurer, whom I had met once or twice on social occasions. Crikelair was cordial but added nothing to my conversation with Keough.

That evening, as I reviewed the day's events, I reached a conclusion. If Texaco did not now come forth with an acceptable offer, I'd write them off and take the job with the insurance company. I figured that Shelby had been instructed to hire the most overqualified African American woman he could find for Texaco's finance department, but not to offer the kind of money and prestigious assignments that would attract someone like me. To get someone at my level, they needed someone with more authority—Keough. And if he couldn't do it, they'd probably bring in someone even more senior—Crikelair.

It was clear from all this that Texaco really wanted to hire me. The problem was that they didn't have a clue about how to do it, though it was as obvious as the big bright Texaco star that adorned every Texaco service station. All I wanted was a job that fit my experience and credentials, the kind they'd offer me if I were an ambitious white male, not an ambitious black woman. I just wanted to be treated equally.

Why was it so hard for them to figure it out?

I was getting a bit tired of dealing with these white boys who were learning how to deal with black women at my expense. This was their very last chance.

A week later, another letter arrived. It offered me a job as a Senior Financial Analyst—right so far—but at a salary of only $55,000, still $10,000 less than my minimum requirement! I hit the roof. I couldn't believe it. After all that yakking and all those assurances! I'm not even going to call them back, I vowed. Instead, I called the insurance company and accepted the job even though I had some misgivings about it. It would require me to commute to Hartford every day and travel frequently to the company's headquarters in Boston, and I wanted to stay nearer to home for the sake of the girls. If things had worked out at Texaco, my job would have only been fifteen minutes away.

A few days later, Shelby called me again.

"We sent you a letter and you didn't answer," he started off warily. "Aren't you pleased?"

"No, I'm not," I shot back. "Shelby, I am not going to take a job for less money than I was making at Chase." I was almost yelling into the phone. "Obviously, you guys have someone else in mind for whatever bogus job you're offering, not me. I've told you three or four different times what my requirements are. Fifty-five thousand dollars just doesn't do it!"

"What? It doesn't have sixty-five thousand dollars on it?" he interjected.

"No, it doesn't," I said.

"Oh, it must be a typo."

"Typo, schmypo," I sneered.

"Oh my God, Bari, you got the wrong letter. It's supposed to be sixty-five thousand. There's been a mistake."

"Oh yeah?"

"We'll get you out a new letter right away. Oh, Bari, I'm so sorry."

I looked at the letter again. It had been signed by none other than Shelby himself.

The next letter came a few days later. It repeated the offer of a position as a Senior Financial Analyst, but at a salary of $65,000.

A flashback to Greek myth: I felt like Sisyphus would have if that rock he was rolling had finally stayed put at the top of the hill, that an eternal struggle had finally ended. This job finally met my financial needs, and even more important, involved minimum commuting time.

I called Shelby and told him I would accept the offer.

"Great, Bari. We'd really like to get you in here before the end of the year. Can you start before Christmas?"

"What's the big rush?" I asked.

"Oh, uh, if you start before the end of the year we can get

you two additional weeks of vacation. It's really for your benefit."

The sudden hurry-up after the dillydallying over the past few months puzzled me, but I attributed it to corporate quirkiness. What the hell, I figured, I haven't worked in a year. I'm tired of being idle. I'll start in December.

A couple of days later I got a call from one of the people on my master trust team who managed the day-to-day relationship with Texaco.

"Watch your back, Bari," he said. "I know those Texaco guys and I don't trust them. They're a bunch of jerks."

CHAPTER SEVEN

STRANGER IN
A STRANGE LAND

Ðecember 17, 1990: my first day on the Texaco payroll. I got up early after a sleepless night punctuated by alternating bouts of anxiety and anticipation. Office hours at Texaco began at 7:30 A.M. and I wanted to be there even earlier. I checked my appearance in the car's rearview mirror before pulling out of the driveway: dark blue business suit, single string of pearls, straightened, shoulder-length hair arranged in a conservative flip, the perfect invisible corporate uniform.

The drive to Texaco's headquarters in Harrison took exactly seventeen minutes. I drove past the unobtrusive Texaco sign, flashed my brand-new ID card at the guard and proceeded down the long curving driveway to the parking lot entrance at the rear of the building. The Texaco building was a blocky, three-story white stone monolith the size of three football fields, its blank immensity accentuated by the big artificial lake and exquisite landscaping that softened the rolling hills on the one-hundred-acre campus even in the bleak early morning. I had been here many times in the past, but this morning I looked at the building with new eyes. After nearly two decades of experience in corporate America, I was keenly aware of the nonverbal statements big companies send to their workers and customers through the design of their corporate buildings. In my heightened emotional state, this vast and inscrutable edifice struck me as a monument to a corporate colossus obsessed with its power and staggering wealth. It was blunt, expensive, and totally impersonal. It gave me the creeps.

Inside, I was soon to learn, was a corporate Calcutta, organized along caste lines as rigid and implacable as those of traditional Hindu society. The first division between Texaco's Brahmins and the lower castes came at a crossroads leading into the cavernous underground parking facility. Turn right, and you entered the regular lot, where thousands of workers parked their cars, then walked to elevators that rose to their floor. Turn left, and you came to a forbidding garage door that could only be opened with an electronic pass. This was the reserved parking area for a tiny elite of no more than fifteen or twenty top managers and members of the board of directors, complete with its own guarded entrance and private elevators that rose to the exalted Mahogany Suite on the third floor. It was a big change from what I was used to at Chase, where even David Rockefeller used the same entrance and rode the same crowded elevators as everyone else without complaint. At Texaco, the pecking order was evidently so inflexible that it even determined which elevator you rode on.

But maybe I'm reading too much into this, I thought as I made my way to Shelby's office in the finance department. He was in an expansive mood, but got straight down to business. "Let me introduce you to the rest of the team." He led me to a conference room where about a dozen people were waiting. Among them were two assistant managers of the pension and benefits division in the finance department where I would be working, John Dowling and Sigfrid Ciomek.

"This is Bari-Ellen Lewis, whom some of you already know," Shelby began, using the married name I was still known by at the time. "She's our new senior financial analyst and she's going to be overseeing our relationship with Chase Manhattan, working with the actuaries on forecasting, and serving on a task force on banking reform and how Texaco should manage all of its banking relationships. I'd like to officially welcome her aboard."

My new coworkers looked like they were in shock.

It turned out that Shelby had not told them until the close of business on the previous Friday that I would be joining their team. Though I had accepted Texaco's offer weeks before, he had given this close-knit, all-white group no time at all to prepare for the arrival of the first black woman to hold a professional position in Texaco's finance department. They'd not even been given an opportunity to ask such fundamental questions as what my duties would be. To me, the lack of preparation for my arrival was a serious mistake. Even in the 1990s, most white folks who hadn't worked with blacks needed some time to adjust to the idea. Having a black person among their peers—and a black woman at that—had evidently unnerved them.

After a brief exchange of pleasantries, Shelby turned me over to Sigfrid, who was going to be my direct supervisor. She was a small, fiftyish woman who still spoke in the accent of her native Norway. I had known Sigfrid for a while and admired her because she was one of the few women to have worked her way up into the virtually all-male ranks of Texaco management. In fact, I had even thought of her as a potential mentor. But as she led me to my new office, Sigfrid seemed fidgety and distracted. She was obviously uncomfortable.

"Gosh, Bari, I can't believe you're here and that you will be working under my supervision," she said as we walked along. "I mean, you've been a vice president at Chase, managing your own team, managing accounts worth billions of dollars. Gosh, under different circumstances, things could be the other way around: you would probably be managing me!"

My new office—number 1607—was strictly corporate standard issue, and about half the size of the room I had occupied at Chase. But Sigfrid was as gushy as a real estate agent trying to make a sale as she pointed out its features and furnishings: a wooden desk, modest credenza, windows on one side looking out at the beautiful grounds while those on the other side offered a view of the corridor.

"Now Bari," said Sigfrid, pausing for emphasis, "at Texaco, window panes are everything. Managers have three-pane offices. Directors have corner offices with four panes; they also get a couch and more comfortable chairs.

"I started out in one of those," she said, gesturing at the rows of cubicles where lower-ranking employees sat on the other side of the corridor. "And now I've got a two-pane office. You're starting out in a two-pane office. They must really think a lot of you."

As she talked, I was startled by the sight of an odd machine that looked like a small refrigerator on wheels rolling silently down the corridor outside my office. "Oh, that's the robot mail cart," Sigfrid explained. "It's very efficient."

That's not the only robot working here, I thought, but I didn't say it. I was in the early throes of a case of corporate culture shock.

It wasn't just the size of the building, or Sigfrid's obsession with what I regarded as meaningless perks. As I looked out into the corridor I could see only three other blacks—Brian Lewis, a junior analyst, and two female secretaries. There weren't many more among the scores of people Sigfrid introduced me to that morning as we went from division to division in the sprawling finance department. Texaco was the whitest place I had been in since lab school in Cincinnati. The hostile stares I evoked from many of my new white colleagues made it clear that they weren't prepared to accept me. It was as though I were a virus that had invaded Texaco's bloodstream and the corporate antibodies had to attack it. My mere presence was an offense against the nature of things.

For example, in the trading room, I was introduced to Silvanus Chambers, a cheerful extrovert who had been the highest ranking black in the finance department until my arrival. As we chatted, a sarcastic voice emanated from the other side of the trading room.

"Well, they say she was a vice president at Chase Manhattan's master trust department, but I never even heard of a master trust. What the heck is that?"

"Master what?" somebody else said, sounding like a school kid making a crude double entendre. There were a few muffled snickers.

I flinched and so did Sil, but Sigfrid did not seem to notice. This was like the hazing my sixth grade class had endured at that all-white elementary school in Cincinnati, and it called for the same dignified response. Like my teacher Mr. Gaston, I ignored the taunt, told Sil that I was glad to have met him, and resumed my tour with Sigfrid.

The reception was even frostier in the banking department, where a band of good old boys from the back room made no effort to conceal their contempt. They did not stand up to greet me or shake my hand. One of them actually got up and began to question me aggressively about my credentials. I kept my tone cordial as I ticked off some of the highlights of my résumé, including my experience managing accounts worth more than $11 billion at the time I left Chase. That seemed to silence him.

The worst was yet to come. As Sigrid escorted me to the office of Robert Ulrich, the deputy treasurer and second in command of the finance department, she admonished me about another aspect of the bizarre caste structure at Texaco. At this company, no employee could call on an executive who ranked two grades or higher above him or her unless accompanied by his or her direct supervisor. Since I was starting at level sixteen, that meant that any time I wanted to consult with someone grade eighteen or more—for instance, Shelby, the head of our department—Sigfrid had to come along. After my long years at Chase, where staff members had unceremoniously called on whomever they needed to see, regardless of rank, this regimented and inflexible rule struck me as archaic and insulting, almost like being in kindergarten. I couldn't imagine how it had survived into the 1990s.

I later came to realize that Bob Ulrich was a bitter man. Though he was a decade or so older and had been on the job longer, he had been passed over for the influential treasurer's job that had been given to David Crikelair. My first day at Texaco, he dove right into a belligerent, detailed grilling about my résumé, apparently trying to prove I had lied about my previous experiences to get the job. I was taken aback by his aggressiveness, but managed to answer every one of his probing queries as straightforwardly as I could. At the end of the interrogation, Ulrich grunted something unintelligible and waved me and Sigfrid out of his office.

I hadn't even had my lunch break yet and I felt as though I was being treated like a monkey in a cage.

After lunch, as I sat in my new office trying to collect my thoughts, someone knocked loudly on my door. Before I could say "come in," the door burst open and in strode a small, energetic black woman with her hand thrust out in greeting and the biggest and most genuine smile I had seen all day lighting up her pretty face.

"Hi, hi, hi, Bari," the human tornado prattled machine-gun style, as she breezed into my office. "I'm Florence Prawl, from human resources. Call me Flo, girlfriend. I knew you were coming and I want to welcome you to Texaco. If there's *anything* I can do to help you get settled, just let me know and it *will* be done! Do you need *anything?* Are they treating you right? What do you think of us?"

She hadn't been in my office for thirty seconds, but we had already clicked.

Florence walked over to my desk and lowered her voice to a conspiratorial whisper: "Girlfriend, we've got to talk. But we can't do it here. There are some things you need to know."

Florence and I didn't get a chance to speak candidly for several days. By then, word had spread throughout the company that a black woman was sitting in a two-pane office in the finance department, and people from all over the building were actually going out of their way to see this strange alien being for themselves. A steady stream of gawkers from other departments paraded along the corridor, trying to appear nonchalant as they gazed into my office.

I ignored the gawkers as much as I could, but some of them refused to be ignored. On one memorable occasion, as two white men walked past my door, one seemed to notice me sitting behind the desk. Through my window, I could see him take a couple more steps, then execute a Charlie Chaplin— style double take so abrupt he almost fell down. He grabbed his companion by the elbow and the two of them backpedaled to my door.

"Is this your office, or are you an outside auditor?" he asked, leaning into the doorway.

"I'm Bari-Ellen Lewis, my name is on the door, and this is my office," I replied as calmly as I could.

"Well, Jesus Christ, I never thought I'd live to see the day when a black woman had an office at Texaco," he said, and wandered off shaking his head. It was almost comical.

But I ran out of patience when one of Sil Chambers' white coworkers from the trading room got up enough gall to invade my office one day. His name was Bill, and like many Wall Street trading types, he had a twisted sense of humor. One afternoon, he dropped by, ostensibly to share the latest joke about a plane crash that had killed hundreds of people or some other tragedy that he found hilarious.

He started off innocuously enough by asking me what I was working on, and I told him, in a friendly, open way. But then he turned angry and resentful, as he gestured around my office.

"You know, you have my job," he said.

"Come again?"

"I'm the one who's supposed to have this job, not you," he went on, in a bitter tone. "I've worked here for years. I've got the qualifications. I've got an MBA from Saint Johns. I was in line to be promoted and to have this job. But, oh no, they couldn't give the job to a white male because of *affirmative action*. They had to go out and find a *black* and a *woman*! That's the only reason they hired you. See what I mean, you have my job. I deserve it. It's not fair."

That was it. I had endured the stares and fingerpointing and the hush that seemed to fall over the entire cafeteria whenever I went down there for lunch because notoriety is part of the price of breaking the color line in any business. Like Jackie Robinson in his early years in major league baseball, I was determined to conduct myself with dignity and turn the other cheek. But this was over the line and I let him have it. I put down the papers I was working on, and turned to look him straight in the eye.

"Tell you what, Bill," I told him in a voice dripping with false sincerity. "If I were you, I'd go right over to that corner office where Dave Crikelair the treasurer sits and I'd tell him that some black woman has taken over your office and stolen your job. Then, I'd walk to the next corner and I'd tell Dave Keough, the senior assistant treasurer, the same thing. Then, I'd walk over to human resources and tell them. Because if you have a problem with me sitting here, it's your problem. It's not my problem."

By now my voice had risen to nearly a shout.

"And if you think that I, Bari-Ellen Lewis, am going to sit here and defend myself to you, or explain my qualifications or try to explain why I have this job and you don't, you are badly misinformed.

"Now have a nice day and get out of my office."

I turned back to my paperwork and he got up and left without another word. He never troubled me again.

Instead of dining in the company cafeteria where we might be overheard, Florence invited me to lunch "off-campus" in a restaurant in a nearby town. I had been on the job a couple of weeks and had met several other black employees. Some of them had heard about how rudely I was being treated and told me similar horror stories of their own. For the most part, I kept my thoughts to myself because I was so new to Texaco. I didn't really know who could be trusted to guard my confidences and who could be counted on to tattle back to the bosses. My discomfort level was already high, but so was my determination. I had faced challenges since grade school and survived them all, and Texaco would be no different.

I figured Florence could help me understand what I'd gotten myself into. I'd learned a little about her background through the grapevine, and it was enormously reassuring. She was about twenty years older than me and a real expert on equal opportunity from decades of work as a private consultant and at another oil company before joining Texaco about a year earlier. She was cheerful, outgoing, and blunt, as well as a tireless networker.

As we ordered, Florence looked around the other tables to see if any other Texaco workers were seated within earshot. Even though we were off campus, it was clear that she felt that we had to be on guard.

"I'm going to lay it on the line for you, girlfriend," she said, leaning over the table and speaking just loudly enough that I could hear her clearly. "There's a story behind why you were hired, and why some other black folks like Sil Chambers were hired. You need to know it."

Over the next few minutes she explained that the Office of Federal Contract Compliance Programs, an agency that monitors the progress of minorities and women at companies that do business with the federal government, had conducted a survey of Texaco's workforce the previous year. It had been turned over to Allen Krowe, Texaco's third in command just after New Year's Day in 1990—and made him hit the ceiling. Krowe hadn't been at Texaco long and was not really part of its inbred, white-bread culture. He had spent most of his career at IBM, which over the years had worked hard to diversify its workforce along race and gender lines for the best of all reasons: they thought it was good business. Krowe was used to diversity, and, according to Florence, the overwhelming white maleness of Texaco's professional workforce had shaken him as much as it had shocked me.

"Girlfriend, Allen Krowe got one look at that OFCCP report and he was appalled, honey, just appalled. He couldn't believe it. Job after job, department after department—no blacks, one black, two blacks. The worst was the finance department, child. They didn't have any blacks at all in professional positions. Fact is, they'd never had one. He called in the senior finance department people and laid them out, girlfriend. 'How come it's all zeroes in every one of these job categories? What are you doing about it? The next time I see this damn report, I don't want to see any more damn donuts!' I mean, honey, he laid them out!

"So what they did, they went out to hire some blacks lickety split! So first thing, they asked me to stop just being a private consultant and come on full time with human resources for the whole company. Then they found Sil Chambers—you met him already—and brought him into the trading room. And they found you and brought you in here.

"It's all because Allen Krowe said that the next time he saw that damn report he didn't want any more donuts on it!"

A veil lifted. Now I understood why Shelby and his higher-ups in the finance department had been so anxious for me to start work just a week before Christmas, instead of waiting until after New Year's. It meant that I would be included on the employment roles the next time the OFCCP did its annual survey. The next time Krowe got the report, there would be no donuts for the finance department because Sil Chambers and I had been hired. We were exhibits A and B to prove that Texaco was really changing. It seemed so cynical.

As the weeks dragged on, working at Texaco seemed more and more like going to grade school. But instead of Reading, Writing, and Arithmetic, it had four mind-numbing Rs of its own: ridiculous rules and regulations, as well as resistance to anything new. Sigfrid, in particular, had absorbed these principles into every cell in her body during the fifteen or so years she had worked at the company. Despite her small stature and Scandinavian good looks, she had the personality of a drill sergeant whose one mission in life seemed to be to break me down and make me conform.

Take her reaction to the first big project I undertook, a total review of how the pensions and benefits department managed its relationships with Chase and other banks. I wrote a two-hundred-page manual reviewing every aspect of the department's investment and cash management accounts with outside advisers as well as the ones that we controlled in-house. From that information, we could devise a new and much better reporting system that gave us more control over the entire $1 billion fund. Following Texaco's customary procedure, I gave a copy of it to Sigfrid so that she could give it to Shelby. A couple of days later, Shelby sent word back to Sigfrid that he was thrilled with my proposal and would put me up for a prestigious Treasurer's Award because of it. But when she came to give me the good news, she added some nit-picking comments of her own.

"It's a very good plan, Bari," she started. "But I noticed that at the bottom of page two, there's a missing apostrophe in the word *it's* and there are some typographical mistakes on page eighteen. You'll have to make sure those kinds of errors don't creep into your reports. I don't know what you were used to at Chase, but at Texaco we have the highest standards."

I couldn't believe it. I was so surprised by her caviling that I just stared at her in amazement. She was right about the typographical errors, of course; I should have caught them. But to dwell on a few misspelled words in a two-hundred-page report that had the potential to save Texaco millions of dollars struck me as rather misguided.

Not long after that Sigfrid barged into my office to upbraid me for breaking another of Texaco's rules. "Bari," said she, trying to sound stern, "you're leaving your office too much. You should stay at your desk."

This time, I spoke up.

I pointed out to Sigfrid that many of the files and other materials I needed were kept in the library, which was only a few yards away from my office. It seemed more efficient for me to retreive the stuff myself rather than to have a secretary fetch it. But right in the middle of my explanation, it struck me how ludicrous it was for me to have to account for all my movements around the office. What counted was the quality of my work, not something this trivial. For the remainder of Sigfrid's lecture, I sat silently, stifling a bitter laugh about the absurdity of it all.

Sigfrid wouldn't let up. No matter how much Shelby or some other higher up praised my work, she found some little fault to nag me about. By the time I got my first three-month evaluation in April 1991, her carping had gotten on my last nerve.

My conversations with Dave Keough before I was hired had led me to believe that Texaco had adopted a new and much improved approach for rating employees called the PMP. I assumed it would be similar to the system I had used at Chase when I evaluated my staff. There would be a fairly detailed description of my duties and of how important each of them were to my overall evaluation. Overseeing the relationship with Chase's master trust department, for example, might count as fifty percent, while another assignment might count as fifteen percent and so on. Most big companies that I knew about had been using this kind of system for years because it gave workers a clear idea of what their priorities were and what they had to do to turn in an acceptable performance. There was nothing mysterious about it. It was, in fact, business as usual.

So I was shocked when Sigfrid sat down with me to go over my first three months on the job. The two sheets of paper she handed me were devoid of the objective criteria I expected. There were no rankings of my various duties, no priorities, nothing that could be used to reach an overall objective evaluation. The report merely gave very vague descriptions of my assignments with Sigfrid's handwritten opinion of my performance. It was completely subjective. The substance of it was that I was doing fine and meeting all expectations, and that pleased me. But I was alarmed by the possibility that such an arbitrary format could be easily abused.

That afternoon I called Florence Prawl at her office in human resources.

"What kind of review is this, Florence?" I asked. "There's nothing here about what I'm really doing, nothing here about what was expected, nothing about which task is more important. There's nothing but what Sigfrid thinks."

Florence chuckled. "It's better than what they used to have. Used to be that at the end of the year your boss just came in and said your raise would be two percent or three percent or whatever and there was no discussion at all."

That night I lay in bed, staring into the dark, and wondering what kind of situation I had gotten myself into. Texaco wasn't merely different than what I was used to or had expected. It didn't seem to trust its employees or treat them like grown-ups. It didn't seem to value independence or creative thought. You could not really tell where you stood.

But I smothered my doubts in the comforting thought that Texaco was changing. The only thing I was really sure of was that the change could not come quickly enough.

CHAPTER EIGHT

IT'S NOT JUST ME

Isolation is surely the most difficult part of being a token black in a hostile, otherwise all-white environment. Because trustworthy sources of information are so limited, you can never be sure of what's going on around you. You feel terribly alone. You're always on edge.

That is one reason why over the next few months I reached out to Sil Chambers, who was the closest thing to a black peer that I had in Texaco's finance department. The more I learned about him and his situation, the less perplexed I was about the bizarre atmosphere that surrounded us. I began to make sense of it. I began to get mad.

Like me, Sil had stumbled into the gap between what Texaco promised and what it delivered to the handful of blacks it recruited for the finance department in 1990. He had been working as a financial analyst in the securities trading room, part of the cash management division, since the early spring of 1990; until my arrival, he had been the highest-ranking African

American in the headquarters finance department. With four-teen years on Wall Street behind him—half as head trader of the Open Market Trading desk for the Federal Reserve Bank of New York, the rest as an institutional account executive for Prudential Bache, a huge brokerage firm—Sil was a consum-mate pro. He also had strong academic credentials—an un-dergrad business degree and an MBA, both from New York University. On top of that he was one of the most open and likable people I'd ever known, a good-natured Cuba Gooding Jr.–lookalike with a fund of self-confidence so immense that it sometimes came across as cockiness. Sil had an ego, all right, but in the fast-paced, high-pressure line he was in, he needed one to survive. Unlike a lot of bond traders and stockbrokers I had run into, Sil had neither burned out from the tension nor lapsed into just plain craziness. His unshakable optimism was rooted in his devotion to his expanding family and the big Pentecostal church in Harlem where he spent many hours a week in worship and volunteer work.

There were big differences in our approaches. My natural reserve and unwillingness to suffer fools gladly tended to put white people on their guard. I'm the last person in the world they would dare to tell a racially offensive joke because they sense I might hand them their head on a platter. But Sil is so wide-open and friendly that some of our white coworkers mistakenly thought they could take liberties with him. Being thick-skinned is an essential part of a bond trader's personality. Sil knew that and accepted it as part of the game. He was so tolerant and forgiving that he sometimes let them get away with stuff I would never have accepted. For example, the same obnoxious white boy who had barged into my office to com-plain that I had gotten "his job," repeatedly told Sil "the only reason we hired you is because you can play basketball." I would have stifled him right away. Sil just laughed it off for a long, long time.

Yet, as we got to know each other, I was struck by the

similarities in the way Texaco had recruited us. As he put it, he decided to "make that move" out of Wall Street because he had fallen on uncertain times. A downturn in the market in 1989 had caused his earnings at Prudential Bache to plummet by roughly $100,000 from the previous year, and a merger with another brokerage had put dozens of once-secure jobs like his in deep jeopardy. He had sent out dozens of letters and résumés to Fortune 500 firms to test the waters and Texaco had reeled him in. As with me, as with Florence, as with every other recent black arrival in Texaco professional ranks, Sil had been told over and over again that Texaco's changing, that it wanted diversity, that it was performance, not color, that counted.

In Sil's case, the song-and-dance began with a phone call from Bob Ripley, the manager of money market operations in the cash management department, inviting him for an interview.

"Sil, we have a slot for somebody with your background in handling interest rates swaps, specialty items, financial derivatives, " Ripley told him when they met. "We came out of the bankruptcy with a very small portfolio, but now we want to increase it. We're looking for someone to help handle our investments and actually manage the trading room."

Sil was exactly the kind of guy they were looking for because he was precisely qualified for the position they wanted to fill. They wanted to install a head trader with more savvy and skills than the people who were already there. Sil obviously had those credentials, Ripley allowed, but there was a bit of a problem. Though Ripley never referred specifically to race, he left Sil with the strong impression that it was an issue. There was, at the time, only one black professional in the finance department, a low-level financial analyst, and no blacks at all in the trading room. The way Ripley was talking, Sil would have to ease into the place, not break the color line from the top.

"Sil, you know what trading rooms are like. These people have been working with each other for years and they'd resent having anyone from the outside come in and be put over them.

"So what I think we would do is bring you in on the same level as everyone else. Then, with your credentials and experience, you'd quickly prove yourself to them. Once you do that, we could make you head trader. Shouldn't take more than a few months."

This was as close to an explicit promise as ever gets made in corporate America. It clearly pledged that Texaco would bring Sil in and move him rapidly up the ladder.

A few weeks later Sil came back again for a follow-up round of interviews that included such exalted officials as David Crikelair, the treasurer, and Ron Sokoloff, Ripley's boss and manager of the cash management division of which the trading room was an essential part. The next day Ripley called him back and presented an offer that sent a chill down my spine when I heard about it. Just like me, Texaco tried to lowball Sil by offering a starting salary so low it was almost insulting.

"Fifty-five thousand," Sil guffawed. "I apologize for laughing, but that's a laughable offer. I was looking for something in the seventies."

Ripley promised to get back to him, just like Shelby had done with me. He did after only an hour, saying that the highest Texaco could go was $60,000 to start.

"But remember," Ripley added. "In just a few months, you're going to get a big promotion and it normally has an increase attached in the range of eleven percent. So you'll be up around seventy thousand in just a few months."

With that assurance, Sil accepted. I doubt that a white candidate with the same credentials and experience would have been asked to undergo the same kind of test.

*   *   *

By the time I arrived, Texaco had kept its promises to Sil—up to a point. True to his word, Bob Ripley had given Sil a chance to prove himself and Sil came through like a champ. "Everyone in the trading room could see that I had a lot more education, a lot more talent, a lot more technical skills, and a lot more knowledge, so they gathered around me and learned things," Sil told me one day over lunch in the Texaco cafeteria as white coworkers glared at us from adjoining tables. "Ripley was telling the other traders, 'Look to Sil before you do anything.' You could see he was grooming me for a position of leadership in the trading room and they really needed it there. Before I arrived there was a lot of bickering about what they should do and how they should do it. One of the things Ripley wanted me to do was be a kind of peacemaker. They wanted somebody that had the skills to tell the others this is the way it's going to be, and there would be no question about it. That's what I did."

In only a few weeks, Sil was given the title of coordinator of the trading desk, the first among equals. Each day he chaired the morning traders' meeting at which the strategy for executing Texaco's complicated transactions was hammered out. He had clearly proven himself.

But when Sil approached Ripley about the promised promotion, he got an unpleasant surprise: the man who had hired him and made all those promises was on his way out, on a transfer to Brazil. But he promised to tell his replacement about Sil's good performance. Meanwhile Sil remained on the same level, grade fourteen, at roughly the same pay as the white traders he was supervising and instructing. The whole discussion of his promotion was delayed for Ripley's replacement to deal with.

As it turned out, Sil's new boss, Steve Koch, knew next to nothing about bond trading. He had made his mark as an executive in Texaco's international division. It was the sort of lateral management move that I learned was de rigueur at

Texaco, part of a plan to "round out" the knowledge of rising stars by exposing them to a wide variety of assignments. Koch was astute enough to take Ripley's parting advice about relying on Sil; within a week of his arrival in June 1990 he told him, "Sil, you're going to be my key man." Two weeks later he assured Sil that he would put in for the promotion to head trader that Sil had been promised. In July, he showed Sil a copy of a letter he had written to Pete Wissel, the husband of my dear friend Susan, recommending Sil for a jump from grade fourteen to grade sixteen with a corresponding increase in salary. Wissel didn't reply.

Month after month for the next four months, Koch wrote to Wissel recommending Sil for the promotion. Month after month for the next four months, Sil grew increasingly frustrated as Wissel did not reply.

Even by the time I started at Texaco that December, Wissel had failed to act on Sil's promotion despite his outstanding performance.

For months, Sil was asked to be a leader without receiving the financial rewards that should have gone along with his responsibilities. He was overworked and underpaid. If I had known how he was being treated, I might not ever have come.

Meanwhile, my relationship with Sigfrid had become like a bad marriage: the more she harassed me, the more I pushed back. In addition, a nasty racial undertone had crept into our increasingly testy interactions. My work, which mainly consisted of overseeing Texaco's dealings with my old colleagues at Chase, wasn't challenging. I had time on my hands I thought could be better used learning new skills that could benefit both me and the company. But when I asked for more demanding assignments, Sigfrid declined.

Thus, when my six-month PMP review drew near in June 1991, I was very concerned. I figured that Sigfrid would have considered my strong reaction to her three-month evaluation of my work as back talk of the sort that simply wasn't heard of—or allowed—at Texaco. She seemed to want me to kowtow to her instead of speaking my mind. She continually harped on my tendency to leave my office to do research or simply learn more about the huge building I hadn't really had time to explore, instead of sitting there trying to look busy. She continued to pick on trivial typing errors that occasionally slipped into reports that were conceptually flawless. It was like being disciplined by my mother.

Finally the big day came. Sigfrid summoned me to her office, and invited me to sit down on the opposite side of her desk. This time, the written PMP report was all about my work and my grades were very good. When she finished going over the written material, she laid aside the papers, folded her hands, drew a deep breath, and leaned toward me.

"Bari," she began in her thick Norwegian accent, "there are some things I want to tell you that are not on this written report. I didn't include them on it this time because you objected so much to my personal comments the last time I evaluated you.

"As your supervisor, I have to inform you that you are too much of a rebel.

"You are too direct with your superiors.

"You ask too many questions.

"You speak at meetings when you haven't been spoken to.

"You should watch how other people here conduct themselves and try to do as they do.

"This is for your own good."

I was astounded. Once again, a conversation that was supposed to concentrate on my work had instead honed in on Sigfrid's complaints about my personality.

"Sigfrid," I said to her, "would you do me the favor of putting those comments in writing, please?"

"I'll think about it," she said.

*　　*　　*

It took me a few minutes to compose myself after that bizarre confrontation. The first thing I did was to reach out to Florence Prawl in human resources. I told her what had happened as dispassionately as I could, but my blood was boiling. By the time I had gotten it all out, my course of action was clear.

"Florence," I vowed, "I am not going to work for this woman anymore. I'm not quitting the company because it has a lot to offer and I have a lot to offer. But I am not working for Sigfrid another minute if I don't have to.

"All I hear from people around here is that Texaco's changing. Sigfrid's just the kind of person who can keep change from happening."

It took nearly a month, though, before I could put my plan into action. I had to wait for Sigfrid to go on vacation so I could talk to Shelby without including her in the conversation. The delay gave me time to think carefully about how I would broach my desire for a change. In the end, I decided to handle it the same way I had handled my similar showdown with a supervisor at Chase more than a decade ago. I would keep race out of it.

"I've been here for six months or so," I told Shelby when I finally got into his office, "and it's just not working out between Sigfrid and me. The assignments she gives me are way below what I'm capable of doing and she keeps the best work for herself. There's not the kind of teamwork and inclusion that I would have expected from someone in her position. I really don't think there's a whole lot I can learn from her."

Shelby looked shocked. In my experience white male executives always look surprised when a black colleague criticizes the work of a white superior.

"I've known Sigfrid for fifteen years and I have the utmost confidence in her," he said. "I've always found her to be totally competent and one of the most knowledgeable people in the finance department."

I stood my ground. "I'm sure she is knowledgeable and

competent. But to me that's not the issue. The issue for me is that I feel that I'm being underutilized and I think I can contribute more with a different supervisor."

By now Shelby looked affronted as well as surprised. "Well, Bari, part of this is my responsibility because I told her to bring you along slowly since you're brand-new here and we wanted to make sure you were on solid ground."

"That would have been fine if I were a less experienced person," I replied, with a bit of an edge.

There was silence for a moment while Shelby seemed to regain his equilibrium. "I have to think about it. I reorganized the department just a few weeks before you arrived and I'm reluctant to do it again.

"I'll get back to you."

Short of quitting right on the spot I had no choice but to wait him out.

Over the next few months while I awaited Shelby's actions, my career at Texaco went into suspended animation. Sigfrid and I spoke only when it was absolutely necessary—with one jarring exception.

On one crisp Indian summer day three months after I had asked for a transfer, I took an after-lunch walk on the path around the huge artificial lake outside the Texaco building.

As I strode along I suddenly found myself walking alongside Sigfrid.

I don't know how the conversation got started, but after a few steps, she came to a sudden halt and turned toward me.

"Until you got here, this place was lily-white," she said. She was almost whining.

Before I could muster any response, Sigfrid turned away and resumed her quick shuffle along the pathway.

I stood there watching her disappear down the path, as speechless and deeply offended as I have ever been in my life. That night, after Staci had gone to bed, I sat alone in my living room, lost in thought and in as deep a funk as the ones I'd experienced during my childhood. I was overwhelmed by despair. Without realizing what I was doing I picked up the phone and put through a call to my father. When he answered, I was Cootsie again.

"Daddy, everything in my life has gone wrong," I sobbed. "Vence and I are getting divorced. The kids are having a tough time. I quit a job that I really loved and now I'm working with a bunch of racists. I don't know what I'm going to do."

Daddy had no specific advice, but he was calm and willing to listen as long as I was willing to talk. We stayed on the line until five A.M., when I finally collapsed. When Staci got up for breakfast the next morning, she found me, tangled up in my clothes, asleep in a living room chair.

CHAPTER NINE

HIGH POTENTIAL

I faced an age-old conundrum: how in the world does a black person constructively deal with bald-faced prejudice like Sigfrid's? After her off-the-wall remark, I could have quit on the spot or protested to Shelby about it, but I didn't think either would do any good. During those first few months at Texaco, I had become vested in a different approach that did not depend on either running away or complaining. In a fragmentary, slowly evolving way, I had begun to see my problems with Sigfrid as part of a much larger picture, and myself as an agent of change—the kind of change Texaco claimed that it wanted but could never achieve as long as it clung to its hidebound and oppressive traditions. Even now I'm not certain exactly how or precisely when the shift in my self-image occurred; I only know it was major. Texaco had promised me—and by extension all of its black employees—something when it recruited me. I was determined to make it live up to its word.

The rebirth of my assertiveness had less to do with Texaco than with serendipitous developments in my personal life. My divorce from Vence was not yet final in the legal sense, yet it had become a fact of my life psychologically. I was becoming accustomed to being on my own for the first time since I was a teenager, and though it was lonely, it was immensely liberating. My little apartment became a quiet haven for redefining myself, where I could immerse myself in books, conversation with friends, or my own thoughts. No longer did I have to suffer through Vence's carping about the way I was handling things. Brooke had gone to Chicago to visit with relatives for a few months because she was still angry with me. So except for Staci's, the only voice I had to listen to was my own. My physical strength had finally returned after the long struggle to cure my intestinal lesion. I was as robust and healthy as I had ever been, not to mention wide-open to change and new possibility, and amazingly happy.

Whatever life—or Texaco—brings, I was convinced, I can handle it.

That's probably why I let my girlfriend Laverne talk me into taking a five-day self-empowerment course down in New York early that fall, even though it sounded like the kind of pop psychology that I had always regarded as mumbo jumbo. True to my preconceptions, the course was studded with hokey clichés like "Today is the first day of the rest of your life," but its message got through to me. Perhaps it was the way that the slogan at the entrance to the hotel ballroom where the lectures were given—"IF YOU WANT CHANGE, YOU HAVE TO CHANGE"—was written in larger and larger letters at the start of each successive session. Perhaps it was the evangelical zeal of the lecturers. More likely it was simply that I was ready to hear that I could get back in control of my fate, no matter who was delivering the message. Whatever it was, I was so affected that I signed on for a second, more advanced session that led to one of the oddest but emotionally stirring epiphanies in my life.

While the first session had focused on how we looked out at the world, the second concentrated on how the world regarded each of us. In addition to rousing lectures we were given assignments outside the classroom, the last and most important of which was to eat a meal with a perfect stranger— not simply a stranger, but the sort of person we most feared and tended to shun. By now I was really into the course, and I took the assignment to heart. I chose a scary-looking, incredibly foul-smelling homeless man I had seen several times panhandling at Grand Central Station.

Course or no course, it took a huge effort not to wince as I timidly approached him and invited him to lunch. He, of course, was skeptical about my offer, but cagily agreed. I had to bribe the waiters in the café inside the station to seat us, a long distance away from the rest of the customers, who gawked at the two of us with looks so similar to the hostile stares our white coworkers shot at Sil and me when we had lunch in the Texaco cafeteria that I almost shuddered. As we perused the menus, I realized that he was holding his upside down: he couldn't read. To help him without embarrassing him, I read off the names of some of the items as though I were considering ordering them for myself.

After some awkward moments, I finally settled on a salad and he on a ham sandwich and a beer. When I asked the waiter, who was practically holding his nose as he took our order, what kind of beer was on tap, my shabby guest loudly asserted himself. "Gotsta be in a bottle," he said firmly. "That way I can drink some here and save the rest for later. Can't do that with no draft beer."

Over the hour or so that we spent together, my guest slowly and painfully told me his life story. He said he had been the victim of sexual abuse as a child, and hadn't ever gone to school. In his late teens he had run away to New York where he eked out a miserable existence as a male prostitute until a woman from Harlem took pity on him and invited him into her home. For a while he had tried to settle down with her and had taken jobs as a janitor. But when she got pregnant it had been too much for him and he fled back to the streets. Now he specialized in hustling change from commuters by assuming as intimidating a posture as he could manage when he approached them. A lot of them, especially women, would gladly pay to get him out of their sight.

"Why you ask me to eat with you?" he asked at the end of his tale, which I had listened to in growing but silent horror. I explained about the self-empowerment course.

"Oh," he said, a tad disappointed. "I thought you was going to pay me for sex."

It's difficult to put into words the effect his remark had on me. I didn't know whether to laugh or to cry. How could this derelict get the idea that an obviously professional woman like me, with her trim business suit, string of pearls, and attaché case might be so hungry for male companionship that I would reach out to a shabby urchin like him?

The encounter put my vulnerabilities into a new perspective. For the rest of the day, and many days after, I mused about the way I came across to other people—a bit distant, a bit formal, even a bit haughty. Did I also seem desperate and weak? Had I done anything to invite the enmity of my white coworkers? I couldn't think of a thing except being black and female. What did I really want from my colleagues and superiors at Texaco and how was I going to get it?

It came down to two things: respect and the rewards for excellent work that Texaco had promised when it recruited me. My white coworkers like Sigfrid seemed to assume that black folks like me and Sil had only been hired because of our race, not for our ability, and were being judged by a different and lower standard. Our mere presence in their heretofore all-white ranks seemed to unsettle them; we were members of an inferior species. It was even more dismaying for many of them when we upset their patronizing assumptions by doing our jobs as well as or better than they did instead of flopping as they had predicted. Well, that was the white folks' problem, not mine. I couldn't stop being black and a woman, of course; I wouldn't stop being myself. I was not going to alter my basic approach or hobble my dreams to fit into Texaco's stultifying regimen; that would cost me too much of my self-respect. The company's leaders had assured me over and over again that Texaco was changing. If they hadn't, I would not have come to work there. I didn't think of myself as a second-class citizen, and damn if I was going to be treated like one.

And then there was Waldo.

I'd been out on a few dates while waiting for the divorce to become final, but between the pressures of my new job and trying to cope with Brooke's and Staci's emotional swings, I wasn't ready for anything serious.

My cousin Vivian had flown in from California and I took her to Greenwich Village to see the sights and hear some music at a jazz brunch at the Blue Note. Afterward, as we strolled through Washington Square, I spotted a group of men intently watching a game of speed chess, and we wandered over to join them. I had recently begun to play again for the first time since high school.

The players—I think they were Russian emigrés—were highly skilled and kept up a running commentary as they moved their pieces and banged their time clocks. Watching them was completely engrossing. Then I heard a male voice asking me if I played. I turned and looked into the face of a tall, athletic young man with an engaging smile. We chatted for a few minutes until it was his turn to play—and get wiped out in just a few moves by one of the Russians. His rapid defeat, however, didn't seem to have any discernible effect on his confidence.

"I'd be happy to give you lessons," he said.

"After that thrashing, I don't know how much you can teach me," I laughed.

"Oh, I just wanted to get the game over with so I could come back and talk to you," he grinned. I just laughed and started to leave.

Vivian and I hadn't gone far when he ran up again and just started gushing:

"Please, give me your number. I've never done anything like this before, but I just have to see you again."

I replied, "Get the heck out of here."

But Vivian would have none of that. "Oh, Bari, just give him your number. What harm could it do? It might be fun, girl!"

I settled for giving him the number at work, and Viv and I headed home to Connecticut. As we made our way out of the park, Waldo was standing there, clutching the card with my number on it and gazing in my direction.

I know he was looking at me because I was looking back at him too.

My job situation was also improving. A few weeks after I had made it clear that I would no longer accept Sigfrid as an overseer, Shelby assigned me to a cross-departmental task force with a wide-ranging and challenging mandate: to study the impact of new federal banking regulations on Texaco's business and make recommendations for the best way to deal with them. As the pension and benefits division's representative to this rather high-profile committee—which was headed by Pete Wissel—I worked alongside people from all of the branches of the finance department, not just my own little group. My detailed knowledge of how banks operate quickly made me a valuable part of the team. I had sources of information—old friends at Chase and other banks—that I could tap for inside information about emerging trends in the industry, which at the time was reeling from the huge savings-and-loan scandal. For the first time since I had joined Texaco, I felt that my abilities were being tapped to the fullest. I actually started to have fun.

In a while I began to receive feedback about my performance. Our final report won raves from the highest Texaco officials like Allen Krowe, and Wissel gave me a fair share of the credit for what we had done. Sil Chambers told me that some of the most hostile white boys in the trading room were even saying that I really seemed to know my stuff. They had begun, grudgingly, to respect me. Technically, Sigfrid was still my boss, but I just stopped dealing with her. Ignoring the dictates of protocol, I went straight to Shelby when I needed to without getting her consent. As far as I was concerned she was out of the picture.

At Texaco, there were two staggered schedules for annual PMP reviews and salary increases, in October and April. Since I had started in December 1990 I fell on the October list. That meant I would get my first annual evaluation in the fall of 1991, a few months short of a full year on the job, and I was actually looking forward to it. I knew that my work, especially on the banking reform task force, had been more than satisfactory, so I wasn't concerned about it. The main question on my mind was whether I would get a raise and how much it would be.

But as the review season got underway, I found some aspects of it unsettling. Unlike many Texaco workers who had never worked anywhere else, I had something to compare it to. At Chase, I had learned that giving workers a clear and objective idea of their strengths and weaknesses was in the best interest of both the company and its employees. I had delivered evaluations of my staff for years and knew that criticism could be delivered to workers in a way that either encouraged them to try harder or destroyed their morale. Texaco's methods seemed to belong in the second category. For example, employees were never told in advance exactly when their review would take place, only that it was pending, so they had no way of knowing how long they'd have to wait. Your supervisor would just call you in one day and deliver the message cold turkey. To my mind, withholding something so basic as the timing of a review was another demeaning example of Texaco's despotic management style. Like so much in the Texaco culture, it could not have been more nerve-racking and intimidating if it had been designed to be. It struck me as a means of controlling people instead of getting the best out of them.

At least Sigfrid would not be delivering my evaluation all by herself, as would have been customary. Because of my protest about her, she took me to Shelby's office so he could be in on it. As far as I know I was the only analyst in the finance department to be accorded such singular treatment.

At the meeting, I used all I had learned about corporate one-upmanship and running business meetings from my long years at Chase to take control of the situation. I wanted to signal both Sigfrid and Shelby that she no longer had any authority over me. I knew that she would be too uncomfortable to sit next to me, so I carefully selected one of the chairs next to Shelby's desk, leaving Sigfrid no choice but to plunk down on the sofa on the far side of the room, beneath the four window panes that were Shelby's due as financial director of the P&B division. Shelby sat behind the desk, with his back to a big étagère overflowing with items from his noted collection of Texaco memorabilia—miniature gasoline trucks, service stations, oil tankers—he was Texaco to the core. By occupying the central position in the room, I had in a subtle way taken control of the session: I could choose to give Sigfrid attention or direct my comments to Shelby by merely turning my head.

She handed copies of my review to Shelby and me, then started reciting my ratings—overall, a G+, the third highest rating on a scale that went from O for "outstanding," S for

"strong," G for "good," N for "needs significant improvement" to U for "unsatisfactory." At Texaco, getting a G+ on
your PMP was extremely good news. If you got two G+ ratings
in a row, you would be in line for a promotion. When we
turned to the things I should focus on in the coming year, I
did most of the talking—all directed to Shelby. I made clear
my desire to expand my work with the actuary who was forecasting the pension plan's future needs. I also wanted to introduce some new investment products that Chase was offering
to help improve the performance of Texaco's master trust. I
concluded by telling them that I agreed with my evaluation
and that I was gratified that we had resolved some of the
problems we'd had—a vague but unmistakable reference to
the way Sigfrid had tormented me. They told me to return my
signed copy of the PMP to them in a day or two and the
meeting was over.

As I neared the door, I thought I heard Shelby mutter,
"Now, if you could just keep quiet."

The meeting ended so abruptly that I was almost back at
my desk before I realized that a vital piece of information was
missing, namely would I get a raise? I had heard through the
grapevine that salary increases were tied to your PMP rating,
but I didn't know what percentage a G+ translated to. Nor did
I know when the higher pay rate would start showing up in
my paycheck. These issues were of vital concern to me because
I had so many responsibilities for Staci. I wanted a bigger
apartment that would seem more like a home. Now that I was
driving to work every day instead of taking the train, I also
needed a more reliable car. But days passed after the review
with no word from Shelby or Sigfrid.

Finally, in some frustration, I went to Sigfrid and asked as
pleasantly as I could, "What's my raise?"

"I have nothing to do with that. Shelby will tell you if you
are getting one on the day it kicks in."

"But that doesn't make much sense," I said. "How are people supposed to make any plans?"

"He will give it to you when he's ready."

End of conversation.

That didn't work for me. I wanted—no, needed—to know now. I put myself through a quick self-evaluation of the kind I had learned in the self-empowerment course. If I just went to Shelby and demanded that he tell me, was I being rebellious? Was I being antagonistic? Was I going outside of protocol? The answer to all three was yes, but I still wanted to know.

So I walked past Shelby's secretary and leaned into his doorway, put on my broadest smile and chimed, "Is this a good time?"

He squinted furiously as he turned from his paperwork to face me. Once again, I had broken the rules by coming straight to him instead of coming through Sigfrid. His voice was almost a snarl: "What is it now?"

"May I close the door?"

He warily nodded assent.

"I'm very pleased with my evaluation," I began, "and I understand that based on my review I'm due for a raise soon and I'd like to know how much it is."

I could see him struggling to keep his temper. His mouth tightened. His cheeks puffed up. He quivered as he drew a deep breath.

"I give people that information on the day the raise shows up in their paycheck. That's the way I've always done it."

"I understand," I replied, "and perhaps that's comfortable for the rest of the people in the department, but it causes some problems for me. I really need to know exactly how much money I am going to have to deal with this coming year and I need to know soon. I'm requesting that you give me that information today or tomorrow."

By now the veins in Shelby's neck were bulging and the

fingers of his intertwined hands were locked so tightly I thought his knuckles would crack.

"I'll think about it."

Two days later Shelby called me in. After I was seated, he slowly reached under his desk blotter, pulled out an envelope and looked inside it, like a gambler peeking at his hole card. Then he placed it facedown on the desk and slid it to me. I picked it up.

"This is your raise, seven point five percent. Increases for G+ ratings this year were between seven and eight percent. I awarded you seven point five because of your above-average work. Congratulations."

It was a watershed. By merely insisting on receiving the respectful treatment I thought everyone was entitled to I had broken a ridiculous tradition. In small things at least, Texaco was changing, and I was helping the change.

Defying Texaco etiquette and getting away with it had consequences that spread like a ripple on a pond. I came to be seen as a person to be reckoned with, to be taken seriously and dealt with accordingly, to be listened to with respect. I felt like I had survived an initiation. I was obviously not one of the good old boys who dominated all aspects of Texaco life, and I never wanted to be one. But I had shown, to anyone who wanted to see it, that I could be part of the team without mindlessly kowtowing to all of its rules.

I stood out. And so I was sought out.

It started in February 1992, Black History Month, when Florence called me on behalf of her boss, Ron Boilla, the director of human resources. Texaco had bought a table at the United Negro College Fund Dinner and Boilla wanted me to attend. I quickly agreed.

But a few days later Flo called back with a second request.

Could I send Boilla some background on myself and my date, so he'd be familiar with everyone at the table?

"Sure," I replied. "Is he going to send me the background on himself and his wife?"

Florence laughed in surprise. "Bari, what are you saying?"

"I'm saying that if I give him the background on myself and my date I want his. That's reciprocity."

"Oh, Bari. That's not the way things are done here. He's not gonna like it."

"Well, unless he sends me his background I'm afraid I can't accept his invitation. That's the way I do things. Otherwise, I'm not gonna like it."

I don't know if Flo ever passed on my request to her boss or wrote it off as too outrageous. I did not see it as an act of rebellion, but as yet another call to be treated with dignity and respect. Moreover, I was wary of being used as a "twofer," whose highly visible presence at the dinner would give the misleading impression that blacks and women were well-represented in Texaco's workforce. Flo never got back to me about Boilla's background and I never went to the dinner.

It didn't seem to have negative consequences. A few weeks later Flo contacted me again on Boilla's behalf. This time he wanted to have lunch with a few fairly senior level black professionals to discuss Texaco's campaign for racial diversity. She, Sil, and I would be the only guests.

The lunch took place in a small but elegant dining room adjacent to the basement level cafeteria. Our host, Boilla, turned out to be a born-again Christian and a bore. He recited the standard spiel that Texaco was changing in a thick Texas twang that made my teeth grind. But a touch of genuine enthusiasm came into his voice when he talked about the company: he had worked there for thirty years and couldn't imagine anyplace better.

I sat quietly, keeping my counsel, while Boilla droned on

about a new initiative that the company was launching: the Texaco Award for Excellence teams—known as TAFE teams—that were being set up to reward fresh thinking and innovation throughout the company. There were going to be TAFE teams in every department, and they would reach out to every employee. Regardless of race, creed, or color, Boilla wanted everybody to be part of the process.

Could he count on us for support?

We all said he could. What else could we say?

Well, okay then, Boilla concluded. This has been a very good meeting. In a few weeks I'd like all of you to join me again for a session with my boss, John Ambler, the head of human resources for the entire company. I'm sure he'll be very interested in everything you have to say.

Later Sil, Flo, and I got together to analyze Boilla's remarks. We were all encouraged. Boilla seemed to be saying that human resources really wanted some input from blacks about making diversity succeed. If so, we must be prepared. We'd do some real research on what other big companies were doing to attract and retain qualified minorities. We'd take their best ideas, combine them into a list of suggestions, and present it to Ambler.

To us, it seemed like a grand opportunity and we were eager, even anxious, to seize it. We could have a voice. We could be part of the team. We could bring about the change that we wanted by working through the Texaco system. What more could we possibly ask?

I was deeply immersed in preparing for the meeting with Ambler when Allen Krowe, Texaco's chief financial officer, invited me to pay a call on him in his office. It was an invitation I had been hoping for because making a good impression on Krowe was vital to my future prospects. I had learned from Florence and the grapevine that Krowe, more than anyone else, was responsible for pushing the idea that Texaco's changing.

He was still a bit of an outsider despite his enormous power. And he evidently believed in diversity.

I made sure that Shelby knew that Krowe had summoned me.

"Do I need to be there?" he asked.

"Did his secretary call and invite you?" I asked back.

"No, she didn't."

"Well, I guess you don't need to be there."

Not five minutes after I left his room, I saw Shelby on his way to the office of Bob Ulrich, who had become Texaco's treasurer a few months earlier after Dave Crikelair moved on to another assignment. I have no doubt that Shelby wanted to make certain that Ulrich, a notorious control freak even by Texaco's rigid standards, was aware of my summons from Krowe. If there was one thing a cautious bureaucrat like Shelby wanted to avoid, it was having his boss be surprised.

When the big day finally came that February I dressed with even more than usual care—my most conservative suit adorned with a demure string of pearls. As I rode the elevator to the third floor where Texaco's top management was ensconced behind thick wooden doors that led to the so-called Mahogany Suite, I ran through the lessons I had learned in the self-empowerment course about dealing with potentially life-changing choices. The key was to be direct, state clearly what I wanted to accomplish, and be prepared to live with the answer. If it was yes, I would take on the new opportunity and exploit it to the maximum. If it was no, I would figure out ways to make it harder to be turned down the next time around.

Krowe did not disappoint me: he was quality. Unlike the managers in the finance department, whose fidelity to rigid rules was a mask for timidity and a lack of imagination, his every gesture exuded deep-seated self-confidence. And he looked the part—a big, burly man with weight lifter's shoulders under a perfectly tailored dark gray business suit. His charisma was palpable. He gave me the impression that talking with me was the most important appointment on his calendar, at least for that day. He steered me to the couch and he took a seat in an adjacent armchair.

"I've been hearing good things about you," he began in a fantastically well-modulated baritone, and then ran through a quick and well-informed summary of my recent endeavors. "Now tell me, how have you been treated? How are you finding things here."

For the next fifteen minutes or so, we chatted about my experiences. I focused exclusively on the work I had been doing, without a word about my relationships with Shelby and Sigfrid. I hadn't come up there to whine, but to pose a big question!

"What would it take to become your assistant?"

"You know, I handle my assistants differently from the other top people around here," he replied. "Al DeCrane (Texaco's president) and Jim Kinnear (the chairman) usually keep someone with them for two years, but usually I only keep them for six months, and expose them to everything. I believe in giving a lot of people a chance to get that kind of exposure rather than just one person for a couple of years. Maybe you should talk to my last two assistants and see what it's like."

He had not shut the door.

"You may not know this, Bari," he continued, "but you're on the high-potential list—people who are strong candidates for advancement. People on that list get high-profile assignments. Sometimes they get to travel on the corporate jet with me or DeCrane, things like that."

I had never heard that before. I didn't know there was a high-potential list, or imagined that I might be on it. To my surprise, my normal reserve slipped a little, and I blurted out how complimented I was by what he had told me.

He hadn't agreed to make me his assistant, but then he

hadn't ruled it out either. I left his office a few minutes later, practically walking on air.

I couldn't wait to tell Florence the news.

"Yeah, girlfriend, I saw that," she said, "but I thought you should hear it from Krowe and not me. There have been a few other blacks on that list but none of them have really gone anywhere. "

"Well, I think I nudged him a bit by asking to be his assistant."

"Girlfriend, no, you didn't," laughed Florence. "Go ahead for yourself! Who knows, maybe in your case the dream will come true."

You bet it will, I thought. Because Texaco's changing.

I completed my research for the meeting with John Ambler in a mood of anticipation bordering on euphoria. He was an important figure in the Texaco pantheon, the vice president in charge of human resources for the entire company. If we could impress him with our suggestions it could reverberate from one end of Texaco to the other. I devoured books and articles in *Black Enterprise* magazine about the best affirmative action plans in corporate America, called friends at other companies to get their ideas, and consulted constantly with Florence and Sil. Given the fragile racial climate at Texaco and the ingrained resistance to change, we knew we couldn't recommend anything radical. We'd stick to programs that had been tried at other big companies and proven to work—-like basing managers' bonuses in part on how well they implemented diversity, or starting a black employees association, or beefing up recruiting from black colleges. Conservative and obvious as these approaches seemed, Texaco hadn't adopted even one of them.

John Ambler made me uneasy from the moment he walked in the room. He was a big-boned, dark-haired man with a scowl that penetrated right through his phony smile. He did not greet us. Instead he walked across the room to a side table, grabbed a handful of peanuts from a bowl, and loudly popped them one by one into his mouth. When Boilla introduced Sil, he reached across the table to shake Sil's hand. When Ron introduced me, he just sat there, and nodded slightly in my direction. He evidently did not believe in shaking hands with females.

Then he started talking, in a thick Virginia drawl. How he had been at Texaco for thirty-three years and it was a really great company. How the bankruptcy had forced Texaco to take a hard look at itself. How the TAFE teams were the key to the quality initiative that would bring the company all the way back and make it even better than ever before. And how he was counting on us to be part of the process.

After we ate, Ambler got down to business. "What do you think of Texaco?"

My turn. "I'm glad you asked that," I said. "Sil and I have both been here for a while now and we can see that Texaco's changing. We're really thrilled by the quality initiative and the TAFE teams and we want to be part of that process. We thought that today we could offer some ideas of how to speed up the change and make the quality initiative work better with respect to diversity.

"In fact," I added as I passed out copies of the list of suggestions that we had prepared, "we'd like to present a few ideas that we think will work. All of them have been adopted at other major corporations and Texaco might want to consider taking a similar approach."

Sil and I then began an animated presentation of our report. But we weren't very far into it before I noticed Ambler's growing discomfort. He was leaning back from the table, looking up at the ceiling, drumming his fingers on the table.

Then, suddenly, just as Sil was in the midst of explaining why Texaco should increase its advertising in black-owned media, Ambler exploded. He slammed his hand on the table, lunged toward us, and bellowed:

"You people must have lost your minds! I think you're a bunch of militants! I've been here for thirty-three years and I can tell you right now that Texaco will not even consider any of these crazy proposals! We'll never do any of these things! The next thing you know we'll have Black Panthers running down the halls or around the circle in front of the building! We're not having that here!"

Needless to say, we were appalled.

"What do you mean, militant?" I demanded. I had lost my cool, and so had Florence. "Heck," she interjected, "we don't even know any Black Panthers! What in the world are you talking about?"

"As far as I'm concerned this meeting is over," Ambler shouted, then leaped up from the table and stalked toward the door. "Come along, Ron."

CHAPTER TEN

THE DIE IS CAST

If John Ambler hadn't acted like a racist bully, the case of *Roberts v. Texaco* might never have been filed. His insulting surprise attack on Flo, Sil, and me changed everything. In a very real sense it was the first shot fired in an epic legal battle over racial discrimination that ultimately would cost Texaco $176.1 million in settlement costs, millions more in legal fees, and catastrophic damage to its carefully guarded reputation. It needn't have happened. Ambler's explosion was merely the first of many occasions when Texaco could have averted humiliation by keeping the lofty promises contained in the company's official statement of its visions and values: *to treat each employee with dignity, to provide opportunities for development and advancement, and to maintain an environment where employees feel free to provide input into business decisions, to improve the system and to make a difference.*

Texaco did not live up to those words, so it wound up eating them.

*   *   *

Right up to the moment of Ambler's rant, I had been willing to give Texaco the benefit of the doubt about whether it really was changing. I had tried to work through the system. I had gone out of my way to keep the gratuitous prejudice I had encountered from my first day on the job from becoming an issue in my dealings with coworkers and managers. Indeed, I had borne it in silence except when the behavior was so obnoxious I was forced to speak up. I had never complained to Shelby or Allen Krowe about Sigfrid's offensive remarks or the snide taunts from white coworkers that I overheard when I walked down the halls or sat down in the cafeteria. I had never filed a protest with management about the unbelievable jerk who invaded my office and assailed me for taking "his" job. But after Ambler's screaming fit, the issue of race was on the table and could no longer be avoided. It had been raised in the ugliest and most destructive way possible. This was no random racist remark by a mid-level manager like Sigfrid. Ambler was the vice president in charge of the very department that was supposed to make Texaco change, speaking on behalf of the entire company.

The mystery was how someone so crude and intolerant could rise to such a sensitive position at a Fortune 500 corporation like Texaco during the 1990s. Though corporate America, like the rest of society, still has more than its share of whites who hate blacks, at most major companies overt expressions of racial hostility are extremely rare not just because they are wrong, but also because they are bad for business. By the time they reach Ambler's level, most executives who harbor racist attitudes have long since learned to conceal them behind a facade of phony politeness and code words. At Texaco, a different standard seemed to apply. Ambler had spent more than three decades at the company in other departments and had little formal training in human resources. His hostility toward diversity was unmistakable. Yet Texaco's leaders had elevated him to a position in which he could affect the destiny of thousands of people from all racial groups. It was obvious that they didn't care enough about human resources to put a qualified person in charge.

Sil, Flo, and I were not militants or Black Panthers, we were believers in the American Dream and the corporate system. We had come to the meeting—at Ambler's invitation, relayed to us through his deputy Ron Boilla—to help Texaco improve its diversity, not to pick a fight over race. Every idea we brought to the table had been tried and proven effective at major corporations like IBM, AT&T and Levi Strauss. Every initiative we suggested had been written about in business publications and newspapers, discussed on TV, debated in Congress and state legislatures—and even, I'm quite sure, in Ambler's own human resources department. Yet Ambler acted like he had never heard such outlandish notions, let alone taken them seriously. He treated them like a Marxist manifesto, not a moderate proposal drawn from the mainstream of corporate America. The man was not just a racist, but an ignoramus. How dare he, or anybody at Texaco, question the qualifications of blacks when he was so poorly prepared for his own job?

From that moment on, I believed that John Ambler's growl, not Allen Krowe's honeyed baritone, was the true voice of Texaco. It was the voice of George Wallace standing in the school house door bellowing "segregation forever," the voice of the mob heckling my sixth grade class as our bus pulled up to an all-white school, the voice of the white cop dragging my father away to beat him and rob him, the voice of the bank vice president telling me I could not be promoted because white customers would not accept me. I could almost hear it every time I reported to work:

"Texaco will never do any of these things!

"Never!

"Never!

"Never!"

*   *   *

Once the initial shock of the meeting wore off, I started to worry about my future. My gravest concern was that Ambler would poison the well against Flo, Sil, and me at just the time when I thought that the worst of my troubles with Texaco had begun to fade. Only a few days before, I had received a good PMP, a decent raise and the exciting news that I was on the high-potential list with the promise of high-profile assignments and speedy promotions. Now, in what seemed like a blink of an eye, all of that was in jeopardy. Waldo and I had been dating regularly for a few months, and found that we had a lot in common because we both worked in finance. That night over dinner I told him, "I guess I can forget about the high-potential list. Ambler's going to tell all the good old boys that I'm a Black Panther and it will be all over." Hearing my story made Waldo as depressed as I was. We hardly touched our meal.

Sil bounced back quicker than I did because so many exciting things were happening in his career. Shortly before the fateful lunch, the promotion and raise he had been waiting for all those months had finally come through; he was now a grade sixteen senior financial analyst, the same level as me, and making about $70,000 a year. He'd led a team that won a Texaco Treasurer's Award for executing a program of interest rate swaps that had saved the company millions of dollars: two shares of stock and his name on a plaque on the wall of the trading room. He was getting along extremely well with his boss, Steve Koch, the manager of the trading room—so well, in fact, that Koch declared he was grooming Sil to succeed him as manager when he moved on to another job. As a first step, Koch had recommended that Sil be promoted to assistant manager, with a grade increase to level seventeen. Then, after Koch moved on, becoming manager would be a natural progression; in one of Sil's favorite phrases, "a piece of cake."

Bob Ulrich had other ideas. In February 1992, he invited Sil to his office along with senior assistant treasurer Dave Keough to discuss Sil's future. In contrast to his usual gruff demeanor, Ulrich was warm, almost avuncular. He was clearly trying to give Sil the impression he had Sil's best interest at heart.

Rather than stay in the trading room, Ulrich said, he wanted Sil to transfer out of cash management to the corporate finance department as part of the regular departmental rotation. It would expose Sil to a new aspect of Texaco's finances and enhance his résumé. "If you are going to progress, you've got to do a little of everything," Ulrich told him. "You just can't stay in cash management and expect to move up. Transferring to corporate finance will be better for your career."

Even so, Sil had to think about it. If he stayed in the trading room, his promotion to assistant manager and eventually manager appeared to be a virtual certainty, if Koch had his way. But if Sil declined the move to corporate finance, he might be turning his back on an even brighter long-term prospect—and offending Ulrich unnecessarily. Sil had enough confidence in his skills to believe he could meet any challenge corporate finance might throw at him, and he wanted to move up, so he agreed to the transfer.

Under his new boss, Peter Meade, the manager of corporate finance, Sil got off to a very fast start. His responsibilities expanded enormously. He was no longer simply executing trades, he was plotting money market strategy. He was put in charge of the "corporate revolver"—a two billion dollar line of credit with several banks which Texaco used to make highly profitable short-term loans to other companies. In addition, he had the not unpleasant duty of buttering up officers from the banks Texaco dealt with. He'd bring them up to Harrison every three or four months for a lavish lunch, and sit in when they hobnobbed with Ulrich or Keough. It was a perfect assignment for a man with Sil's gregariousness and transparent sincerity. He ate it up. He was terrific.

*   *   *

His new team was a different story. Three financial analysts were assigned to report to him, but only one of them—a young white man named Don—was a top-notch performer. Debra*, the white woman in charge of bank administration, always seemed to be tired, probably because in addition to her demanding job in corporate finance she was working a second job in a restaurant owned by her family. Her reports were so filled with mistakes that Sil had to almost redo them from scratch to make them acceptable.

Finally, there was Larry Barnes. Larry was a young black man who had climbed up from Chicago's South Side ghetto to attend Howard University and Duke University, where he earned an MBA. He had only been at Texaco for a few months, but he was already in serious trouble. Despite his utter lack of experience, corporate finance had given him responsibility for a $750 million interest rate swap program so complex that it would have tested the skills of a savvy Wall Street veteran. Larry knew that he desperately needed coaching and training to stand any chance of succeeding and he had repeatedly asked his bosses to provide it. But until Sil arrived, every one of his requests had fallen on stone-deaf ears.

Sil's team remained intact only until mid-1992 when Meade moved on to another assignment. Sil's new boss was Robert "Bob" Gordan, who transferred up from the Texaco operation in Coral Gables. Gordan had a reputation of being a tough, even ruthless manager, but he quickly set Sil at ease. He told him that he had heard good things about him from Peter Meade, and was sure they would work well together.

But within days, Gordan made a move that undercut Sil dramatically. He removed Don from Sil's team and placed him under his own direct supervision. Losing the only first-rate analyst on his team put Sil in a pickle. The people left on his staff were two of the weakest performers in the entire depart-

---

* pseudonym

ment. That was a recipe for disaster because supervisors were held accountable for the work of their underlings.

To a less trusting soul than Sil, Gordan's personnel moves would have looked like a set-up. They sure looked like one to me. During my fifteen years in corporate America I had seen white executives set up black folks to fail by giving them a difficult job, denying them the resources and training they needed to do it, and then judging them—and by implication all other blacks—by the harshest possible standard when things didn't work out, as inevitably they didn't. Indeed, something like that had been done to me during my first years at Chase Manhattan. It was not really anything new.

But what Bob Gordan did to handicap Sil over the next few months took sabotage to a new level. Of all the weapons he could have employed, Gordan chose Larry Barnes.

In my experience before coming to Texaco, senior managers often took a deep personal interest in the fate of young people they brought into their companies, and often became their mentors. Since Gordan himself had recruited Larry, he hoped that Gordan's arrival in corporate finance would mean that he would finally get the hands-on counseling and training that he so desperately needed. But instead of coming to Larry's aid with advice and support, Gordan totally ignored him. He left Larry to sink or swim on his own.

Sil already had his hands full with restructuring the corporate revolver, a huge and complicated transaction that demanded all of his time and attention. Yet he had to take time to correct Debra's error-filled reports and back-stop Larry. There were not that many hours in the day.

So Sil suggested to Gordan that Larry should be brought up to speed by sending him to special short courses that various banks and business schools conducted around the country. It would be an investment in Larry's future.

Over and over again, Gordan turned him down.

The reasons were varied. There was no money in the budget for Larry's tuition. There was no money in the budget to fly Larry to out-of-town courses. Larry should find cheaper alternatives. Larry should find free alternatives. I'll think about it. Maybe next year.

The heartbreaking long and short of it was that Larry's morale slumped as it became clear that Gordan was unwilling to invest anything in his training. Sensing his frustration, Sil took to coming in on weekends to tutor Larry on his work. He even set up meetings between Larry and some old friends from Wall Street who knew swaps inside out.

But despite the marked improvement that Sil noticed in Larry's work, his young subordinate had been targeted by the finance department for failure. In November, Gordan called Sil into his office.

He told Sil he was not happy with the quality of the work from his team. He'd had to hand back some reports that Larry had done because they were unacceptable, and one of Debra's reports contained a mistake that had slipped through the cracks and made it all the way to Allen Krowe.

He wasn't happy either, Sil replied. Debra's work had gotten better, but she still made so many errors he'd be better off doing the work himself in the first place. Larry desperately needed training and he could not seem to get it. Maybe they ought to move him to a new area where he could do better.

"Well, I know you've been given bad people to work with," said Gordan. "Do the best you can with them. We won't hold it against you. Your own projects are going just fine."

A few days later Sil sat down with his wife and kids for a prayerful Thanksgiving dinner. But even as he thanked God for his manifold gifts he did not count having a boss like Bob Gordan among them.

The other shoe dropped after New Year's as corporate finance began its annual round of PMP evaluations. Larry, Sil figured, deserved an overall G because in Sil's view he was hardworking and productive and his work had improved. He would have rated Larry higher if his technical skills had been better.

Gordan disagreed. When he and Sil sat down to go over Larry's PMP, Gordan dropped it at least a notch—from G to G− and, from G− to N, for "needs significant improvement"— in virtually every category. By the time Gordan was through, Larry's overall PMP rating was G−, the third from the bottom. With such a blot on his record at that early stage of his career, Larry had no real future at Texaco. Indeed, he was doomed. It broke Sil's heart.

Over the next two or three weeks Sil tried over and over again to persuade Gordan to change his mind about Larry's rating. But as with Sil's pleas to get Larry some training, Gordan was adamant in his refusal. Not long after that, Larry was transferred to pensions and benefits, where I became his second black supervisor. But even though Larry was no longer in corporate finance, his shadow loomed over Sil's career like a haunt he could never escape.

That March, Gordan called in Sil for his own PMP. He thought he had nothing to worry about. His work on the corporate revolver and accounts receivable had gone well. He had even gotten a letter from Bob Ulrich commending him and his team for their work on a difficult project. But as he listened to Gordan rattle on, Sil became increasingly uneasy. Gordan had hardly mentioned Sil's own work—only the less than sterling performance of his subordinates.

"We have to lower your rating because the people under you had bad ratings," Gordan said. "You're getting a G-minus."

For once Sil didn't smile. At last he saw through Gordan's game. With a G− PMP his hopes for advancement were dashed. He would not get the best assignments. His career would go into a tailspin. He exploded.

"I disagree with everything on here. It's a pack of lies. It doesn't say anything positive at all! This PMP doesn't say anything about the good work I've done that you praised me for!

It doesn't say anything about the letter I got from Bob Ulrich! Why'd you leave all that out?

"All this year we've talked about the problems with my team and you said you understood and wouldn't hold it against me! If I'm getting a bad rating because the people under me have a bad rating, you should get one too, since I work for you!

"G-minus!

"This is baloney!

"Why are you doing this, Bob?"

NOB—Nancy's Out Box. That's what my colleagues in P&B started calling me after Shelby finally decided to respond to my request for a new supervisor in the spring of 1992. Her name was Nancy Nakovick.

Nancy was no racist, but she had some issues. She was a brilliant woman with degrees from the prestigious Wharton School of Business and M.I.T., but had only been an assistant manager for a few months when I joined her team. I found her to be moody and insecure, inclined to boss all of her subordinates around instead of managing them. We did not get along.

One afternoon she stormed into my office waving some papers and yelling at me and I set her straight. "Just close the door and leave right now," I told her as calmly as I could. "I'm not putting on a show by getting into a screaming match. This is an office, not an asylum. Nobody yells at me at work."

After several similar confrontations, Nancy stopped talking to me altogether. She'd just leave my assignments in my out box and stalk off without a word—hence my derisive nickname, NOB. Our clashes continued until Nancy finally got the message that I expected to be treated respectfully and started to chill out. After that, our relationship slowly began to improve.

Domesticating my new boss, however, was not my topmost

concern. I was still waiting to see what the repercussions would be from the catastrophic luncheon with John Ambler. There wasn't anything I could put my finger on except a subtle change in the atmosphere. Shelby, who had always been friendly enough in the past, even when I annoyed him, seemed to have trouble looking me straight in the face and resorted to oblique glances. But I could not really tell if Shelby was backing away from me, because he also saw to it that I got tougher, more challenging assignments. In addition to working with the actuary and Chase, I was given responsibility for some of the equity futures transactions we were exploring as a hedge against downturns in the economy. It was a new area for me, more visible than my previous tasks, and I was excited. After I heard from Florence that the only thing Ambler had said about the meeting was that it had not been what he expected and that he had been disappointed, I let down my guard just a little. Maybe, just maybe, I thought, there won't be any repercussions after all.

There was only one way to find out—by making some requests. I was nearing my fortieth birthday, and was anxious to move up the ladder. I had taken the measure of my coworkers and knew that my work was at least equal to theirs. If Nancy could move up from senior financial analyst to assistant manager, I didn't see why I couldn't or shouldn't. Dave Keough had told me when he was recruiting me that it was possible that someday I could be sitting where he was sitting, in a four-pane office with the credenza and nice artwork that went with being an assistant treasurer. I knew I was not going to get there, or anywhere near there, unless I got more exposure, the kind of high-profile assignments that would allow me to work closely with senior management and become more to them than a face and a name—in short, the opportunities that were a benefit of being on the "high-potential list." To use army slang, I had to get my ticket punched in a number of demanding jobs before I could expect to move up. I wasn't looking to skip over several grades in one leap, but to steadily climb the ladder by doing well in a variety of jobs in different departments.

But at Texaco, it was the nature of things for those plums to fall to white males who were part of the good old boy network, or to a few white women who belonged to its ladies auxiliary. Exciting opportunities were rarely posted publicly, so you couldn't even apply. When I managed to get wind of something interesting it had usually been filled by the time I heard about it. I put in for those opportunities anyway—the prestigious annual Texaco conference at which select employees from all of the company's worldwide branches got to hobnob with the company's highest officers and brainstorm about Texaco's future; a task force that was going to London to work on international financing; even missions as mundane as traveling to dreary Bakersfield, California, to review a high-priority alternative energy program. Sometimes I simply asked Shelby to consider me, sometimes I put it in writing. I made a point of stating that I wanted to be considered for promotion to assistant manager and international assignments on the formal career self-assessment form that I filed that May. I even indicated that I would relocate without limitation in order to get it.

I don't know if anyone read it.

Regardless of how urgently I made my requests, or the form in which I expressed them, the answer was always the same: It was always no.

Of course I would not accept that. If the path before me was barred, I would search for another. I had tamed Nancy. Once she figured out that she couldn't cow me, our testy relationship evolved into a de facto alliance based upon the quality of my work. I made a point of congratulating her whenever she did something that impressed me, which appealed to her pride in her intellect. She began to relax. I still had to watch her. More than once she praised some report I had prepared, then tried to take credit for it when she gave it to Shelby. Her growing reliance on me did not preclude her from occasionally trying to stab me in the back. On a few occasions, I put an end to the deception by letting Shelby know who was actually responsible for the work.

At the same time I eagerly sought opportunities that were not directly related to my work to enhance my reputation as a team player. For example, when Florence suggested me as Texaco's representative to the United Way Campaign for the New York, New Jersey, and Connecticut area, I leaped to accept. It was not only a good cause but a chance to wow prominent managers from other big companies with whom I'd be working. It paid off. In September, the president of United Way wrote to Texaco's chairman, praising my work on the charity's finance committee and thanking him for lending them the services of one of Texaco's "best and brightest." The chairman passed it on to me with a warm handwritten note thanking me for "your willingness, your dedication, and your success with this great cause"—which naturally went into my official employee file where my bosses would notice it when the time came for my next PMP.

More important, I plunged into the Texaco Award for Excellence campaign that had been top management's hottest priority ever since I joined the company. I served on a four-member task force on human resources in the finance department with two men destined to play a pivotal part in this story—Rich Lundwall, the human resources manager for the finance department, and James Link, who, like Dave Keough, was a senior assistant treasurer. Our task was to suggest ways in which the finance department could improve its use of human resources, including diversifying its workforce. If our ideas were good, there was a chance they'd be adopted by the entire company—and I'd get a share in the glory.

I immediately ran into trouble. As we sat around discussing how to answer one of the questions on the elaborate TAFE form, Link leaned back from the table and barked in an authoritative tone:

"How did we answer this one last year? Let's just use that again."

That made no sense to me, so I asked a question in what I thought was a constructive and sensible tone.

"Did the way we answered it last year win an award?" I asked.

"No," Link replied.

"Well, if it didn't win last year, it probably won't win this year," I said. "I think we need a new approach."

Dead silence, until Lundwall cleared his throat, took off his glasses, and fixed me with a stare of the sort that a parent directs at a misbehaving toddler.

"Bari," he said, in a tone suggesting he couldn't believe what he'd just witnessed, "we don't do that here."

"Do what?"

"Speak up."

Now I understood. As Lundwall had reminded me, I had committed the unpardonable sin of disagreeing with the opinion of a high-ranking good old boy. It was a crime Texaco would never forgive.

Shortly after Christmas I took my first real vacation in years, a ten-day trip to Egypt with a group of friends. In Cairo, I visited the Sphinx. I realized as I gazed into its face that I was having as much trouble trying to solve my problems with Texaco as ancient wise men did trying to solve the riddle of the Sphinx.

In January 1993, it was PMP season again and time for my annual review. Nancy summoned me to her desk with such a big smile I knew it was going to be good.

"Bari, your work has been excellent across the board," she began. "Ss in some areas, nothing less than a G-plus in any category. Overall, I rate you as an S. You're probably in line

for promotion. Congratulations." Nancy was beaming, and so
was I.

That night Waldo and I celebrated what now seemed to be
the end of my ordeal. I'd been told repeatedly that two strong
PMP ratings—G+s or better—in a row would put me in line
for a promotion, and now Nancy herself had confirmed it. I
was sure that the high-profile work Allen Krowe had promised
me would materialize now that I'd got an S.

Two days later my smiles turned to rage.

I knew something was up when I saw the pained, embarrassed look on Nancy's face as we sat down to talk. At first
she was too choked up to speak. Finally, as she handed me
my PMP, she managed to get out a few words, in a voice so
halting that it verged on a stutter.

"I don't know how to tell you this, Bari. But your rating's
been changed.

"Instead of getting an S, it's been lowered to G-plus."

At first I couldn't believe it. I looked at the PMP in stunned
incomprehension and slowly leafed through its pages. Some of
the S ratings Nancy had given me had been erased and replaced with G+s. On the last page my overall mark had indeed
been changed to a G+. I could see the erasures. I sat there
gritting my teeth and then asked Nancy, "Why?"

She fidgeted around in her chair.

"I don't know if I should be telling you this. Management
had a discussion and Jim Link said that when you were working with him on the TAFE team you were uppity. So they
lowered your rating."

I didn't say anything, and Nancy went on, "Oh, Bari, this
is not so bad. You still got a G-plus, that's still a good rating.
It could have been so much worse.

"You should hear how they talk about blacks in those meetings! There's all kinds of racial jokes and stuff. My family's
from Poland and I know they probably tell Polish jokes if I'm
not in the room. I even heard Dave Keough call you a 'little

colored girl!' That's just the way it is here. You can't do any-thing about it. I have to sit there and listen to that junk, but I can't do anything.

"I know you're hurt and I know you're angry but I've got to ask you to sign this. I think you're a terrific human being now that we've gotten to know each other, and I would never do anything to hurt you. Please, Bari, don't get too upset. Please sign this thing and get it back to me soon. I have to have it."

"No, Nancy, I'm not going to sign it," I replied. "This is wrong, just plain wrong. I'm not going along with it for a minute."

I left Nancy's office in a near trance and made my way to a quiet room near the cafeteria. First Ambler had called me a Black Panther. Now Link was calling me "uppity." Now they were pressuring me, through Nancy, to go along with a racist downgrade in my rating without so much as a peep of com-plaint. They might as well have called me a nigger and told me to stay in "my place." Now I understood why at Texaco PMP's were so often written in pencil—to make them easy to fiddle with.

It wasn't a glass ceiling I was up against.

It was a brick wall.

CHAPTER ELEVEN

DESPERATE HOURS

I didn't realize how defeated I felt until tears started rolling down my face as I drove home that evening. My long-standing vow never to cry at work or about work had been washed away in a flood of contradictory emotions. One moment, I was raging at Texaco for the sucker punch it had hurled at me, the next I was kicking myself for ever believing that the company's good old boys would ever be fair in the first place.

I got home to a dark and empty apartment. Brooke had moved away and Staci, now a spunky tenth-grader, had stayed after school to run in a track meet. Under normal circumstances, I would have reveled in the few rare moments of solitude the girls' absence provided, but after the traumatic events of the day, the last thing I needed was to be alone. Still weeping uncontrollably, I raced to my room and flung myself on the bed. It took a while for me to collect myself enough to telephone Waldo.

After our last upbeat conversation about getting an S on

my PMP, he was expecting more good news, maybe even about the promotion Nancy had hinted was coming. I could almost hear his jaw drop as I told him what had actually happened.

"I don't understand. How can they just lower your rating like that?" he asked, in an incredulous tone. "Didn't Nancy check it out with her bosses before she gave it to you?"

"She told me she had shown it to Shelby and he didn't have any problems with it," I said.

"I've never heard anything like that before at a big company like Texaco," said Waldo. "I can't believe it."

"Neither can I."

After we hung up, I retrieved a copy of the evaluation that Nancy had given me less than forty-eight hours earlier and laid it next to the one she'd given me that afternoon. Not a single word of Nancy's complimentary remarks about my performance had been changed, only my rating.

She had written, for example, that my "thorough and effective presentation to management" about Texaco's possible participation in new securities lending programs had produced "ongoing, substantial savings" for the company—that was still there.

She had praised my "ongoing and timely execution" of a monthly market update that the company's financial strategists used to plan our investment decisions—that was still there.

She had complimented my "good progress" toward developing a thorough understanding of the technical aspects of pension fund asset allocations and funding methods—that was still there.

There were no criticisms at all.

The good old boys had not even bothered to inject any negative comments, no matter how bogus, about my work into the report as a pretext for lowering my rating.

The message was clear: I was not being punished for my work, but for my attitude.

I had just finished reviewing the documents when Staci burst in, proudly brandishing a blue ribbon she had won in the 4×200 meter relay. When she saw the stricken look on my face, her bubbly joy gave way to tears of her own. "Mom, what's wrong? Are you sick? Did something happen to Daddy? Is Brooke all right?" she demanded, urgently grasping my shoulders. "Tell me what's wrong!"

Filling Staci in on the story helped me to calm down a bit, especially when she interrupted me to ask, "What do they mean by uppity?" I could tell from her bewildered expression that she had never heard the word used in such a context before and had no idea what it meant. It brought me up short. It suddenly struck me how thoroughly Vence and I had protected our children from racial prejudice; we might even have done too good a job. In Stamford, outright bigotry was almost unheard of, but there were only a tiny number of black residents. In our sheltered, overwhelmingly white environment, the big problem for black middle-class parents like us was assuring that our children did not lose touch with their racial roots, not battling antiblack remarks.

Vence and I had worked hard to make sure that Brooke and Staci were prepared to cope with the racial challenges they were likely to experience once they left our suburban cocoon. We had filled our home with books about black history, given them black dolls to play with, and taken them to black cultural festivals and concerts. I'd even put aside my misgivings about the snooty reputation of Jack and Jill, a national organization for upper-middle-class black children, and enrolled the girls in the local chapter to make sure they had some black playmates.

Because of our diligent efforts, the girls were undeniably knowledgeable and proud of their racial heritage. But, as Staci's innocent question reminded me, it is one thing to know intellectually about being black in America, and quite another to understand, deep down in your bones, about the devastating impact of racist acts like the one I had suffered that day.

Staci, thank God, had never felt the sting of bigotry in her own life, and I prayed that she never would. But, sadly, black children have to learn things white children don't. Learning to cope with discrimination remains an essential part of their education for psychological survival, even on the brink of the twenty-first century. Staci had to understand fully what had happened to me that day. She needed to share my anguish and rage. She did not need protection anymore. She needed the truth.

"What they mean is that I'm an uppity nigger," I explained, filling my voice with disgust, "They think I'm a black person who doesn't know how to stay in her place. Since the days of slavery, they've been calling black people who stand up for themselves 'uppity' and there are still people who believe it."

Staci looked stunned by my use of the "N-word," which I loathe and which I'd never said to her before. "But, Mom, that's wrong. It's so racist," she exclaimed. "You've got to fight it."

"Don't worry," I said, hugging her tightly. "I will." I sounded more confident than I felt.

Later that evening, I sat alone in my bedroom, studying myself in the mirror. I looked terrible. My tears had carved rivulets into my makeup; my clothes, which I hadn't changed, were in disarray, and the shoulder-length braids I had been wearing for a few months were a tangled mess. But beneath the wreckage I could discern a strong resemblance to my beloved grandmother, whose patient love and calm reassurance had bolstered me through the worst days of my childhood. I could almost feel her comforting embrace and hear her soft voice as I drifted off to sleep: "Things will look better in the morning."

They didn't. I awoke the next day with a pounding headache. The thought of going to work in what I now considered to be enemy territory nearly made me throw up. I thought of quitting. I had actually picked up the phone to call in sick when Staci poked her head in my door.

"Mom," she said, quietly, "I thought about it all night. You have to fight this."

Staci was right: for the sake of my self-respect, I could not run away. I could not let Staci down. I could not let the good old boys beat me. I had to fight back. The question was how.

My options were limited. At Texaco there were established procedures for appealing a PMP, but all of them seemed pointless. Why bother complaining to the human resources department when its head was John Ambler, who had labeled Sil, Florence, and me as black militants? How could I expect justice from the heads of the finance department, when Nancy had told me that Ulrich, Link, and Keough were the perpetrators of the offense that had been committed against me? What confidence could I place in Shelby when I was sure that he, too, had sat in on the meeting? Why put Nancy on the spot, since she lacked the power to reverse the decision even if she'd had the courage to do so? Before I could really decide on a course of action, I needed some reliable information. I needed to consult with Florence and Sil. With that fragmentary strategy in mind, I got dressed and went into the office, feeling like I was on my way into battle.

I could sense a change in the atmosphere as soon as I entered the corridor. For months Nancy and I had started the workday by going down to the cafeteria for coffee. But on this day she buried her gaze in a newspaper and did not even look up at me as I walked past her office, doing my best to hold my head high and act normally. Once I got to my desk, I put in a call to Florence and arranged to meet her in the cafeteria.

By the time I got down there Florence was already pacing the hall with a worried look on her face.

"Girlfriend, I can tell from your voice that something is wrong. What's going on?"

I pulled out a copy of Nancy's first review and gave it to Florence to study.

"You got an S! I don't think I've ever seen an S next to a black person's name before. You're probably going to be promoted!" she said.

"Now take a look at this," I said, handing her the second review.

"Oh my God, Bari, they lowered your rating," she said, as she flipped through the pages. "I've never seen anything like this. It's ridiculous. What are you going to do?"

"I'm not sure yet," I replied. "But I need a big favor. I need for you to find out if I'm still on the high-potential list."

Florence looked around nervously to see if anyone could overhear us. "I'll get back to you as soon as I can."

My next stop was Sil. As usual, he was in a jovial mood when I arrived at his office in corporate finance. When I asked if I could close his office door so we could talk privately, he gave me a typically flippant response, "Oh, go ahead, but I warn you, it's a little bit early in the morning for me to cheat on my wife."

"Sil," I said, "this is no laughing matter. Something terrible has happened with my PMP. Two days ago Nancy gave me an S . . ."

"An S," Sil interjected, cutting me off. "What's terrible about that? I never heard of a black person getting an S around here. You ought to be happy about it."

"But, Sil, wait till you hear me out. Yesterday they lowered it to a G-plus because Jim Link said I was 'uppity.'"

He looked at me thoughtfully, but didn't say anything as I told him the whole story.

"Sil," I said, trying to prod him to be as open with me as I had been with him, "have you ever heard anything about Ulrich, Link, Keough, and the other seniors telling racist jokes at their meetings?"

"Not really, Bari, but it wouldn't surprise me," Sil replied.

"A while ago I told one of the white managers over here that I thought some black people ought to be in on those meetings and he just laughed it off. He said I didn't have to worry because he was the resident Liberal and he would speak for us. I asked him how he could speak for us when he doesn't even speak to us! They could be doing anything in there and we'd never know it."

Sil said nothing to me at all about his own situation, but I could tell he was troubled. I returned to my office to await the next word from Florence.

Florence seemed agitated, but she said very little as we drove to a restaurant far from the Texaco building. Once we were seated, and she'd checked out the room to make sure we were not overheard, her words tumbled out in a rapid stream.

"Girlfriend, you would not believe what these white boys are doing. Sil came to see me last week and he's very upset. He got a bad PMP the last time around and he thinks it was racist. What's happening to you and him is just the tip of the iceberg. I've talked to lots of blacks who've been working here for years who aren't even being paid the minimum salary for the grade they're in. If they ask for a promotion, they get turned down. The government comes in once in a while and finds violations and Texaco promises to fix them, but absolutely nothing gets done. Most of the blacks are too scared to complain. It's a disgrace.

"A few weeks ago, I got booted out of my office into one of those cubicles where anybody can hear whatever you're saying. There's no way anybody who wants to make a complaint can talk to me confidentially anymore. They don't feel safe. When I told Ambler about it, he said I wasn't entitled to an office because I wasn't a grade sixteen, just a fifteen! And I said, that's ridiculous. I can't do my job under these circumstances. But they're not doing anything about it. It's sickening."

She paused and looked at me grimly.

"I pulled up the latest version of the high-potential list. You've been dropped. Your name's not on it."

As it turned out, Sil had good reasons for not sharing the details of his plight with me. Unbeknownst to me, he had found someone besides Florence to confide in, who had advised him to be tight-lipped. His name was Jerry Leaphart.

Florence had told me a little about Leaphart a few months before, but I had not met him. I knew only that he was one of the few black staff lawyers in Texaco's legal department and had returned to headquarters in late 1992 or early 1993 after spending many years at Texaco's branch in Angola. According to Florence and the rumor mill, Leaphart was an intelligent, highly skilled lawyer and no pushover. If that were true, I thought to myself, he might be able to help me fight Texaco. He might even be a mentor.

Sil had already beat me to him. Not long after getting his disastrous PMP rating from Bob Gordan, Sil was assigned to lead a corporate finance team that would arrange new financing for Texaco's billion-plus accounts receivable. It was a huge undertaking requiring close coordination with the controller's office and the legal department. It was also, from Sil's point of view, a make-or-break deal: his future was riding on it. He was desperate.

That may explain why Sil had poured his heart out when he walked into Leaphart's office and discovered that the attorney he would be working with was black. Here, for the first time since Sil had come to Texaco, was another African American male professional of roughly the same age and stature, with whom he could discuss his plight. He trusted Leaphart instinctively and threw discretion out the window. Before he had even taken a seat, he had started telling Leaphart his story.

"This is not just another deal to me," Sil declared plaintively. "This is my whole future. I got a bad review last year and I don't think I deserved it. These white guys are ganging up on me. They're trying to screw me. I really need your help, brother." He went on to describe how his PMP had been lowered because of the poor performance of his subordinates, his blowup at his boss, Bob Gordan—the whole nine yards. It was a one-sided conversation. Leaphart listened impassively, then clapped Sil on the back, and ended the meeting with a reassuring comment: "We'll make sure you get a good review out of this deal. Don't worry. I'll be with you every step of the way."

The next day he phoned Sil and invited him to lunch in the Texaco cafeteria. This time he had a lot of questions. He pumped Sil for every detail about the times when he had requested training for Larry Barnes and been turned down, for every nuance of his conversations with Gordan, for every loaded comment on his PMP. He seemed to take an especially keen interest in Sil's observation that the young white analyst who had assumed Larry's duties after he was transferred out of corporate finance had been given the training that Larry had been denied.

"There's a reason why I'm asking you all these questions, Sil," Leaphart said when he'd finished the interrogation. "I've only been back from Angola for a few months and I've been talking to lots of African Americans who work here. And, brother, every black person I talk to is having the same problems as you. They are all getting these G-minus ratings, just like you. They're all being told one thing about their performance during the year, then being judged by an entirely different standard on their PMP, just like you. They're all being denied promotions.

"We need to do something about this, man. We need to take some kind of legal action, maybe a class action because this looks like a pattern of discrimination. Don't say anything about it yet. Keep it to yourself."

It was the first time anyone had raised the prospect of filing a lawsuit charging Texaco with racial discrimination.

* * *

A week later, Sil, Florence, Leaphart, and I had lunch at the Cobblestone Restaurant in Rye, New York, where we could talk more freely. By now, each of us had learned enough about the other's difficulties to realize that our own travails were pieces of a much larger and more disturbing mosaic.

On the way to the restaurant, Leaphart told us his story in a machine-gun style that did not allow interruption. He talked the whole time it took to drive there and for fifteen minutes after we were seated at a table. In Angola, a manager had falsely accused him of some sort of wrongdoing—he didn't say what—and he'd been given a low PMP rating. When he complained about it he had been transferred back to Harrison "because they want to keep an eye on me." None of the challenging assignments that he thought suitable for a lawyer with his vast experience and sixteen years with the company had been given to him since his return; he was wasting his time on routine legal work that he thought was below his station.

"Texaco is a crazy place. Texaco is filled with racists," he rattled on, clearly enjoying the sound of his own voice. "I've filed a complaint with the Equal Employment Opportunity Commission because of what they're trying to do to me. I'm not gonna let these racist bastards get away with it. I'm going to teach them a very expensive lesson for messing with me. Bet on that."

Sil, Florence, and I looked at each other in surprise. This was the first any of us had heard that Leaphart had already taken legal action against Texaco. Why hadn't Leaphart disclosed that significant information to Sil at their earlier lunch? I wondered. What the heck is going on with this guy? I decided I didn't trust him.

That evening when I returned home I started keeping a journal. I knew, somehow, that the day would come when I would need a record of events.

*   *   *

The next day Shelby called me in for the first time since my PMP had been gutted. "You've been here long enough now to take on some supervisory responsibilities," he began. "Starting tomorrow, we want Larry Barnes to report to you."

My alarm bell went off. By now Sil had told me the whole sad story of how Larry had been used to undermine him in corporate finance. Did Shelby plan to try the same thing with me?

"Am I being promoted, Shelby?" I asked.

"No, this is just part of your regular duties," he replied.

"Tell me this. There have been two white MBAs in P&B for a while and neither of them reports to me. Why is it that when a black MBA comes into the department, I become his supervisor?"

"Well, I think he needs a mentor."

End of conversation.

That night, over a bottle of wine and some dinner with Florence, I poured out my suspicions about Shelby's latest personnel ploy. "They're trying to set me up just like they set up Sil. They either want to use Larry's performance to lower my ratings, or they want me to give him a bad rating so they can fire him and blame it on a black woman. Either way it stinks."

"That's not the half of it, Bari," Florence said. "I found out today that the other black MBA, Steve Block, also got a G-minus rating. You know, they haven't given him any real work at all since he came to the company. They're trying to shaft him."

"Florence," I said, growing angrier by the moment, "this is craziness. They are going to ruin both these young guys before they even have a chance to get started. They bring them in here, they don't give them a chance, and pretty soon, they'll push them out the door. We cannot let this happen."

Things were reaching critical mass. I might be able to thwart Texaco's plot against Larry Barnes by helping him to resurrect his career, but such individual action was no substitute for the bold offensive on discrimination I was now convinced that we needed. Texaco was harming its black employees as a group. We had to fight back in concert.

For the moment, there was only one option available for defending ourselves. Jerry Leaphart had invited a group of black Texaco employees to meet with the lawyer who was handling his individual case, a well-known woman attorney. Despite my qualms about Leaphart's judgment, I had to at least explore the idea that his approach might be productive.

I wasn't impressed with Leaphart's lawyer. She crouched over the papers on her cluttered desk, chain-smoking and coughing as she fired questions at the eight or nine of us who had gathered in her office in midtown New York on a sunny Saturday morning in May 1993. What grade level are you? What's your salary? Do you think you're being mistreated? How do you know that race has anything to do with it? If you think you've been denied a promotion because you're black, what's the evidence? If you think you're paid less than your white counterparts, how can you prove it? Are you considered a professional?

It was the last question that bothered me most. In contrast to Florence, Leaphart, and me—Sil hadn't been able to make it—the majority of the other people who had summoned the courage to come to the meeting were relatively low-level black employees—maintenance workers, clerks, and secretaries—who had been stuck in their positions for many years. They were up against the same brick wall that I was, whether they wore blue collars or business suits. I wanted us to stick together, not be divided into groups. After all, race was the issue, not rank.

The lawyer did not see it that way. After a half hour or so of questions she rubbed her eyes, took another drag from her cigarette, then waved it at Leaphart, Florence, and me. "I'm really interested in this group, the professionals in grades twelve and above. I can't do anything for you," she said, gesturing at my lower-ranking coworkers. "Texaco already has plenty of blacks in low-level jobs, so trying to include you in the case would really mess up the soup, know what I mean?" The disappointment was tangible. It got worse as the lawyer went on.

"Equal opportunity cases are long, tedious, and expensive affairs," she said. "They often take seven years or more. I need a retainer. You guys are going to have to start a legal fund to defray the costs. Everybody who joins the case can pay a certain sum into the fund every month, say two hundred dollars, till we get enough to get started."

That was enough for me—and everybody else except Leaphart. As we rode down in the elevator together, all I heard was grumbling from my lower-ranking colleagues. "Oh, that's nice," sneered one of them. "You professionals get to have your lawsuit and win a lot of money and us blue collar types don't get nothing. Reminds me of the house Negroes and field hands back during slavery." Instead of unifying us for collective action against Texaco, Leaphart's lawyer had left us divided and mutually resentful. The meeting had been a disaster. I did not want her to represent me.

Jerry did not seem to notice my discomfort. "Bari," he said, "we need to get that fund started. Do you want to be treasurer?" It was so absurd that I laughed in his face. "Well, think about it and let's talk next week," he said. He would not be deterred.

Our next caucus took place after work the following Tuesday night. Leaphart, excited and fidgety, had another outlandish proposal. "We've got to come up with at least twenty-five people who want to be in on the suit by the middle of next week if we're going to proceed," he announced. "I've got a list of all the black people who work at Texaco. Why don't we divide it up and each call some people and ask them to join us? There's no time to waste."

I thought he was crazy. "Jerry," I said, "What are we supposed to do? Call up somebody out of the blue and say, 'Hi, I'm Bari-Ellen Roberts and I'd like to know if you want to file suit against Texaco'? It's ridiculous. I'll talk to people I know and trust face to face, but I'm not calling anybody I don't know. It's too risky." Sil and Florence felt the same way.

"Okay," said Leaphart. "I'll call them myself."

He was as good as his word. During the next few days he placed dozens of long-distance calls to black Texaco employees all over the country, asking them to join the lawsuit. And just as Sil, Florence, and I feared, his indiscretion quickly backfired. One of the black workers Jerry had contacted couldn't wait to tell his white supervisor about the conversation. A day later, the head of Texaco's legal department summoned Leaphart to his office and summarily fired him. We heard that he had been given fifteen minutes to collect his personal items and was then marched out of the building by security guards. I never saw him again.

CHAPTER TWELVE

DARK DAYS, WHITE KNIGHTS

Jerry Leaphart's abrupt dismissal landed on us like a bomb. As word of it ricocheted around Texaco's headquarters, our little band of conspirators started running for cover. Our gravest worry was that whoever had snitched on Jerry might also have ratted on us. I was convinced that Texaco would wage a ruthless campaign to track down all the people suspected of collaborating with Leaphart and expel them from the building. Other than Florence and Sil, I didn't trust anybody.

In the weeks that followed, Texaco's black employees sunk into a paranoid coma. Though only our jobs, not our lives, were in danger, the atmosphere resembled the oppressive gloom over a Southern town in the aftermath of a lynching. All talk of filing a discrimination suit came to a screeching halt. Nobody wanted to be seen huddling with anyone else in the hallways or cafeteria for fear of attracting attention from white coworkers, some of whom seemed to be glaring at us with even more hostility than usual. Nobody laughed out loud.

Nobody used any slang. Nobody wanted to admit ever having laid eyes on Jerry Leaphart, much less having consorted with him about any lawsuit.

I have to admit that I was among those most consumed by anxiety. My reputation for outspokenness and flouting Texaco tradition made me a natural suspect. The downgrading of my PMP and the removal of my name from the high-potential list suggested that I might already be on some kind of management hit list of "uppity" blacks. Though Leaphart, Sil, Florence and I had been careful to conduct our meetings "off-campus," away from the Texaco building, to reduce the odds of being detected, any number of people, black or white, might have spotted us together and reported their suspicions to management. I assumed it would only be a matter of time before beefy security guards appeared in my doorway, gave me fifteen minutes to clean out my desk, and threw me out of the building.

Had it not been for Staci, I probably would have quit. After promising her that I'd fight back against the racism I was encountering on my job, there was no way I could just cut and run. From time to time, I filled her in on the latest revolting development at Texaco and my fear that I would be fired. No matter how dire the situation seemed to me, Staci never wavered in her belief that I had to fight for my rights, regardless of the cost. She implored me, in her idealistic, suburban, teen-aged way to "hang tough, Mom." Her unshakable confidence in me was a source of renewed courage and determination. She was my rock and my salvation. Yet, despite the strength I borrowed from her every day, there were times when the tension at Texaco became so thick that I nearly crumbled.

For the life of me I can't remember exactly what triggered my sense of dread on one particular day a few weeks after Leaphart was ousted. It may have been something as innocuous as the way Shelby looked at me or something Sigfrid said at a meeting. Whatever it was, I was suddenly seized by a wave of panic so strong that I almost shivered. *I'd better get a grip on myself*, I thought, *or I'm going to go out of my mind.*

That night, after Staci went to bed, I sat in the living room with the lights off, mulling over the situation. We were locked in a war of nerves with Texaco and the company was obviously winning. By striking Leaphart from the picture, Texaco had decapitated our incipient movement and the body had died. We were utterly leaderless. Maybe I should just leave before my health began to slide.

And then, from somewhere in the back of my mind, came a powerful image from *Glory*, the movie about runaway slaves who joined the Union Army during the Civil War to fight for their freedom. In one especially inspiring scene, the character played by Denzel Washington picks up the flag and charges ahead after its bearer has been shot down. If our forebears could show such courage in the face of certain death, I thought, how could I even think of abandoning the struggle for justice at Texaco? As I had learned in my self-empowerment class two years before, if I wanted a change, I had to make it. I still didn't know what I was going to do, but I knew I was going to do something, even if it cost me my job. Jerry Leaphart had been cut down, but I could pick up the banner.

To steel myself for the uncertain future I picked up the phone in a familiar ritual. The phone rang for a long, long time before I heard my father say "hello," his voice still groggy with sleep. I told him about the decision I'd made.

"I want to take these guys on, Daddy," I said. "If it doesn't work out, can I come home?"

"Of course you can, Cootsie," my father replied, laughing affectionately "But you won't have to because you're going to win."

Now I was ready.

There was no change in the uneasy status quo at Texaco until mid-September. Nancy and I had reestablished our working relationship, but not our budding friendship. After the lowering of my PMP, I could never be really comfortable with her again, and she, too, was obviously embarrassed. Some subjects, notably my review, Jerry Leaphart, or discrimination, were strictly taboo.

The only thing I looked forward to was working with Larry Barnes. When he had arrived in pensions and benefits a few months before, his morale had been totally shattered. He was tall, physically fit, and not yet thirty years old, but he walked with the stoop of a much older and broken man. He needed a fresh start and rehabilitation. I insisted to Shelby that Larry's lousy PMPs in corporate finance should not be held against him, and to his credit, Shelby agreed: "Okay, he's got a clean slate. You mentor him."

I did my best, employing what I had learned from the tutelage of Henry Tucker, my first black boss at Chicago's Continental Bank. I invited Larry into my office regularly for closed-door chats about projects I was working on as well as his own assignments. I prodded Nancy to allow him to make presentations to the senior managers to give him a chance to shine. Slowly, as the months passed by, Larry started standing up straight again. Even Shelby noticed the difference. Larry became proof that blacks could thrive at Texaco if they were only given a chance.

Despite the satisfaction I took from Larry's revival, I remained frustrated and edgy about my inability to breathe new life into a larger legal assault against discrimination. I had spoken to a few lawyers I knew, but none of them had an interest in taking the case. Texaco, they pointed out, was a huge corporation with enormous financial and legal resources. It could keep throwing lawyers at us until we were exhausted. So far, amid all the fear that had settled over my coworkers and me after Leaphart's termination, we had not even been able to agree on a battle plan, let alone come up with the funds to finance a case that was likely to last for at least five years with no guarantee of a victorious outcome. The struggle seemed so unequal even I began to feel that it might not be worth fighting.

I had just about given up hope when Florence called me one afternoon and told me to meet her right away at our usual rendezvous point near the cafeteria. I could tell from the excited tone of her voice that she had some really big news.

When I got there, Florence had a gleam in her eye that I hadn't seen since the day Jerry Leaphart was fired. "Girlfriend, have you ever heard of this group called the Interfaith Center for Corporate Responsibility?" Florence whispered excitedly as we paced the corridor, constantly checking to make sure no one could overhear us. "It's a church group down in New York that buys shares of stock in big companies so they can attend stockholder's meetings and raise hell with management over stuff like the environment and affirmative action. I saw some of them at the last annual stockholders meeting. They've been tangling with Texaco for years.

"Somebody down there called me and they want to meet with some black people from Texaco. They know what happened to Jerry. Would you be willing to talk to them?"

I couldn't wait.

"You're really taking on a tough customer," Timothy Smith laughed from the other side of the conference table where Sil, Florence, and I were seated. "Texaco is one of the most intractable companies we've dealt with. They talk glibly about making changes, but they don't implement them. You should have been at the annual meeting."

For the next few minutes, the tall, graying leader of the ICCR regaled us with an account of how several people from ICCR had gone toe to toe with Texaco's chairman Alfred DeCrane at the yearly stockholders' meeting that had been held back in May. Following its long-standing strategy of trying to meld investment with religious responsibility, ICCR had submitted a bevy of resolutions for various reforms to Texaco's stockholders for their approval. Among them were proposals to replace staggered terms for members of the board of directors with annual elections, so the directors could be held more accountable. Another was to set a definite date for Texaco to name a black to the board; in the nearly hundred years of the company's existence, there had not been even one.

"We made a powerful case to them for diversifying the board," Smith went on. "Lois"—he gestured at Lois Dauway, a black woman in braids similar to mine who was sitting to his left—"pointed out that since forty-five percent of all major corporations already have at least one minority on their board, we wonder what's keeping Texaco? And you should have seen Gary here in action." He clapped the shoulder of a dark-haired intense-looking man with a bushy mustache seated at his right. "All the resolutions failed, but we'll try again next year, won't we, Gary?"

"Are you aware of all the lawsuits for sex and race discrimination that Texaco has pending?" asked Gary Brouse. "More than fifty people have been in touch with us in the past year alone to complain about discrimination. At least eight cases are pending with the Human Rights Commission here in New York. And there are at least three more in New Orleans—not to mention a lot more we don't know about yet. Texaco has wasted millions of shareholder dollars fighting these cases instead of settling them and putting in reforms that would stop discrimination from being a problem."

He paused for effect.

"I'll tell you what their attitude is. When we had a discussion back in February with some of Texaco's top managers about naming some women and blacks to the board of directors, the corporate secretary, Carl Davidson, just yelled at us, 'We are simply not seeking skirts or a black face to put on our board!' He actually admitted that Texaco didn't want any and wasn't looking for any! Can you imagine a top executive of a major American company talking about blacks and women like that?" Brouse concluded with a weary shake of his head.

Unfortunately, I could easily imagine it, if the major company was Texaco.

"You know about the Janella Martin case out in California," he went on, becoming even more agitated. "She sued Texaco for sex discrimination nearly ten years ago and it took her eight years to win. She was awarded $17.7 million because they denied her a promotion she was entitled to and gave it to a man instead! After she filed the suit, somebody smashed the windows of her office. Her husband's car was broken into, her home was burglarized, and evidence she was using for her case was stolen! Now Texaco has convinced the judge to knock down the award and she'll probably wind up with a lot less. I know for a fact that she tried to settle the case before it went to court, but Texaco flatly refused.

"Al DeCrane," Brouse continued, referring to Texaco's chairman, "would rather fight these cases and lose them all than admit Texaco has ever discriminated."

Brouse talked so passionately and so knowledgeably about antidiscrimination lawsuits that I thought he was a lawyer.

"Would you be willing to take our case?" I asked.

"I'm just the head of ICCR's Equality Project, not a lawyer," Brouse replied, "but I can put you in touch with one."

In the aftermath of the meeting with ICCR, Florence, Sil and I each faced a momentous decision. Initiating legal action against Texaco would place not only our current jobs, but our entire careers at enormous risk, since many companies are reluctant to hire anyone who has ever filed a lawsuit against an employer. I was determined to carry on despite that possibility and Sil seemed equally committed. But over the next few days Florence had anguished second thoughts.

"Oh Bari, I haven't been able to think about anything else but this lawsuit for days," she told me in a telephone conversation about a week later. "But I just can't be a part of it. I'm so close to retiring. Texaco might take away my pension. I don't know if I can stand the strain." She sobbed. "Girlfriend, if I were younger, I'd be right there with you and Sil. But I just can't do it. You two will have to fight this battle without me. I feel like I'm letting you down."

If we had been talking face to face, I would have embraced her. Instead, I said to her, "Florence, you've already done more than your share. I don't feel let down at all." The truth was that I did.

I had nearly drifted off to sleep a few hours later when the telephone rang again.

"Is this Bari-Ellen Roberts?" a woman inquired in an urgent whisper.

"Yes, it's Bari," I said.

"I work at Texaco and I've been talking to some of the same people you have," the woman went on. My suspicions were immediately aroused because no one besides Sil, Florence and I was supposed to know about what we'd been up to.

"Like who?" I demanded.

"Like Gary Brouse," she said. "He told me to call you. If you really want to do something about Texaco, I can help you."

I hesitated for a moment before I replied. "There's going to be a meeting soon. If you're serious, you will be there."

"I'll be there," the woman responded. Then she hung up. As I put the phone back on its hook, it dawned on me that she had not told me her name.

It was the next to the last night of October 1993 when we finally got together with the lawyer Brouse had recommended in a church basement in suburban Connecticut. Besides Sil and myself, only two other people were there. One was Katherine Malarkey, a Texaco secretary who had contacted us at Brouse's urging because she had filed a sex discrimination suit against the company. The other was a woman clutching a briefcase so stuffed with papers I thought it would burst. "I'm the one who phoned you that night," she said. "Just call me 'Dora.' "

"Dora's" secretiveness was only one of the things that contributed to the spookiness of our clandestine gathering. The church—to which Malarkey belonged—was festooned with Halloween decorations. "Reminds me of corporate finance," Sil quipped, as we walked to the church door past a legion of kids dressed up as black cats, goblins, and witches.

Cyrus Mehri was already waiting for us when we arrived. My first look at him was disappointing. I had been expecting two members of the Washington, D.C., law firm of Cohen, Milstein, Hausfeld & Toll, including a senior partner, not just this thirty-something young guy who looked a bit like the actor Andy Garcia on a bad hair day and seemed almost as flippant. I angrily surmised that the law firm didn't think enough of our case to send the first string to an initial meeting. I was wrong. Mehri quickly demonstrated his commitment to our cause by shooing Katherine Malarkey out of the room over her angry objections.

"Miss Malarkey, you have to leave or this meeting cannot continue," he firmly explained as Katherine sulked. "I'm here to discuss a potential case alleging racial discrimination with these folks, who might be plaintiffs, and you obviously can't be part of that. Moreover, if you stay here it might compromise you as a witness. If you really want to help these people, you'll let us have some privacy so we can talk frankly." Somewhat mollified, Katherine left.

As soon as she did, Cyrus—as I was already calling him— gave us some background about his firm. "If we take the case, the legal team will be led by Mike Hausfeld, one of the name partners in the firm, whom you may already have heard of. He's known as 'the Toxic Avenger.' "

Sil let out a whistle. "You gotta be kidding me," he said.

"Isn't that the guy who sued Texaco for letting oil seep into these people's backyards down in Virginia? I think he got a couple of hundred million dollars or something. I know about it because corporate finance put together a bond issue to defray the cost of the cleanup."

"Not just some people's backyards," said Cyrus. "It was Hausfeld's own neighborhood. He took it very personally." It was my turn to whistle.

"If we take the case," Cyrus continued, "it will be on a contingency basis. That means the firm will bear all the costs of the litigation and recoup it, along with our fee, if we produce a settlement. If we lose, you owe us nothing."

I whistled again.

Cyrus spent the next few minutes telling us about himself and some of the other cases his law firm had handled. His parents, both liberal intellectuals, had fled to the United States to escape political persecution in their native Iran. He had been born in New York and had grown up right here in suburban Connecticut, not far from the church where we were meeting. Before becoming an attorney, he had spent several years as one of Ralph Nader's Raiders. Indeed, the famous consumer advocate had been his role model until he met Mike Hausfeld. "Our firm is one of the few around the country that specializes in class action suits on behalf of plaintiffs. It's our only business. Mike Hausfeld is one of the best plaintiff's lawyers you'll ever see. He doesn't believe in the law as an end in itself, like some lawyers do. He believes it's a way to get justice. He won't take a case for a client he doesn't believe in. He's no hired gun. He's practicing the kind of law I wanted to practice when I started law school." In one of his many cases, Hausfeld had brought a class action suit seeking millions of dollars in compensation for Native Americans after the disastrous Exxon Valdez oil spill in Alaska. He had also filed the first successful sexual harassment suit against the U.S. Justice Department.

Someone from the church came in and said there was a

phone call. It turned out to be Hausfeld, calling on a cell phone from a limousine stuck in traffic just outside New York. "I'm trying my best to get there before the meeting breaks up, but I don't think I can make it," Hausfeld explained. "From what I know about your case, it's a strong one and I'm definitely interested. If we all decide to go forward together, we need to make it as broad as possible."

I was impressed, and more important, so was "Dora." Up to this point, she had sat quietly, looking skeptical and clutching her bulging briefcase. Two factors had tipped the scale. First was the way Cyrus had spent so much time selling his law firm to us, instead of peppering us with questions as had Leaphart's uninspiring attorney. The second was that this law firm had indeed thought enough of our cause to send its very best man. These lawyers seemed to want to persuade us that they were worthy to take our case, not the other way around. "Here," said "Dora" quietly, opening her briefcase, "I have some things that might help you."

Among the documents she handed to Cyrus were Texaco's highly confidential response to the Mobil Salary Survey, an annual comparison of minority pay scales and employment at major oil companies conducted by the Mobil Oil Company. I'd never seen it before. The detailed statistics showed that when it came to diversity Texaco was the worst in the industry. At every level Texaco had far fewer black employees than the industry average and the disparity grew by an alarming degree the higher up the scale you went. For example, blacks constituted only 5.9 percent of Texaco employees earning between $51,000 and $59,000 compared with 7.2 percent in the industry as a whole. In my pay grade, $77,600 to $86,099, the black percentage was only 1.8 percent compared with 3.2 percent for the industry. And at the top of the scale, at $128,000 or more, Texaco had only 0.4 percent blacks, four times less than the industry average of 1.8 percent. This was dynamite—hard numbers that proved that Texaco had clamped a lid on its black employees, gleaned from the company's own files. With this kind of evidence we might be able to show that discrimination was deeply entrenched at Texaco, a part of the company's culture, not merely the result of occasional misguided acts by a few individuals.

It was Cyrus's turn to whistle.

We spent the next two hours briefing him on our individual grievances, the meeting with John Ambler, the Leaphart saga, and the intimidating atmosphere inside Texaco. It was exhausting. When we finally petered out, Cyrus looked at us and declared, "It looks like we've got a case here."

And, I thought to myself, *it looks like we've got a lawyer*.

Two anxious months passed before we heard any more from Cyrus and Mike. As it turned out, within their firm there was strong opposition against taking our case. Cohen, Milstein, Hausfeld & Toll had not handled a major civil rights case for two decades, and during that time both the political and legal climate had changed for the worse, as far as blacks' rights were concerned. White America was in the midst of a backlash against affirmative action led by conservative ideologues who branded any attempt to level the racial playing field as a noxious "quota" or "racial preference." A similar trend had taken hold in the federal courts. Ultraconservative judges selected by Ronald Reagan and George Bush were steadily rolling back the tenuous gains blacks had made during the Civil Rights Movement. The more Cyrus dug into recent developments in the field, the more depressed he became. Over the past twenty years dozens of law firms had gone bankrupt trying to win racial discrimination cases. They took years to conclude, were awesomely expensive to litigate, and the evidentiary standard was constantly changing to make it more difficult to prove that discrimination had actually occurred. Predictably, Mike's hardnosed partners took one look at our case and concluded that the firm shouldn't touch it. A case like this took a lot of attention and a lot of thought. It involved moral principle. And in the end, you didn't get paid very much even if you won. Why spend millions of dollars and long years fighting this fight when easier and far more lucrative targets, like product liability suits and securities fraud cases, were so readily available?

It sounds sentimental, but to Cyrus, the simple answer was justice. As he told me some months later, he became committed to our cause the moment that he was convinced that Sil and I were telling the unembellished truth about what Texaco had done to us; he wanted to right a wrong. He thought of Cohen, Milstein as a kind of private law enforcement agency doing battle against crimes that the government either ignored or could not handle. He was a crusader. He was determined to develop a strategy through which the firm could fight for justice and make some money in the process.

He and Hausfeld finally focused on a provision in the Civil Rights Act of 1991 which allowed victims of racial discrimination to collect damages up to $300,000 apiece. Prior to that they had only been able to win the actual amount of wages they had lost because they'd been victimized, almost always a far lesser sum. If the lawyers could put together a large enough number of black employees at Texaco—a "class" in legal terminology—and win the maximum award for each of them, it would amount to a fortune. If, say, there were one thousand people in the class, the total award would be $300 million. If Cohen, Milstein could collect even a tenth of that sum, its fees would be a quarter of that, $7.5 million. Not bad for a few years' work!

Mike made a passionate appeal to his partners for accepting our case at a closed-door meeting over the Thanksgiving weekend. He approached it in the same way he would have summed up a case for a jury. "You have to understand what this case could mean, not just for us, but for the principles this country is based on. America has been through the stages of opening the doors so that blacks could get hired by these companies. Now the question is, What do you do when the doors open? No one has successfully looked at what happens to blacks once they get inside the company, to make sure they are treated fairly. It's clear to me that despite the progress that has been made in bringing minorities in, there is little to no progress being made in elevating them to the levels they merit based on their qualifications and hard work. Just getting them in the door is not enough. We have to smash the glass ceiling, too.

"We have a chance to make that point by bringing a nationwide class action suit against Texaco, a company that already has a bad record on the environment, on employment, on every issue of social concern. It's the worst company in a very bad industry. We have strong and credible clients who have put their jobs on the line for the sake of justice. If there ever was an opportunity to make a change in the law that would have a dramatic impact on corporate America and the way it treats minorities, this is it. There may never be a better opportunity. We've got to take it, or we won't be able to live with ourselves." All his partners' objections were blown away by his passionate logic.

After the holiday, Cyrus called Sil and me and said, "Fasten your seat belts, we're going ahead."

If there is a God, She sometimes has a backhanded way of accomplishing miracles. Almost from the day Sil and I and the lawyers began the feverish work of drafting our initial complaint, the Devil ran wild at Texaco, unleashing a fresh plague of racial insults worse than the ones we'd already endured. Oddly, the new assaults did not damage our morale or weaken our commitment to filing the lawsuit. On the contrary, they made us too angry to turn back. Every time a new incident occurred, we simply added it to the case.

For my part, the new difficulties started in mid-March 1994, when Nancy announced she was leaving Texaco to take a job with an investment bank. I had now been at Texaco for more than three years and had earned three consecutive G+ ratings, which I had been told was more than enough to put me in line for promotion. Perhaps to make sure that we parted on a high note, Nancy informed me that if she were grading my performance right then, she would give me an S on my PMP for my solid performance across the board. She even told me that she thought I should get her job because I had earned it. I immediately rushed into Shelby's office and told him I wanted the position. I also filled out a formal application.

A few days later, Shelby called me into his office, closed the door, and asked me to sit down.

"Bari, I'm moving Jack Butler into Nancy's job."

I gasped in astonishment.

I knew who Jack Butler was: an assistant manager in another branch of the finance department who had no experience working with pensions or equities, the two most vital components of the assistant manager's job. From what I knew of his record, and given my direct experience in the department, I was clearly better qualified to hold down the position. And I said so.

"Why is Jack Butler getting the job instead of me?" I was furious. "What are his qualifications? What does he know about pensions? What does he know about equity investment? What does he know about actuarial assumptions—all the stuff I've focused on?"

Shelby said he didn't know the answers to any of those questions. He squirmed around behind his desk for a moment, then said, "Look, I wanted to let you know about this before I told the rest of the department." He got up abruptly and walked into a nearby conference room where the other analysts were gathering. Silently smoldering I dogged his heels every step of the way.

The larger meeting, if anything, was even more infuriating.

I was determined to get answers to my questions and so I posed them again, in front of the entire group.

"What is Jack Butler's background with pensions?"

None, Shelby replied.

"What is his background in equity investments?"

None, Shelby replied.

"Then why is he getting this job, since those are the things that we deal with in this department?"

"Well," said Shelby, "because Jack is a long-time Texaco employee."

And he's a white man, I could have added.

At that point, a young analyst named Brad Lawson voiced an anxiety-ridden query of his own.

"Well, what's going to happen when he gets here, because a lot of us are new to the department and we don't know very much about the pension industry either?"

"Don't worry," said Shelby. "Bari will help train him. Bari will help on that end."

I just about lost it. A white man with fewer qualifications than me had been given a job that I thought should have rightly been mine and now I was actually expected to train him so he could boss me! Where did Texaco get such unmitigated gall? I am not a violent person at all, but it took all my control to keep from throwing things.

Sil's story was more complicated but equally vexing. In January, Gordan and Wissel suddenly informed him that he was going to be sent back to cash management to work on the trading desk, the department where he had started when he first came to Texaco. The transfer, which Sil rightly considered to be a serious setback to his career, came as a total surprise. "How can you send me there when my performance is so much better than it was last year?" he asked Wissel. To which Wissel replied, "It isn't. I know what your rating is, and it's a G-minus."

Sil was flabbergasted. This wasn't even his scheduled PMP

meeting. He thought he had been doing well. Only a couple of months before, Wissel had complimented him on his improved performance. "What's going on here, guys?" he spat out, "Déjà vu or something?" A year earlier Gordan had rated Sil poorly because of the weak performance of Sil's subordinates. This time around Gordan blamed the low grade on Sil's own performance, ignoring the improved output of his team. "It's crazy," Sil told me. "It's just a shell game. Last year when my team was doing lousy work, Gordan told me it was on me. Now, when even 'Debra' is doing solid G-plus work, they say it has nothing to do with the way I supervised them and trained her. It doesn't make any sense."

Sil was even angrier about Gordan's outrageous claim that he had made only negligible contributions to three major deals he had worked his heart out on. Because of his desire to improve his PMP rating, Sil had gone out of his way to keep Gordan informed about the deals' progress every step of the way and not once had Gordan voiced any criticism. On the contrary, he had praised him. Now Gordan was not only knocking Sil's performance, he had given him a G– for poor communication! Within moments after he heard Wissel and Gordan out, Sil decided to appeal the rating.

The PMP appeals process at Texaco should not have been dignified by such a high-sounding name. It required an aggrieved employee to first make his case to his direct supervisors, the very same people who had issued the disputed review in the first place. In Sil's case that was Gordan and Wissel. In spite of the futility of it all, Sil dutifully submitted to the process. I helped him draft a letter of protest, which he submitted to Wissel in February. Wissel's reply came back in early March just as we expected: appeal denied.

By now, Sil's racial antennae were extremely inflamed, perhaps because of the impending lawsuit. He escalated his appeal to the head of the finance department, treasurer Bob Ulrich, and his top assistant, David Keough—and, after consulting with Cyrus, he put his belief that he had been subjected to a "pattern of (racial) discrimination" by Gordan in writing. To support his charge, he added that several other African Americans, including a banker who had visited Texaco to try to drum up some business, had also complained of having been insulted by Gordan.

Sil's memo touched off one of the weirdest examples of race relations I had ever heard of. Ulrich, slipping back into the avuncular guise he sometimes used when he was trying to manipulate people, told Sil the whole mess could be straightened out if Sil would just delete the paragraph charging Gordan with discrimination from his memo. "If you'll do that, I think we can see about giving you a more favorable review in August and a salary increase in October." Insulted, Sil turned him down.

Three days later Ulrich repeated the offer, coupling it with this entreaty: "Sil, I'm really upset about this and so is Bob Gordan. Having a charge like this on his record could damage his career."

To which Sil replied with admirable wit: "Bob, what about *my* career?" For the second time he turned Ulrich down flat.

These incidents were still fresh in our minds when our lawsuit was finally served on Texaco on March 23, 1994.

"This is a class action brought by two individual plaintiffs on behalf of themselves and other individuals similarly situated against Texaco Incorporated," it began. "Plaintiffs seek declaratory and injunctive relief and monetary damages to redress the deprivation of rights . . . under the Civil Rights Act of 1871, as amended in 1991, and Section 296 of the New York State Human Rights Law. The plaintiffs are African American employees who are victims of racial discriminatory employment policies and practices. The plaintiffs are qualified employees who have been denied the opportunity for promotion because of the disparate impact and treatment caused by Texaco's racially discriminatory policies."

The language was clunky and legalistic, but to me it was poetry. The case was placed under the supervision of U.S. District Court Judge Charles Brieant, who in turn assigned Magistrate Judge Mark D. Fox to handle pre-trial issues such as the gathering of evidence.

Because my name was first on the list of plaintiffs, the case became known as *Roberts v. Texaco.*

CHAPTER THIRTEEN

IN THE TRENCHES

I was driving home from the grocery store when a bulletin flashed over an all-news radio station. "This just in. Two black employees of Texaco, Inc., filed a class action lawsuit yesterday charging the giant oil company with racial discrimination. Bari-Ellen Roberts of Fairfield County, Connecticut, and Sil Chambers of Rockland County, New York, say that Texaco has violated civil rights laws by denying blacks . . ."

I was so riveted by the report that I almost lost control of the car. Until this moment, the existence of the lawsuit had been a secret shared only by Sil, me, and our lawyers. If I had decided, even at the very last instant, to back out, there would have been nothing but pride and my vow to Staci to stop me. Now that my challenge to Texaco had been relayed to hundreds of thousands, maybe even millions, of people, turning back was no longer an option. I would simply have to hang on and see it through to the end. A confusing tangle of conflicting emotions—excitement, relief that the battle at long last had been launched, totally unexpected jitters—swept over me as the gravity of my commitment sunk in. What would going to work be like now that the whole world knew that Sil and I had thrown down the gauntlet? How would Texaco react? Was I prepared to be in the spotlight? Would my coworkers support me or shun me? I gripped the steering wheel tightly and concentrated on driving to stop myself from becoming completely consumed by my reverie.

Staci was jumping up and down in the living room when I got home. "Mom, Mom, you and Sil are on the news!" she shrieked. "This is so exciting!" I joined her in front of the TV just in time to watch the tail end of a brief announcement about the case. "I am going to have me a *famous* Mom," Staci exclaimed, smacking me playfully on the shoulder. The telephone rang. It was Florence. "G 'head, girlfriend. It should be an interesting day at work tomorrow," she said, with an ironic chuckle. I agreed. As soon as I put the phone down, it rang again. This time it was Waldo calling from New York to say that he'd heard the report on TV and did I need anything? I invited him to come up for dinner. As soon as I hung up, the phone rang again; this time, it was a black coworker calling to tell me that I had been on TV, as if I didn't already know. It kept up like that until I took the phone off the hook after Waldo left, so that Staci could get some sleep. I knew I wouldn't get any.

Many of the calls had been from black people at Texaco whom I barely knew, telling me how excited they were when they heard the story. A brief mention of my name on TV had made me an instant celebrity. Only a handful asked me about the case itself or what they could do to help. Naïvely, I had hoped that word of the suit would be a battle cry that would rally scores and scores of our black coworkers to our cause. But judging from what I had heard tonight, most of my black coworkers would be content to remain on the sidelines. I felt disappointed and very alone.

The next morning *Roberts v. Texaco* was on the front page of the local newspaper that I read at the breakfast table, and on the radio and TV news updates that I listened to as I dressed for work. Texaco had, of course, issued a statement vehemently denying the charges. I winced at the thought of what might await me when I arrived at the office. The story would be all over the building. From my very first day on the job, the enviroment at Texaco had felt like enemy territory. Now it felt like stepping into a minefield. In our complaint, the lawyers had spelled out in great detail the intolerable treatment that Sil and I had experienced, naming the names of the managers involved—Bob Ulrich, Dave Keough, John Ambler, and Jack Butler, the white man who had gotten the assistant manager's job that I thought I deserved. How would these powerful white men react to being accused of bigotry? Would they want to discuss the complaint? Worst of all, would Texaco retaliate against me for standing up for my rights?

My fear of a backlash was based on more than speculation. Even though the company's official policy stated that "unwelcome, hostile, offensive, degrading, or abusive" conduct would not be tolerated, people at Texaco often turned the lives of employees who challenged the company into a living hell. Out in California Janella Martin had been threatened with bodily harm after she filed her lawsuit. Jerry Leaphart had been summarily dismissed and frog-marched out of the building for merely trying to stir up interest in a suit—Sil and I had actually brought one. In a case that was still pending, Charlene McGowan's job responsibilities had been taken away after she filed a sex discrimination suit against Texaco; ultimately, after months of alleged harassment, she had been fired. The judge in Katherine Malarkey's sexual harassment suit had even written that Texaco's legal tactics had seemed designed less to win that case than to scare off other potential plaintiffs. What vindictive measure might be in store for me?

By the time I parked my car in the Texaco lot, my whole

body was shaking. It took a tremendous effort to collect my belongings, walk to the underground entrance, and board the elevator that would take me to the finance department. Thinking of my sixth grade teacher Mr. Gaston, urging our class to hold our heads high and ignore the taunting mob that had surrounded our school bus so many years ago back in Cincinnati, I willed my back to be straight, my shoulders to be set, my strides to be firm and determined. I forced myself to smile. I could feel the pressure of hostile stares as I walked down the hall to my office. All the hustle and bustle that usually attended the start of the workday was replaced by an ominous silence. By the time I collapsed into my office chair, I was a nervous wreck.

I was still recovering from the ordeal when the phone started ringing again. It did not stop for days. Nor did the angry glares from black workers as well as white ones. For every black who gave me or Sil an approving wink or black power salute when they passed one of us in the hallway, there seemed to be scores who were shying away. Most of our black coworkers seemed to have given up hope that Texaco would ever change and they were fearful of rocking the boat.

Others were sheer opportunists. A worker from Texas called to say he was very interested in joining the case, but wanted to check it out with his white boss before making a final decision. He phoned back a couple days later to inform me that since his boss had given him a $2,000 raise and invited him to a barbecue as soon as he brought up the lawsuit, Sil and I would have to get along without him.

"Don't worry, I got your back, sister Bari," a smooth-talking black professional in another department assured me, adding that "you and Sil can be Mr. Outside and I'll be Mr. Inside. You tell me what you're up to and I'll tell you what they're up to." It was obvious that he was trying to wheedle some secret out of me that he could turn to his own advantage.

After I told him that I needed someone to stand beside me, not in back of me, I never heard from him again.

In the ladies' room an older black woman who had worked for many years in another department assailed me with a barrage of furious questions. "Why are you stirring up all this mess?" she bellowed at me, clenching her fists and coming so close that I thought she would strike me. "How long have you worked here anyway? You're sitting up there in a two-pane office starting all this crap without thinking about anybody else! What do you have to complain about? You're just going to mess things up for everybody! I don't want no part of this, you hear me!"

With so little hope of gaining support from our coworkers, Sil and I optimistically reached out to civil rights groups for assistance. Surely groups whose sole reason for existence was fighting bigotry would respond to our cause! We fired off letters and e-mail messages to Jesse Jackson's Rainbow Coalition, the NAACP, and Urban League and other black organizations, telling them about the case and asking for any help they could give us. Not a single one of them answered. Except for "Dora" and our lawyers, Sil and I were still very much on our own.

"Pay those Negroes no mind at all," Florence admonished me over lunch at a nearby restaurant to which we had fled a day or two later for some respite from the tension inside the building. "They've been beaten down so long they're used to it. They got that slave mentality. They've got a little white voice inside their heads controlling them. It'll take them a while to stop listening to it and realize that you and Sil are right to do what you're doing. Right now, most of them are just scared. Some of them will come around. You just have to be patient. What else you gonna do, girlfriend?"

Meanwhile, Texaco seemed to be deliberately ignoring Sil and me. Apart from the ritualistic denials it had issued when the story broke, the company had been ominously silent. None of the finance department managers we had named in the suit made any mention of it. Indeed, they seemed to be going out of their way to act as though the suit was of no concern to them at all. Their feigned nonchalance and business-as-usual attitude struck me as arrogant and contemptuous, an extension of the war of nerves that the company had waged against its black employees since the Leaphart fiasco. I had to suppress the urge to barge into Shelby's office, grab him by his lapels, and demand, "What do you think about this?"

The tension was as thick as fog by April 1, when Jack Butler arrived to take over the assistant manager's job that had been denied me. When he called me into his office I braced myself for what I presumed would be a testy encounter.

"Bari, I'm new over here," he began, after the two of us sat down. "I don't know the language, I don't know the products. I need help from the team.

"I'm going to rely very heavily on you in particular to help train me, and help me get up to speed about this department."

I had to stifle a cry of frustration as Butler prattled on about his previous assignment at Texaco's alternative energy research and development project. He had just confirmed what Shelby had told me about his complete ignorance about the work of the P&B department. If I, a black woman, or Sil, a black man, had applied for a job about which we knew so little, Texaco would have laughed in our faces. For a good old boy like Jack Butler, this astonishing lack of experience had been no hindrance at all. By the time our meeting broke up, I was burning.

The uneasy calm finally burst on April 4, the anniversary of Martin Luther King Jr.'s assassination. Late on the previous afternoon, as I was preparing to leave work for the day, Jack Butler had come into my office with a long list of questions about a recent meeting of the pension committee and some other work I had done. Knowing that it would be a lengthy discussion, I asked if we could postpone it until the next day.

"Fine," he barked at me, "we'll meet at eight o'clock in the morning."

I left home in plenty of time to be at work for the meeting with Butler. But as I sped down the highway toward Harrison, I heard the telltale thunk of a flat tire. I nursed the car to the nearest gas station, but I could not get the tire fixed right away because the mechanic had not yet arrived. So, as had long been the custom in the finance department when there was an emergency, I phoned the secretary in charge of keeping attendance and told her that I would be late, but expected to arrive no later than nine.

I was still a bit flustered when I got to the office at 8:45. I was unpacking my bag when Butler suddenly loomed in my door.

"So," he said, sarcastically, "Let's start our eight o'clock meeting."

"Jack, can I have a few minutes to unpack my bag and get a cup of coffee?" I replied, with a little smile, adding that a flat tire had delayed my arrival. "I can come down and meet with you in about ten minutes."

"No," he shouted. "We're going to do this right now! I'm tired of waiting!" Then he started rattling off questions. "What's the PBGC? What's this securities lending program all about? When is your next meeting with the actuary?"

I interrupted. "Jack, what makes sense is for me to give you copies of some of the reports that I've done so you can read them. Then I'll be happy to answer any questions you have."

"I'm not reading anything," he shouted again, even louder. "You are going to tell me everything I want to know right now."

"No, I'm not, Jack," I replied. Though I kept my voice low, I had become as angry as he was. "I will give you some stuff to read, you can develop some questions based on that, and we can discuss it."

"Bari, you have to do what I say when I tell you to do it," Butler screamed. His eyes were rolling and his face was scarlet. "I'm your superior."

"No, you aren't, Jack," I fired back.

"You obviously don't understand anything about organization, do you?" he said in a voice laden with contempt. "Allen Krowe is up here, Bob Ulrich is here, Shelby Faber is here, I'm here," he said, lowering his hand as he ticked off each name to indicate where each person stood in the Texaco hierarchy. "You," he said, pointing to the floor, "you're down here."

By then I had had enough of this obnoxious and totally unnecessary confrontation. "Jack, leave my office right now," I yelled at him. "This conversation is going nowhere. Why don't we both get some space right now."

"I'm not leaving until you give me everything in your desk! It's Texaco property and I want it right now!"

"Jack, I'm not giving you anything!"

"Oh yes, you are! If you don't start taking out your files right now, I'm going to come around there and get them!"

"Come on," I yelled, thrusting out my jaw in defiance. "You just come on!"

Very deliberately, Butler strode around my desk and stood over me clenching his fists as I quivered with rage in my chair. When he reached down toward the desk drawer, I pushed my knee against it to block him.

"So now what are you going to do?" I seethed, looking directly into his face. We locked stares for an instant that felt like an eternity. He looked away first, then walked back to the other side of the desk and sat down. I rose on unsteady legs and escaped as quickly as I could into the corridor, brushing past a small band of coworkers who had been standing outside my door listening to the argument.

When I returned after about twenty minutes or so, Butler was still sitting there, still red-faced and scowling. Unbelievably, as soon as I got through the door, he started demanding answers to the very same questions that had triggered our previous brawl. What's the PBGC? What's the securities lending program? When is your next meeting with the actuary?

I'd had enough. I stopped him in midstream.

"Jack, this is insane. This is not how I operate. I can't believe it's how you operate. We need to break this off right now and talk about all this stuff later."

I don't know if my imploring tone or the dismayed look on my face had anything to do with it, but Butler seemed to come to his senses. Yet he could not resist pointing a finger at me and firing a parting shot as he walked to the door. "The next time you are going to be late, you call me and tell me directly, understand? Don't just call in to the secretary."

"But calling in to the secretary has been the policy since I've been here," I sputtered back. "Are you saying that I have to meet a different standard from everyone else?"

"Exactly right," he said, "You call me, not the secretary."

About an hour later, I went to Shelby and told him what had happened.

He gave me an incredulous look and blandly asked, "What in the world did you do to get Jack so upset?"

It was such a classic good-old-boy response that I almost laughed.

Florence's advice to be patient turned out to be right on target. Over the next few days calls from scoffers and mere curiosity seekers declined to a trickle. Gradually, other blacks who believed that Texaco had violated their rights stepped forward to join our cause. The stories of these long-suffering men and women made my heart break. Some of them made the ordeal I had gone through seem like a picnic. Their pain practically screamed.

There was a ship-to-shore call from the only black worker on an off-shore oil rig somewhere in the mid-Atlantic, tearfully complaining about the constant stream of racist vilification that was hurled at him by his white shipmates.

There was one from a man who had worked for Texaco for eighteen years, claiming that he had experienced a nervous breakdown because of the company's noxious racial environment. As he recounted his pathetic and moving story of racist taunts, physical threats, and being passed over for one promotion after another, I could hear his wife imploring him to get off the phone and take his medicine. There was another from a Filipino who said he was fed up with the racist wisecracks of his white coworkers at a Texaco outpost in Singapore and wanted to know if our lawsuit was for blacks only.

Some of the stories were so outrageous that even I had trouble believing them. Marsha Harris had recently been transferred to the Texaco controller's office in Universal City, California, after working for the company for nineteen years in Houston. Her troubles with Texaco had begun as soon as she applied for a job with the company after graduating from Spelman, a prestigious black women's college, with a degree in economics. She wanted to be stationed in Atlanta for personal reasons, but was told by a Texaco manager that it would not be possible because "we already have enough blacks in Atlanta, and we need some more in Houston. That's where we want you to go." Like me, Marsha felt that she had been passed over for promotions and high-profile job opportunities because of her race.

But what really riled her, she told me, was "NIGYYSOB."

Short for "now I got you, you son of a bitch," the acronym had appeared in the instructional materials for a Texaco in-house training course that Marsha had taken. It was Texaco terminology for a management style that should be avoided. Merely printed on the page, it had struck Marsha as just another example of the catchy management jargon that had become so popular during the 1980s and 1990s. It wasn't until she heard the instructor, Patricia Guard of Texaco's human resources department, refer to something called "nigger-sob" on the first day of the course, that she knew how the term was pronounced—the "N-word" followed by sob, as in "cry." Marsha shook her head in disbelief. She was sure she could not have actually heard what she thought she had. But after Guard repeated it several times, Marsha knew she was not mistaken. She was shocked and offended by the use of a term with such an insulting racial connotation. It seemed totally insensitive. Even some of the good old boys taking the course seemed to share her discomfort. One volunteered to Marsha that "you could not pay me to say it."

Marsha approached Guard before the second day's session to express her concern. She told the instructor that she felt that the term was totally inappropriate in the workplace because it sounded too much like the N-word. According to Marsha, Guard replied that she had been using the acronym for quite a while and no one had ever objected. But she promised to pass Marsha's complaint on to higher-ups in HR and get back to her. Despite Marsha's repeated attempts to follow up on the conversation through Texaco's electronic message system, she never heard anything further. Indeed, the insulting term had been used in at least one other class two weeks to a month later.

I got Marsha to send me a copy of the instructional materials and put her in touch with Cyrus Mehri.

Though *Roberts v. Texaco* was only a few weeks old, being a plaintiff in a racial discrimination suit had already proved to be one of the most stressful and demanding roles I had ever played in my life. It affected everything from my relationships with my family and friends to the way I performed on my job, to my health (which was getting worse) and the size of my phone bill (which was soaring). The most difficult aspect was coming to terms with the undeniable fact that I had surrendered control over certain basic decisions that could profoundly affect my life to a group of people whom I trusted implicitly but did not know very well: the outcome of the case, and my destiny, rested with our lawyers. Sil and I had a role to play as conduits of information, and we would, of course, have a big say in the extremely unlikely event that Texaco made an offer to settle the case. But when it came to shaping strategy or making day-to-day decisions, the matter was entirely out of our hands. Cyrus kept us up to date on major developments as the case proceeded, but that was not an entirely acceptable substitute for being in the room when major events transpired. Sometimes, frustrating weeks would go by with no major action. It was like being a soldier in a remote outpost far from the main battleground. I could only hear the distant thunder of legal artillery; I was not calling the shots.

One reason that I felt so out of the loop was that our legal team had greatly expanded. In addition to Cyrus, Cohen, Milstein had assigned a young associate named Beth Andreozzi to the case. Hausfeld's old friend, Charles Mann, Ph.D., a wisecracking statistical expert, had also come on board to analyze whatever data the lawyers could pry out of Texaco's clutches. To give us a legal beachhead in New York and share the enormous upfront costs of the litigation that we all thought would last for years, Cohen, Milstein enlisted Daniel L. Berger and Steve Singer of Bernstein, Litowitz, Berger & Grossman, a venerable law firm whose offices were located on Manhattan's Avenue of the Americas not far from the Chase Manhattan building where I had spent so many satisfying years. Finally, to compensate for its own lack of recent experience in civil rights and racial discrimination suits, Cohen, Milstein secured the assistance of Richard T. Sampson, a flamboyant Baltimore lawyer with a fondness for cowboy boots, who had handled a lot of discrimination cases. It was a formidable team with an equally formidable mission.

In order for *Roberts v. Texaco* to go forward as a class action suit, the lawyers had to establish four basic facts:

1. That the affected group was so numerous that it would be impractical for all of its members to become individual plaintiffs;

2. That there were questions of law or fact that all members of the group had in common;

3. That the claims being made by the name plaintiffs—in this case Sil and me—were typical of those of the group as a whole;

4. And that we could fairly and adequately represent the interests of all of those we wanted to fight for.

Moreover, and this is what made the challenge especially daunting, we were planning a broad-based assault on discrimination throughout Texaco, not just in the finance department where Sil and I worked, which meant delving into the operations of a company with tens of thousands of employees in dozens of locations all over the country. In recent years, one conservative court ruling after another had made it next to impossible to win certification for a class as all-encompassing as the one we were trying to assemble; judges were always whittling them down. You might succeed in obtaining class certification for, say, blacks employed in grades seven through nine in the accounts receivable division of the accounting department of the company, but that would not include blacks working right next door in the accounts payable division of the very same firm. The things that Texaco had done to Sil and me were certainly egregious acts of bigotry, but they did not by themselves provide sufficient proof of a company-wide culture of discrimination. We needed a whole lot more.

To back up our claim that the company was guilty of *systematic* discrimination, we needed blacks from other divisions of Texaco to step forward and join the suit, proving that racist employment practices existed beyond the confines of the finance department. Sil and I could help on that front. We gathered the names of the people who had reached out to us, and passed them along to our lawyers. Then Cyrus flew out to interview them, in all debriefing more than thirty potential plaintiffs. Four became name plaintiffs when the lawyers filed an amended and expanded version of our complaint on June 30, 1994.

One of the plaintiffs named was Marsha Harris, who had brought the astounding NIGYYSOB story to our attention. Another was Janet Leigh Williams, a marketing consultant at a Texaco subsidiary named TRMI in Orange County, California. Janet had won a handsome collection of plaques for her extraordinary performance, including the "Superstar 1992 Award for the Pacific Region," that TRMI's president described as the highest honor in the company's pantheon, and "The Star of the American Road" as the best marketing consultant in the region. In 1992, she learned that despite her stellar sales record she was being paid $850 a month less than whites who held the same position. When she complained about the discrepancy to her supervisor, a white man named Scott Bratt, he had brushed her off with the comment, "There's nothing we can do about it." The following year, after a transfer to another TRMI branch in Orange County, she took up the matter again with her new boss, Milton Price, who was even more brusque, telling her that, "Management doesn't have to pay you the same as everyone else." As if that weren't enough, Janet said that Price had a penchant for making racist wisecracks. He had once admonished her to "stop all this Anglo-Saxon dialogue," which Janet assumed to mean that she should stop speaking grammatical English and talk like a character out of *Amos 'n' Andy*.

Beatrice Hester had worked for TRMI since 1989 as an administrative systems secretary in the marketing division. After about a year on the job, she asked her supervisors what it would take for her to win a promotion to marketing consultant. She was told that she needed a college degree. After she got her bachelor of science from University of Redlands in 1992, she formally applied for a vacant marketing consultant's job, only to be informed by a coworker that it had been set aside for a white male employee who hadn't even been interviewed for the position. When she complained to her boss—the same Milton Price with whom Janet Williams had tangled—he told her that management "wanted to hire a certain type of person" for the job.

Last was Veronica Shinault, who had recently quit her job as an assistant in Texaco's human resources department and gone to work as a manager at Gannett newspapers. She said that instead of giving her a promotion and pay raise that her manager promised, Texaco had given her a new title, but at the same salary.

I had never met any of the new named plaintiffs face to face, but they felt like old comrades-in-arms. Sil and I were no longer out there alone. I wanted to hug them all.

Adding the four new named plaintiffs to the complaint went a long way toward satisfying the human dimension. But we also needed hard, detailed statistics that Charles Mann could analyze for evidence that throughout Texaco blacks as a group were paid less or promoted less frequently than their equally qualified white counterparts, to back our claim that the PMP process was being applied in a racially discriminatory manner across the board. There was only one place to get that information: Texaco's own files. It was going to be a tough nut to crack.

In lawsuits like *Roberts v. Texaco*, both plaintiffs and defendants are allowed to go after that sort of information in a process known as discovery. They submit requests for documents that the other side must comply with, unless it has compelling reasons not to do so. Deliberately withholding or concealing requested evidence is a violation of the law. The problem was that our lawyers were not exactly sure of what they should be looking for. As financial specialists, neither Sil nor I had a clue about the manner in which Texaco maintained its payroll records or hiring data. We had no idea of what went on in the secretive meetings where high-ranking good old boys doled out promotions and plum assignments. Some of the black Texaco employees who had stepped forward to help our cause had tidbits of information that filled in a few of the yawning gaps in our incomplete picture of how Texaco operated. But beyond those fragmentary leads, the lawyers were flying blind. They had to ask Texaco to produce *every-thing* that might conceivably be relevant in the broadest possible terms, or else something could fall through the cracks. The downside of the strategy was that it might provide Texaco with a pretext for weaseling out of supplying the data on the grounds that our requests were too ambiguous or unduly burdensome.

The lawyers knew they were in for a fight over every single scrap of information, no matter how innocuous it seemed. As Gary Brouse of the ICCR had cautioned us, Texaco's chairman, Al DeCrane, had a well-deserved reputation for continuing to fight legal battles long after any reasonable person would have concluded that Texaco did not have a leg to stand on. He was, as one of the lawyers described him, "one bull-headed, litigious s.o.b."

To defend itself in our case, Texaco had selected a law firm as tough and combative as DeCrane himself: New York's Kaye, Scholer, Fierman, Hays & Handler. They were really tough customers and awesomely effective. Just six months before *Roberts v. Texaco* was filed, they had persuaded a judge in the very same courthouse where our case would be fought to deny class certification in the sex discrimination suit that had been brought by Charlene McGowan. In the words of *The American Lawyer* magazine, Kaye, Scholer had squashed McGowan's suit "like a tank rolling over a tin can" by, among other things, destroying her reputation. Kaye, Scholer's unmitigated victory in the McGowan case made it certain that the firm would adopt identical tactics in *Roberts v. Texaco.*

The Kaye, Scholer lawyer in charge of Texaco's defense in *Roberts v. Texaco* was Andrea Christensen, who had been deeply involved in grinding McGowan's case into the mud. Christensen's objective would be to challenge our case on every possible ground. She would attempt to discredit Sil's and my individual claims of bias by waging personal attacks on our credentials and performance. She would argue that even if our individual complaints were valid, they were not proof of widespread discrimination in the company. Even if they were, she would contend Sil and I were not fit to serve as representatives of Texaco's blacks. In short, she would attack and attack and attack. As Cyrus warned Sil and me, "From here on, it's going to be scorched earth, legal trench warfare. And both of you are going to be targets."

In some ways a lawsuit is like war. These are also elements of espionage. Our key secret agent was "Dora," the source of Texaco's confidential response to the Mobil Salary Survey that had given the lawyers their first hard evidence of widespread discrimination within the company. Over the next few months, several anonymous envelopes stuffed with vital information from company files were delivered to Cohen, Milstein's office in Washington. A copy of the affirmative action plan for Texaco headquarters. A report from the Office of Federal Contract Compliance Programs reprimanding Texaco for discriminating against blacks at its facility in Houston in 1994. Pages and pages of stuff.

She and a few other sympathetic coworkers kept it up until Texaco flew into a rage and changed the access codes on its computers. "Dora's" sources dried up. But by then, it didn't matter. She had provided us with a trove of damaging evidence that Texaco and Kaye, Scholer never wanted to fall into our hands.

For Christensen, learning "Dora's" identity became a magnificent obsession. For our side, protecting her—and other black employees who supported us—was a top priority. We feared retaliation by Texaco that much. It became the issue that overshadowed everything else in the early phases of the battle over discovery.

Someone should write a whole book about our legal team's efforts to pry evidence that we were clearly entitled to out of Texaco and the outrageous techniques that the company and Christensen used to conceal it. It would be a very large tome. Our lawyers knew that fights over providing evidence were run-of-the-mill. But the resistance they got from Texaco was extreme. Whenever our lawyers sought to get hard data about Texaco's employment practices, the company stalled and switched the subject to our sources of information. It seemed to me that it was the only thing they ever wanted to talk about. Even after Magistrate Fox told them to knock it off, they persisted. Over the next eighteen months they demanded that our lawyers disclose "Dora's" identity at least ten times. Meanwhile, they were stonewalling our requests for documents every step of the way.

One of the most vital pieces of information we sought was the so-called Texaco Interactive Personnel Payroll System database, a computerized employment database covering every worker in the company—TIPPS for short. This was the raw material Charles Mann needed to determine whether or not blacks had been underpaid or promoted less frequently than similarly qualified whites. Though every legal precedent our lawyers could come up with established our right to the TIPPS database, Texaco and Christensen refused to turn it over, offering one mind-boggling rationale after another as an excuse for failing to comply with our repeated demands.

It would cost too much to run off a copy of the data.

The data was being moved from one Texaco facility to another.

It would take Texaco's computer staff ninety days to run off a tape.

Our lawyers might give it to computer hackers who could use it to break into Texaco's database.

Whatever it took. They were shameless.

Texaco's refusal to turn over copies of the high-potential list was even sillier and more infuriating. Being on the high-potential list was the ticket to the top at Texaco. It guaranteed high-profile assignments and promotions. Allen Krowe, the company's chief financial officer, had personally told me that I was on it. It turned out that one of Veronica Shinault's duties in the human resources department had been to keep it updated. She told the lawyers about it in great detail. There was an HP-5 list of employees who management thought could be promoted by three grade levels or more in a five-year period. There was an HP-10 list of those who might make the leap over a decade. Only a tiny handful of blacks had ever been on either one. In a sense, the list was the embodiment of the good-old-boy network, the means through which the all-white, all-male company elite took care of its own.

But when our lawyers asked Texaco for copies, Christensen wrote back on July 17, 1994, that "Texaco has no responsive information." She was, in effect, denying that the high-profile list that Texaco had been using for years even existed!

The wrangling took a turn that would have been funny had it not been so serious, when a few months later Veronica made an astonishing discovery. With the permission of her supervisors in Texaco's HR department, she had frequently brought home documents from the office, so she could work on them on her personal computer. Among the items she had worked on at home was—you guessed it—the high-potential list. When she first got involved in the case, she had forgotten the list was still on her hard drive, so she didn't tell Cyrus about it.

*   *   *

Unlike Texaco's, our lawyers did not stonewall or delay when Texaco made requests for documents in our possession. So when the company demanded that the name plaintiffs turn over copies of any documents about Texaco that were in their possession, Veronica checked her computer. Lo and behold, the high-potential list was still there. She printed a copy and gave it to the lawyers, who in turn produced it to Texaco.

Christensen went through the roof. She fired off a furious screed, dated September 12, 1994, to Magistrate Fox who was overseeing the discovery process, demanding that he issue a court order "compelling plaintiff's counsel to disclose how they obtained highly confidential documents that were taken from Texaco's offices without permission or authorization. . . . They included lists of Texaco employees who have been identified as having high potential for advancement. . . ."

Christensen had put herself in the ridiculous position of trying to find out who had given us a document whose very existence she had denied only two months earlier!

Then she went even farther. She added that the fact that our lawyers even had a copy of the supposedly nonexistent document raised "issues concerning the qualifications and fitness of the proposed class counsel."

Though she was the one who had just been caught in a big fat lie, she was accusing our lawyers of unfitness.

It was arrogant. It was vindictive. It was dishonest and totally absurd. It was so Texaco.

CHAPTER FOURTEEN

DUELING DEPOSITIONS

Hair is a statement. A few weeks after *Roberts v. Texaco* was filed, I wanted to look like a warrior in the hope that it would help me to feel more like one. So I consulted with a "locktician"—a specialist in cultivating the natural Rastafarian hairstyle known as dreadlocks—in a heavily West Indian-populated section of Brooklyn. She called herself Ona the Locksmyth and her slogan was, "we don't just lock hair, we unlock minds." She cut off the braided extensions I had been wearing for several months, and twisted my kinks into a cap of spiky, ear-length coils—a perfect, bristling look for going into battle. "Oh Ma," Staci exclaimed when she saw me, "you look awesome." I thought so, too.

One of the reasons for my defiant attitude was that Texaco had started rooting around in my past in an attempt to do the same thing to me and Sil that it had done to Charlene McGowan—win its case by destroying my reputation. Christensen had also started a witch hunt to find out the names of the black Texaco employees who were in the least bit sympathetic to our case, especially "Dora."

Starting on June 16, 1994, Christensen fired off one letter after another to Magistrate Fox demanding that our lawyers turn over the names of "putative class members," which included, by implication, any black employee at Texaco who had ever asked Sil and me why we had filed the case. Our lawyers refused to comply with these demands, for what I thought were very good reasons. Apart from Sil and I, no black employee of Texaco had at this point stepped forward and become a plaintiff. We saw no reason to expose anyone who was merely seeking information about the case to the very real threat of intimidation.

Prospective witnesses needed to look no further than Sil's and my experiences to know that Texaco's lawyers would try to drag their names through the mud if they came forward. In early July, Christensen blasted off subpoenas to every employer that Sil and I had ever worked for, and to every college or graduate school we had ever attended. She did the same to the other four name plaintiffs after they joined the suit. It was harassment on a grand scale. Texaco had had ample opportunity to check the references and school records both of us had supplied when we applied for our jobs. Insofar as *Roberts v. Texaco* was concerned, the only work experience that mattered was the three-plus years I had spent in Texaco's finance department. I had received three consecutive above average ratings, which was surely a better indication of my competence and qualifications as a senior financial analyst than some dusty archive from the insurance company in Chicago where I held down my first, very low clerical position.

In retrospect I'm not sure if Christensen's fishing expedition into my past was really designed to produce any new and damaging information about me, since there wasn't any. It was probably part of her strategy for rattling me on the eve of my deposition, which was set to take place on July 14 and 15 at

Dan Berger's office in Rockefeller Center. I was already nervous about testifying under oath for the very first time. I didn't know what was expected. Moreover, Hausfeld, the lawyer in charge of our legal team, had another commitment and would not be present. Herb Milstein, a senior partner in Cohen, Milstein, would be filling in, along with Cyrus. I'd never met Milstein. "Just keep in mind that this is not a trial. She's going to try to upset you. You should answer most questions yes or no. If you don't understand a question say so. And if you need to take a break, you can always take one."

Milstein's advice was reassuring, but only up to a point. I was jittery when the questioning began, which is precisely what Christensen wanted. It is impossible to fully convey in words what it is like to be interrogated by her. You had to see her in action to appreciate the spectacle in all its malevolent glory. To begin with, she was dressed to intimidate—all black clothes, stringy blond hair, and a contemptuous curl on her lips. She did not even say good morning, but plunged right into her attack. She never looked at me directly, but with a sidelong glare and a sneer. Her fidgety movements and frequent snarls suggested that she was on the verge of bursting with rage. She was a master of innuendo by mere inflection. She could talk about the most innocent aspect of your life in a tone that made it seem like a deep moral failing.

We hadn't been into it for more than five minutes when we had our first clash, during a review of my education and previous work.

"All right, I'm going to ask you to look at Defendant's exhibit number one, page fourteen," she growled, flinging a document down on the desk. It was a copy of our amended complaint.

"If you'll note there, it states 'Ms. Roberts graduated from Loyola University of Chicago in 1978 with a bachelor of arts degree.'

"Why do you state in your complaint that you graduated from Loyola University and on your application that you graduated from Mundelein College?" A fierce expression crept over her face that translated into, "Aha, I've got you now!"

As I explained simply that Mundelein had become a part of Loyola after I graduated, Christensen eyes bulged and a look of total incredulity spread over her face. She turned her head slightly and clicked her teeth as though she had never heard such a preposterous story before.

It was like that all day. The insinuations got really thick when she turned to the sick leave I had taken from Chase Manhattan just before coming to work at Texaco.

"At what point in time did you conclude your disability with Chase?" she demanded.

"Around the first of November, around the first of November," I said, wondering what would come next.

"So, prior to November first, you received from your physician a statement that you were capable of returning to work?" She was really boring in, jabbing her pencil, quivering like a Doberman.

"I'm not sure when I received that—when I received the— as a matter of fact—I'm not sure when I received that statement. It may not have been November. I'm saying around November or December," I sputtered, trying my best to figure out where this might be leading.

"When you filled out your application to seek employment at Texaco, which was signed November 29, 1990, had you been certified as capable of returning to work?

"I can't remember. I'm not sure that I was certified. I know the doctor and I were in conversation about it. But certified, receiving something from him, I'm not sure of that date."

"Well," she said, leaning back, and shaking her head skeptically, "did you return to work at any point during 1990 at Chase Manhattan?"

"No."

"Did you continue to receive disability checks up until the point at which you started work at Texaco?"

I said I couldn't remember.

She turned to other subjects for a while, then suddenly honed in again on the question of my sick leave.

"Were you perfectly comfortable with Chase Manhattan Bank knowing that you were looking for another job while you were on disability leave from the bank?"

"I was not uncomfortable with that."

"You weren't concerned that Chase Manhattan Bank might think that was an act of disloyalty, to be receiving disability payments and at the same time interviewing for another job with another employer?"

We had not even gotten to the lunch break yet, and she had already implied that I had inflated my résumé and ripped off Chase Manhattan. I wondered if we were ever going to get around to talking about racial discrimination at Texaco.

At the very end of the first day, Christensen returned to her obsession to learn the names of any black employees who might be sympathetic to my cause.

"Can you give me a single instance of an individual who complained to the Texaco affirmative action officer and as to whom no—"

Herb Milstein leaped in before she could complete the question. "I think we're into an area here that, of sort of naming names, that has been raised with the magistrate. . . . I think she knows, but she doesn't want to identify who it was and whom she knows, and I think that this information is privileged."

"Can you tell me how that information is privileged?" Christensen snarled.

Herb was cool. "Well, I'd be happy to, but this woman [referring to me] really wants to go home, and she's really tired."

"Well, we'll start off the morning with a call to Magistrate Fox," Christensen intoned sarcastically.

"That's fine," Herb blandly replied.

*   *   *

The next day began with the promised call to Magistrate Fox, but he was busy in court and could not come to the phone. So the big question of whether I could be forced to give up the names of our sympathizers would not be answered until he called back. Herb Milstein offered a compromise that would allow me to keep testifying until the issue could be resolved. He said that I could give Christensen the answers she wanted provided they were placed under seal, meaning that they could not be disclosed to anyone—including Texaco—except the lawyers working on both sides of the case, unless and until the magistrate ordered otherwise. After checking with the company, Christensen agreed.

Thus, when she asked me the names of workers who had complained about being discriminated against by Texaco, I had no choice but to name them. When she demanded to know who had gone with me to discuss our grievances with the federal Equal Employment Opportunity Commission, I had no choice but to name them. When she asked who besides me had attended the meeting with Brouse, I had to name them. It was one of the hardest things I had ever been forced to do in my life.

But for some reason, Christensen never directly asked me the question that I was most reluctant to answer: the identity of the person who had given my lawyers the Mobil salary survey that had gotten our whole case off the ground.

Christensen had missed her golden opportunity.

I did not have to identify "Dora."

Her true identity remains a secret to this very day and I pray that it always will.

A bit later, Christensen started going after the names of the Texaco employees who had attended the meeting with Leaphart's lawyer.

"After careful consideration, I'm going to instruct the witness not to answer that," Milstein interjected. "I think the identity of those who attended that meeting and what was said, it was seeking legal advice and I think that's fully protected."

Christensen snapped back. "The names are not protected under the attorney-client privilege or any other privilege."

"I think under these circumstances, it is," Milstein replied.

"No," snapped Christensen. "The court told us to proceed with the deposition, and as a matter of fact, Magistrate Fox made it quite clear on the phone that he viewed that the names should be disclosed."

"No," Cyrus piped up, with a look of total astonishment. "He didn't say that."

Christensen smiled condescendingly. "See, that's one of the problems with having so many different law firms handling this. We both, John Howley [a young Kaye, Scholer lawyer] and I were on the phone and as far as the names were concerned, he made it quite clear that he viewed that was information which should be disclosed."

"Well, I was there and I didn't get that impression from him at all," Cyrus shot back.

"Well, why don't we call him and ask him?" said Christensen.

It took a while to get through to the magistrate. "What's the problem?" he asked.

"The problem is that we've asked for the names of putative class members and the plaintiff's counsel has taken the position that that information is confidential and privileged," said Christensen.

"Isn't that under consideration by me right now?" the magistrate said, sounding puzzled.

"It's the precise issue before you right now," Cyrus answered.

"It's our position, and we have substantial case law to support it, that there's nothing confidential about the names," Christensen said.

The magistrate cut her off.

"I have you scheduled to come in on the twenty-eighth [of July]. I'm certainly not in a position, candidly, to give you a ruling on this at this point. I think you should proceed with what you have." His tone suggested that he was annoyed by Christensen's attempt to rush him into ruling on the matter before he was ready. Christensen had tried to pull a fast one and failed.

The judge's rebuke of Christensen revived my confidence. By the time she finally got around to asking me about the racial abuses that had been heaped on me since my first day at Texaco, I knew I was on solid ground. I made no effort to conceal my outrage at Jack Butler's near-physical assault on me nor that my evaluation had been lowered because senior management said I was "uppity." I gave back as good as I got, even when the questions grew completely bizarre. At one point, Christensen even tried to suggest that Sigfrid had been sympathizing with blacks, not insulting me, when she complained that until my arrival the finance department had been "lily white."

"Is the term 'lily white' considered to be derogatory toward a Caucasian?" snapped Christensen.

I was baffled by the question.

"Some Caucasians would tell you that they find that to be a highly offensive comment. So I'm curious as to how you responded to the use of the term 'lily white'?"

"I don't know how Caucasians view it, okay," I replied, throwing up my hands in exasperation. The whole discussion seemed silly and pointless.

At about 6:30 P.M. Christensen spat out, "I have no further questions," and dismissed me with a wave of the hand. I felt like one of Muhammad Ali's punching bags, but at least I had survived.

If it had been tough for me, it was even tougher for Sil when he squared off with Christensen. She seemed to have even more contempt for him than she had for me, perhaps because he is a black man. Whatever its origin, Chistensen's animus immediately got under Sil's skin and he responded with cockiness. He tried to fence with her. Within only a few minutes of the interrogation, he was frankly in very deep water.

His difficulties began when Christensen asked him why he had asked for a starting salary of $60,000 at Texaco after making as much as three times more in his previous job at Prudential Bache.

"In 1989, you earned $185,000 in commissions; 1990, you earned approximately $80,000. Why didn't you ask to earn $80,000 at Texaco?" Christensen demanded, showing Sil a copy of his job application.

"I don't know," Sil replied. "I don't remember, honestly, I don't remember putting that $60,000 figure in there, but it is right there. That's the best I can explain it."

A few questions later Christensen hammered the point home relentlessly.

"Is it your belief that Texaco's decision to hire you at $60,000 a year as an analyst in the trading room was motivated by your race?"

"Could you explain the question?"

"Is it your position that your race had anything to do with the decision made by Texaco to hire you as an analyst in the trading room in March 1990?"

"See, I'm not sure what you mean by the question, that race had to do with hiring me. I don't know what you mean."

"Was your race involved in any way in the decision made by Texaco to hire you in March 1990?"

"Do I believe that race was a factor in hiring me?"

"Right."

"I don't know."

"Do you believe that you were treated differently by Texaco in the manner in which you were hired because of your race?"

"Well, that's what I'm talking about in terms of the salary. I believe that because of race I was started at a lower level."

It was clear that Sil would have a hard time proving that Texaco had discriminated against him by paying him the starting salary that he had asked for. Score one for Christensen.

But as had been the case with me, Sil recovered his balance when the subject shifted to what the case was really all about: Texaco's bigoted employment practices. His account of Ulrich's bald-faced attempt to persuade him to drop the charge of racial discrimination he had lodged against his supervisor, Bob Gordan, in exchange for a raise and a higher evaluation was passionate, detailed, and convincing.

After a shaky start, Sil had fought his way back to a draw by the end of the deposition.

But when our lawyers took depositions from a band of high-level Texaco executives, they had an entirely different objective. Instead of trying to trick the company's witnesses into contradicting themselves or attacking them personally, our legal team was trying to learn as much as it could about the way in which the good-old-boy network really operated inside the company. It was a difficult quest, almost like hacking one's way through a jungle, because most of the witnesses were either evasive or so unknowledgeable about their own departments that their testimony was nearly useless.

The exception was Rich Lundwall, the finance department's senior administrator for human resources. He was pure Texaco, an ex-Marine who had worked his way up from gas station attendant to management during thirty years with the company. He and I had had one memorable and unsettling run-in at Texaco, when he scolded me for taking issue with Jim Link at the TAFE team meeting.

Unlike the other Texaco witnesses, Lundwall seemed willing to give a direct reply to a direct question about the internal workings of the personnel system of the finance department. On August 5, 1994, Cyrus asked him a series of questions about the TIPPS database:

"Let's say that you extracted information from the TIPPS system regarding the finance department for your use as part of your job responsibility. Do you create kind of a separate database that you work with on your own or do you put it on a tape, or what do you do usually?"

"Neither of those," answered Lundwall.

"Can you describe what you do?"

"If it is data we are going to be using at a meeting, it would probably exist somewhere in my master book. There might be a compilation of data that I got from the system. But to keep another system to have the data in it would be redundant since we already have one."

"What do you mean by the master book?"

"I keep a book. We have minutes of meetings."

Cyrus's ears perked up. He had never heard of the master book before, but it sounded promising, so he pressed on.

"In the master book, are there hard copy extracts from the TIPPS system?"

"Oftentimes, yes."

Under further questioning, Lundwall disclosed that the master book was used as the basis for employee development meetings conducted twice a year by the senior managers of the finance department—Bob Ulrich, Dave Keough, Pete Wissel, Peter Meade, Steven Carlson, and Brian Ashley. Among the subjects they discussed were the department's track record and "What we can do to enhance Texaco's position in minority representation at higher position grades, managers, and supervisory levels."

To Cyrus, this master book sounded like an evidentiary gold mine. He turned to John Howley, the young Kaye, Scholer attorney.

"If you can, find out what you have produced, if anything, from this master book, including the minutes."

"If you are requesting the master book, send us a request. We will take it under advisement," Howley replied.

Cyrus sounded unusually excited in a conference call with Sil and me after Lundwall's testimony. "I think we may be onto something," he said, without going into detail.

On August 9, Cyrus sent a letter to Andrea Christensen. To avoid a complaint from Texaco that his request was too vague and burdensome, he carefully specified that he was looking for the "finance department master book and all documents related to or ever contained in such master book" that Lundwall had described in his testimony. You couldn't get more specific than that.

On August 11, Christensen replied by mail that "the additional documents and information that you have requested in your two letters of August 9 are currently being reviewed and we will notify you when the production is available."

It sounded like Texaco was going to turn the master book over. But just to make sure, Cyrus filed a formal request for the documents on August 12.

When the deadline for Texaco to turn over the evidence arrived thirty days later, the company did not produce even a shred of paper, much less the master books. As it had with the TIPPS data base and the high-potential list, the company was stonewalling us again!

Cyrus was frustrated and furious. After consulting with Dan and Steve Singer in New York, he telephoned Howley in mid-September and asked for the master books again. Howley told him they would be sent over the very same day.

They never arrived.

*   *   *

Faced with Texaco's refusal to turn over evidence the plaintiffs were clearly entitled to, the lawyers prepared for another bitter encounter with Texaco and Andrea Christensen. They began work on a request for a court order that would compel Texaco to release the master books and other documents.

But before the battle could be joined, *Roberts v. Texaco* took a totally unexpected twist.

Miguel Hernandez, a mediator who worked with the U.S. Justice Department's Community Relations Service, had read a newspaper story about our lawsuit and had volunteered to step in to help resolve the case before it went to court.

On September 14, Magistrate Fox took Hernandez up on his offer. He ordered a halt to litigation and instructed us to sit down with Texaco in November. He also ordered the company to stop stalling and give us the data from the TIPPS data base because we needed the information to prepare for the mediation.

It arrived only two days before the mediation was scheduled to begin. Charles Mann took a look at it and scratched his head in frustration. The company had deleted all the information about the employees in its highest pay grades—almost surely to conceal the fact that virtually all of them were white. The data it did provide was hopelessly scrambled. Cyrus compared it to shattering a mirror against the floor and expecting us to reassemble it and get an undistorted picture. Even on the brink of an attempt at mediation, Texaco was still playing games.

CHAPTER FIFTEEN

IN BAD FAITH

Though it seems preposterously naïve to have been the slightest bit optimistic after being on the receiving end of six months of stonewalling and deception, Sil and I went into mediation thinking there was a chance that Texaco would settle the case. It would have made good business sense. By entering into an agreement that both sides could support, the company could cut short a potentially embarrassing controversy without admitting any wrongdoing, stop the clock on the mounting fees it was paying Kaye, Scholer, and, perhaps most important, demonstrate that its commitment to equal opportunity was more than a sham. Our side also had good reasons to come to the table with an eye toward reaching a settlement; the main one was time. I had faith that Sil, the other plaintiffs, and I would not give up until we got justice, and that our lawyers would be with us every step of the way, no matter how long it took. But I saw no reason for us to endure a drawn-out legal ordeal whose outcome was totally uncertain if there was a chance to hammer out an acceptable deal in a few weeks of face-to-face bargaining. Such a result seemed imminently achievable, if Texaco negotiated in good faith—a questionable assumption, to be sure, but at least we could hope.

Even Mike Hausfeld seemed to think we might finally be getting somewhere as he outlined our bargaining strategy in Dan Berger's office on the morning the mediation began. "Okay," he said, reading from a sheet of scribbled notes. "The first thing we're going to talk about is changing the PMP process, stepping up minority recruiting, setting up a mentoring program and all the other broad programmatic changes we think are needed." He paused for an instant. "Then, once we get all that out of the way, we're going to talk about money."

He playfully poked a finger at the statistician, Charles Mann, who grunted something in Yiddish, but kept his eyes fixed on the *New York Times* crossword puzzle he had nearly filled out after working on it for only five minutes. "My good friend Charles has exercised his magnificent brain on the inadequate material that Texaco has so graciously deigned to provide us from the TIPPS data base and has come up with what seems like a reasonable figure. We think Texaco ought to pay ten million dollars in back wages to the black employees it has been discriminating against for the past five years and another ten million dollars to compensate. Throw in attorneys' fees and other odds and ends and it comes to thirty million dollars. Sil, Bari, how's that sound?"

It sounded pretty good to me. This was the first time Mike had ever said how much he was gunning for, and I was surprised to learn that he thought we could get so much. "Do you really think there's that kind of money in this?" Sil asked.

"Sure, sure, why not?" Mike answered, slipping into the Jewish accent he used when he was bantering with Mann. "We've got a strong case on behalf of fourteen hundred or fifteen hundred class members. It's a realistic sum. Now, Charles, hand me one of those bagels."

My optimism began to fade not long after the two teams lined up across a shiny oblong table at Kaye, Scholer's offices on Park Avenue. I was seated between Mike and Sil and directly across from Dave Keough and Bob Ulrich, impatiently drumming his fingers and patting his foot as though he couldn't wait to get out of there. Next to Ulrich perched Andrea Christensen, dressed in her usual tight-collared blouse and blue business suit, officiously shuffling through a stack of papers. At the far ends of the table sat two surprises: Ed Gasden, an African American who had been recruited to become Texaco's manager of diversity only a week before Sil and I filed the suit, and, to my shock and dismay, a young black Texaco lawyer named Carolyn Sellers. She was the wife of Sil's coworker and close friend, Johnny Sellers, and was looking extremely uncomfortable. Up to this point, neither Gasden or Carolyn—or any other black—had ever played any part in Texaco's strategy. It was obvious that Texaco had added them to its negotiating team so that it would not be all-white. I knew Carolyn well enough to know that if she had a choice, she wouldn't be sitting on that side of the table. From what little I knew about Gasden, I figured he had volunteered to be there.

There was something gentle and vaguely priestly about the mediator, Miguel Hernandez. Fiftyish, balding and slightly paunchy, he had spent more than two decades reconciling racial disputes. As far as we had been able to learn, he had little experience in dealing with corporate America. He took up station at a rostrum at one end of the table, behind which he had set up two easels. One of them had *Roberts* scrawled across the top, the other had *Texaco*.

"Is this room, we start with a level playing field; everybody is equal," Hernandez began, sounding very sincere. "Mediation is not like litigation, which is adversarial. If one side wins, the other side loses. In this room, we will search for common ground, so that both sides can win. In all my years as a mediator, I have never failed to bring about an agreement. I don't intend for this to be the first time I fail." He passed out some pamphlets, adding "You might find this helpful." It turned out to be literature about meditation and stress relief.

The difficulty of finding common ground became evident as soon as Christensen opened her mouth. In a voice dripping with false cordiality, she welcomed us to Kaye, Scholer's office and then outlined Texaco's view of the case. As far as she was concerned, the only issue was that Sil and I were literally making a federal case out of our career frustrations. When she finished she smirked.

Our side was shocked and disgusted. Our hope disappeared. It was now evident that Texaco had no intention of settling the case on any ground we might find acceptable. Christensen had not even mentioned the names of our four fellow plaintiffs, nor any of the specific allegations in our law suit. "She acts like she hasn't even read the complaint," I whispered to Sil. If that's all we're going to talk about, we might as well leave right now. We're wasting our time." Sil snickered softly, provoking a stare from Christensen that could have cut through steel. It was clear that she loathed him.

I could see that Hausfeld was as outraged as Sil and I were by Christensen's distorted summary of the issues. He took a moment to compose himself, then spoke directly to Hernandez, totally ignoring Christensen. Our view of the case was precisely the opposite. The case was about much, much more than two individuals. We were there to talk about relief for all the blacks who had been denied opportunity by Texaco and a change in its corporate environment.

All the while Hernandez had been scribbling on the two easels, listing the key points each side had made in its opening salvos. "Well, let's see what we have in common," he said, stepping back a bit to look at what he had written. Apart from the desire to resolve the conflict, there was absolutely nothing.

Said Hernandez, "let's take a break."

The sparring escalated when we resumed. The first order of business was to make a list of items that would be discussed. Ours naturally included payments to compensate the black workers whom Texaco had discriminated against. Theirs didn't even mention it.

Hernandez brought the first day to a close on a note that was truly bizarre. "Everyone go home tonight," he admonished us. "Take a nice relaxing bath, light some incense and candles and think about what we've accomplished together today and how we can make progress tomorrow."

Hernandez was clearly so out of his depth that I almost cried. He might as well have suggested that crusty old Bob Ulrich should go out and hug a tree.

The weird combination of New Age philosophy and legal brawling continued for the next two weeks. Every session began with Hernandez cheerfully reading a poetic verse or an inspiring line from Bartlett's Familiar Quotations in the futile hope of establishing a cooperative atmosphere for negotiation. But as soon as he finished Hausfeld and Christensen started duking it out. Texaco was simply unwilling to compromise even on such uncontroversial issues as publicly posting jobs so that not only good old boys would know when an opportunity was available, creating a mentoring program, and reforming the PMP appeals process.

Despite the slow pace of the bargaining, we managed to reach agreement on a few issues during the next couple of weeks. Texaco's men and their lawyers greeted every one of these tiny steps with a burst of self-congratulation worthy of the discovery of a vast new oil field. I thought their reaction was completely inappropriate. So far, all we'd accomplished was getting Texaco to adopt policies toward its employees that many major corporations had been using for years. It wasn't like we were breaking new ground. They were still in the Stone Age. We were not about to be bought off by a few welcome, but insignificant changes.

One day, during a break in the bargaining, Sil and I were engaging in some idle chit-chat on our side of the table. Christensen looked up from her chair and rapped on the table to get our attention. "I don't know what you two are so happy about," she said. "You will both be old and gray and not have any friends, and Texaco will never settle this case. Never." Then she chuckled.

The company's position could not have been more clear.

Finally, about three weeks into the process, it was time to cut to the chase.

As Mike Hausfeld put it, it was time to talk about money.

During the course of the mediation Charles Mann had managed to extract some meaningful numbers from the scraps of data that Texaco had provided. By his latest calculations, Texaco owed its black professionals between thirty million and forty million. "I'm going to go in tomorrow and ask for seventy million and work back from there. If we get thirty million we'll take it," Hausfeld told us during an evening strategy session at Dan's office in late November. This was the moment I had been anticipating for months. I couldn't wait.

When we arrived at Kaye, Scholer the next morning, Hausfeld had on his game face. For once, he did not joke with Charles Mann. Instead he sat quietly at the table in our conference room, intently studying his proposal. "Folks," he finally said, "I am going to do all the talking. Nobody else says anything. Just sit there and look as tough as you can."

As we walked into the conference room a few moments later Hernandez was literally handing out flowers.

*   *   *

When Hausfeld handed over our proposal, Christensen could barely contain her anger. Without a word, she leaped up from the table and stalked out of the room with the rest of Texaco's team falling in behind her. We went back to our own conference room to await their response. About two hours later, Hernandez came in to inform us that Texaco would not be returning to the table that day.

Four days passed before we reconvened. It was back to the impasse again. Texaco did not even want to discuss financial relief for its black employees. To us, it was the only thing worth talking about. As Christensen fumed, Hausfeld delivered a passionate speech about the need to compensate blacks for the harm they had suffered from Texaco's racial bias. It was so eloquent I wanted to jump up and cheer.

When he finished Christensen crossed her arms, looked directly at me and Sil and growled in a slow, deliberate voice:

"Texaco will never, ever throw a bunch of money at a bunch of blacks! You all can forget that."

Christensen leaned back in her chair with a smug little smile. The Almighty had spoken.

If someone had fired a gun across the table it would not have provoked a stronger reaction. The silence was palpable. Carolyn Sellers looked like she was going to cry and even Ed Gasden looked shocked. Cyrus was gasping. So was Hernandez. Hausfeld merely stared at her like a pathologist examining a rare form of malignancy and shook his head.

"I think we need a break," said Hernandez.

The mediation limped on until mid-December, but it had ended for all practical purposes. Absolutely nothing more got resolved. Christmas was only a few days away, but I wasn't merry at all.

CHAPTER SIXTEEN

CAN I GET A WITNESS

The holidays turned out to be even gloomier for the lawyers than they were for me, thanks to another faux pas by the hapless mediator, Miguel Hernandez. He told them that the magistrate wanted them back in court in White Plains on the day after Christmas to explain why the mediation had failed. Cyrus had to fly up from South Carolina, disrupting a visit with his parents-in-law, and Mike Hausfeld came up from his second home in West Virginia. When they got to the courthouse, Richard Sampson was already waiting. So were Christensen and some other Texaco lawyers. But the courtroom was darkened and empty. It turned out that the meeting with the magistrate was not until January 26. Hernandez had gotten the date wrong.

It was a bad way to ring in the New Year. The collapse of the mediation left us with no choice but to head back to court and renew the battle over class certification. Not one of our evidentiary requests had been satisfactorily resolved. Texaco still had not produced the finance department master books that we had been waiting for since Rich Lundwall's deposition. It not had provided a complete version of the TIPPS data-base or the "identifiers" Charles Mann needed in order to correlate the scanty employment data the company had supplied with our copies of the high-potential list. It had not turned over the raw material that a Texaco consultant used to compile a survey of employee attitudes. Or portions of the scores of the affirmative action plans that were supposed to be in effect at different branches of the company. They were still stonewalling, ducking, and dodging.

Hausfeld had lost patience. He wanted to get things moving. At a conference with the magistrate on Valentine's Day he agreed to a frantic schedule for completing the discovery process in the hope of shaking things loose.

Both sides would complete taking testimony from expert witnesses by May. Then we would move to have our class certified by Judge Brieant. It was a tremendous amount of work to be done in a very short time. By now, the magistrate, too, seemed to be fed up with Texaco's dawdling over the evidence. Essentially, he threw out both sides' previous evidentiary requests and started over from scratch. He gave our lawyers only five days to present a new, much more focused list of document requests. Then Texaco would get only a week after receiving our requests to produce everything that we asked for, unless it could show a compelling reason to the contrary. This was a big win for us because we would no longer have to prove why we needed a particular piece of evidence. From this point on, the burden would be on Texaco to prove why they did not have to disclose it. We were on the offensive again. The lawyers renewed our demands for a more complete version of the TIPPS database, the master books, and a few other essential items. Perhaps we would finally get them.

But there was, as always, a downside. Texaco demanded the right to depose all our nonexpert witnesses—the thirty Texaco workers who had supplied information to Cyrus about their own firsthand experiences with discrimination during an earlier phase of the case—during a two-week period in late March and early April. It was a shrewd move on Christensen's part. She knew that our small legal team would be stretched to the breaking point if its members had to fan out across the country to defend so many depositions, while at the same time engaging in hand-to-hand legal combat over documents that Texaco would surely withhold until the last possible moment and taking testimony from expert witnesses. Texaco, on the other hand, had battalions of lawyers at its disposal. She was trying to exhaust us.

Moreover, Texaco's lawyers had resumed rummaging through my personal life. In early March, we found out that Texaco—without notifying our attorneys—had served subpoenas on New York University, Sil's alma mater, and Xavier University, where I had gone for one troubled semester after Brooke was born. Typically, Christensen had resorted to total distortion in her written response to our complaint:

> The Xavier University document is a transcript for lead plaintiff Bari-Ellen Roberts. It indicates that Ms. Roberts received a grade of F for "Failure" in every course she completed and that as a result of her poor performance, she received no academic credit from Xavier University. In this action—where Ms. Roberts claims that her education and experience gave her the qualifications for a promotion—Ms. Roberts' education will be a critical issue. Her less than stellar academic record is a unique, individual issue that affects not only her individual claim, but also argues strongly against her serving as a class representative.

I had never made any secret of the difficult semester I spent at Xavier, which took place during one of the most stressful periods of my life. Nor had I ever felt the need to apologize for it. At the time, I was a teenaged mother locked in a shotgun marriage facing a totally uncertain future. But rather than completely falling apart, I had rebounded and rebuilt my life. I had returned to college and earned a degree with honors, raised two children, and spent nearly two productive decades in corporate America. Even Texaco's racist managers had given me strong evaluations for my performance. How dare this woman insinuate that I was unfit to challenge Texaco because I had suffered—and completely recovered from—a personal crisis? Did she know any limits at all?

Up to that point, I had tried my best, though not always successfully, to keep my personal feelings about Christensen in check, to regard her as a tough lawyer trying to do her job, not just an insulting witch. But this assault on my character and reputation disgusted me. She had gone too far. From that point on, *Roberts v. Texaco* was not merely a lawsuit about racial discrimination. For me, it became a personal battle between Andrea Christensen and me.

As it turned out, Texaco's attempt to drain our legal resources by scheduling all those depositions was a serious mistake in their strategy. It set the stage for the appearance of an unsung hero in the case, Diane R. Williams, a black labor lawyer in Washington. Williams's association with Hausfeld went back to the late 1970s, when he had successfully sued a federal agency for sexual harassment on her behalf. Williams had used the money from the award to pay her law school expenses. Now Cohen, Milstein was hiring her to handle the depositions for the plaintiffs in *Roberts v. Texaco*. She was a tiger. She fended off every devious attempt by Texaco's lawyers to trick our witnesses into revealing the names of black employees whose identities we were still protecting. The witnesses felt safe enough to provide some of the most compelling testimony about Texaco's racially hostile environment to emerge in the case.

They spoke passionately about being passed over for promotion after promotion, about their belief that they were being paid less than whites doing the same job, about being subjected to savage name-calling and harassment, about having their complaints about racial bias brushed aside. Their testimony revealed that despite the company's bold promises about equal opportunity, in branch after branch, in state after state, at Texaco bigotry ran wild.

Johnny Berry, a senior account manager in the marketing department at Texaco's Houston facility, described how his PMP ratings had been lowered after he filed a racial discrimination complaint in 1990. A year or so later he had discussed his concerns with a division vice president and been told that if an African American and a white person were competing for a job, it was "only human nature to give it to the white person." The same vice president had once dressed up as a black Sambo for a company Halloween party.

Eleanor Hunt, who worked in the public affairs office of a Texaco subsidiary in Houston, maintained that after she complained about being discriminated against, her boss told her to see a psychologist and take a drug test.

Paulette East, an associate employee relations administrator at Texaco's Houston facility, had been constantly subjected to racial slurs, innuendoes, and jokes. In her presence, a white manager in the personnel department shared a joke with two of East's white coworkers: "Do you know why black parents don't let their kids play in the sandbox? Because when they go to the bathroom, they can't tell their kids from their shit."

Michael Moccio, a Caucasian who had served as manager of Texaco's regional comptroller's department in Denver until leaving the company in 1994, described being expressly ordered by a superior, Jim Woolley, to fire an African American junior accountant who had filed a charge of discrimination with the local office of the Equal Employment Opportunity Commission, in violation of both federal law and Texaco's official policy. According to Moccio, when he brought the complaint filed by Mary Devorce to the attention of his superior, Woolley said, 'I'd fire her black ass.' " When Moccio pointed out that Texaco should not and could not fire Devorce simply because she claimed that she had been discriminated against, Woolley told him, "I guess we treat niggers different down here [in Houston]." Moccio had refused to discharge Devorce and Texaco had subsequently settled her claim for $60,000.

Katie Green Sampson, a secretary at the Texaco Houston facility, recalled a disparaging remark made by a white division manager about a black Texaco attorney named Malachi Johnson: "With a name like Malachi, what would he know about legal issues in the tax department?"

Larry Barnes, my former protégé in Texaco's finance department, had become so frustrated despite my tutoring that he had quit Texaco. He remembered being told by Dave Keough, in the presence of my boss Shelby Faber and another Texaco executive, "we can go golfing and you can be my caddie."

Jimmy Porter, a terminal supervisor at Texaco's Wilmington, California, facility, provided an extraordinarily detailed portrait of a racially hostile environment. In 1993, he had a disagreement with a black driver under his supervision. They took the dispute to the plant manager, a white man named Wes Boat. Before Porter could even explain why they had come to see him, Boat snapped, "I have an orangutan in charge [referring to Porter] and a dumb truck driver who can't read." Porter complained to Boat's supervisor, Steve Shaw, who made Boat apologize. But after Porter sent a letter about the incident to Texaco's human resources department, he was called into Boat's office, where Boat shut the lights off and said in a threatening manner, "this is what's going to happen to you."

On other occasions, Porter said, his tires had been slashed, racially offensive slurs had been written about him on the bathroom walls, and KKK had been painted on the side of his car. He had overheard Wes Boat say that a black driver named Larry Moppin was "a nigger, nothing but a nigger." He had heard that a white terminal worker in Bakersfield had called a black driver a "porch monkey." Because of the stress, Porter had developed a bleeding ulcer and missed a whole year of work.

I knew what Porter felt like. I seemed to be getting jolts from every direction. Waldo and I were squabbling, over what I wasn't sure. Brooke was in Stamford, but she was still keeping her distance. Staci was preparing to graduate from high school and sail off to the University of Virginia in the fall. Though her departure was months away, I already felt like an empty nester. I was bored out of my mind with my job. *Roberts v. Texaco* seemed to be stuck in an interminable rut for weeks at a time. I didn't think things could get any worse.

But they did. In May Bob Ulrich retired and was replaced as Texaco's treasurer by none other than James F. Link, who I had been told had lowered my PMP because I was "uppity." Talk about stressful. Link's elevation meant that at the very least I would have to see him every day, if not interact with him in a meeting. With every encounter I was transported back to that terrible afternoon when I lost control of myself after Nancy had given me the disconcerting news about the downgrading of my evaluation. It already took all my strength to get out of bed in the morning and come to Texaco. Now that a man who had personally targeted me had taken charge of the finance department, working there would be even more stressful.

Another blow came in April. Cyrus told Sil and me that we would have to reapply to the EEOC for a new right-to-sue letter against Texaco on a company-wide basis because a mistake had been made in our initial complaint to the agency nearly two years before. Andrea Christensen gloated. It meant that there would be another delay in the progress of *Roberts v. Texaco.*

The most alarming news came from my family in Cincinnati. My sisters told me that my mother, who had been living alone for two years since her second husband died, had begun acting strangely. She hadn't cleaned up her house in weeks and the place was a shambles. She'd been in two car accidents. She was forgetting things. Something was very wrong.

I took a few days off from work and drove home to see for myself. Mom was even worse than my sisters had described. She fluctuated between moments of piercing lucidity and complete befuddlement. She sometimes went for days without eating or taking a bath.

I couldn't stay very long, so I arranged for my sisters to take Mom to the doctor. The diagnosis came back a few days later. She was in the early stages of Alzheimer's disease and could no longer take care of herself.

As if that weren't enough, in June we suffered perhaps the most serious setback since the lawsuit was filed. At Texaco's instigation, Judge Brieant had asked the EEOC to investigate Texaco on a company-wide basis. That meant that the case would be on hold for months. Texaco's attempt to drag out the affair for as long as it could had succeeded. More than two years had slipped away and we didn't seem to be any further along the road to justice then when our journey had begun.

Under the weight of all these pressures, my body eventually snapped. I began to gain weight, suffer memory lapses, mood swings, and bouts of depression. Sometimes I could hardly stand. In late summer, just after I had tearfully packed Staci off to college, I discovered a lump in my breast. Because there is no history of breast cancer in my family, I felt absolutely sure that the lump was stress-related.

On October 2, 1995, I underwent surgery. My sister Traci

flew in from Cincinnati to be with me, which was wonderful. The operation was a complete success. The lump turned out to be benign and the surgeon left such a small scar I could hardly see it.

I stayed home to recuperate for ten days. The time off from Texaco was delightful. It gave me a respite from the tension inside the building and a chance to restore my morale. Even better, Brooke sent me flowers and called to wish me well. It was the first time we had had a sincere discussion in months. I could tell that the anger she had felt toward me since I broke with her father had dissipated. I felt sure our estrangement was over.

Waldo put the icing on the cake one night over dinner. He took my hand, looked into my eyes, and said, "I don't think you should be alone any more." A few days later, he moved in.

CHAPTER SEVENTEEN

TALE OF THE TAPES

"Waldo, you'll never guess who came into my office today claiming he had some 'big, big' evidence that could break our case wide open," I said, trying to sound mysterious as we drove home from the train station.

"Was it Bob Ulrich?" Waldo laughed.

"No, guess again," I teased him.

"Dave Keough?"

"Nope."

"I know," said Waldo, really cracking up now. "Andrea Christensen!"

"Oh no, not her, not in a million years!"

"Come on, Bari, give me a hint."

"Remember the guy who was doing the twist at last year's Texaco Christmas party?"

"Yeah . . ."

"You know, the guy who organizes all the tennis and golf tournaments."

"Yeah . . ."

"Come on, Waldo! The guy who told me that I was out of line for disagreeing with Jim Link in a meeting!"

"You have got to be kidding me," Waldo exclaimed. "Not him! That guy is Mr. Texaco!"

It was the evening of July 31, 1996. Waldo and I had been living together for almost a year, and by now he knew almost as much about *Roberts v. Texaco* as I did. With Staci away at college or doing summer internships, he had taken her place as my chief supporter. I had gotten into the habit of picking him up at the train station on days when I had big news to tell him about the case—and sometimes when I just couldn't wait to see him. But the frustrating truth was that for the past year, I had not had very much to report.

Roberts v. Texaco had gone into limbo after Andrea Christensen's extraordinary outburst brought the mediation attempt to a standstill. The plaintiffs, and even our lawyers, had been paralyzed for months while we waited for the Equal Employment Opportunity Commission to complete its own investigation of Texaco. It seemed to take forever, which is just what Texaco wanted. It had been the company, not us, who had demanded the government probe in the first place. Then it had deliberately dragged out the investigation by refusing to cooperate with the agency. The EEOC had been forced to take Texaco to court not once, but twice, demanding that it turn over its employment records.

For both the plaintiffs and our legal team, the biggest problem was keeping up our morale while we waited for the EEOC to finish its work. Meanwhile life had to go on. Veronica moved from New York to Louisiana to take a new job. Beatrice had a baby and so did Cyrus and his wife, Robin Anne. Marsha became very sick with a variety of stress-related ailments. Our conference calls with Cyrus and the other lawyers became a telephonic support group, as we talked each other through our individual causes for celebration and sadness. I still had not met most of the other plaintiffs face to face, but they felt like very close friends.

But when the commission finally issued its report in early June, it turned out to have been worth waiting for. Texaco's stonewalling and deception had blown up right in its own face.

"There is reasonable cause to believe that [Texaco] failed to promote Blacks in grades 7 through 14 as a class throughout its facilities because of their race," wrote Spencer H. Lewis, the EEOC's New York district director. Though the EEOC made no finding about whether employees in higher pay grades like Sil and me had been victimized by discrimination, it issued a right-to-sue letter that would allow us to proceed with our case on a class basis, a big victory. The agency's finding made mincemeat out of Texaco's claim that there was no evidence of a company-wide culture of discrimination, as we had contended. In all likelihood, Judge Brieant would certify Sil, the other name plaintiffs, and me as class representatives of all of Texaco's black professional employees when we went back to court in the fall. We were on a roll.

Typically, Texaco had tried to bury the EEOC's damning finding under a mountain of misinformation. They asked the agency to reconsider its conclusion. And they sent out an open letter to all employees that was so full of self-serving distortions about the agency report that we took out a full page ad in several newspapers to refute it point by point. For example, we noted that the company's bland claim that the EEOC's finding of discrimination against employees in grades seven through fourteen "is based on an incomplete record" failed to mention that it had taken the agency nearly nine months to pry the relevant documents out of Texaco. If the information the company had provided to the agency was incomplete, it had only itself to blame.

Bolstered by the EEOC report, the other plaintiffs and I

could hardly wait for the case to get back in court. Cyrus and Steve Singer were hard at work on a powerful supplement to our motion for class certification that drew upon the dramatic testimony we had obtained from our expert witnesses the previous summer. Everyone's spirits were rising.

And then, on that sunny morning in July, I looked up from work and saw none other than Rich Lundwall standing in the doorway with a loopy grin on his face and his hand plunged deep into his pants pocket as though he was going to pull something out of it.

"Can I close the door, Bari?" he said. "I've got something here that could be really helpful to your case."

My internal alarm went off. I didn't trust Rich at all. He was the man who had scolded me for taking issue with a manager in public, a key moment in the series of events that eventually led to my filing the lawsuit. Though we had sat in offices only twenty feet apart for more than two years and worked together on a few projects, he had never uttered a single word of support for my cause. To the contrary, I thought he disliked me. His unexpected offer to help my case just might be some kind of setup.

"Rich, I can't take whatever it is that you have," I replied. "Get in touch with my lawyer." I extracted one of Cyrus's cards from my purse and gave it to him. He thanked me and left.

I didn't learn until three months later that Lundwall had telephoned Cyrus the very next day. Though they had not spoken since Cyrus had taken Rich's deposition almost exactly two years before, Cyrus remembered him vividly. Of all the witnesses from Texaco our lawyers had questioned, Lundwall had come across as the most honest and forthright, disclosing the existence of the finance department master books that were at the heart of our never-ending evidentiary tussle with Texaco. Why in the world, Cyrus wondered, would this guy be calling me now? The answer was astonishing. Lundwall told Cyrus that he would have said even more in his deposition if he had not been under pressure from Texaco's lawyers. Now, despite his loyalty and long years of service, he was being forced into retirement at age fifty-five and he wanted to fight it. He had information that would help our case. Would Cyrus file an age discrimination suit against Texaco on his behalf?

Cyrus immediately said no. It might be a conflict of interest. But he was intrigued by Lundwall's proposition. He was convinced that Texaco and its lawyers had deliberately withheld evidence that we were entitled to under the rules of discovery. Our informer, "Dora," had seen documents being destroyed, but because of her fear of retaliation, she was not willing to come forward. Could Lundwall possibly have evidence that would help us prove what we strongly suspected?

But Cyrus kept the question to himself because this was a ticklish area. He was not even sure that he was permitted to speak with a Texaco middle manager like Lundwall unless the company's lawyers were present. It might be a violation of rules forbidding so-called ex parte contacts between attorneys and certain witnesses on the opposite sides of a lawsuit. He told Lundwall that he would like to meet with him, but only if it could be done without breaching the ethical and legal rules. Some subjects, especially any conversations Lundwall may have had with Texaco's lawyers, were totally out of bounds. If Cyrus became privy to such information, even by accident, Cohen, Milstein could be thrown off the case and Cyrus might even be disbarred.

Cyrus spent the next four days trying to come up with an ethically acceptable way to follow up this intriguing conversation. He concluded that it would be prudent to wait until Lundwall was no longer an active Texaco employee before he could have a substantive conversation with him. The question was, when would that be?

A few days later, Lundwall faxed Cyrus a copy of a memo

from Ron Boilla of Texaco's human resources department specifying that his last day on the active payroll would be August 31. It concluded with Boilla wishing Lundwall "health and happiness in retirement." Lundwall noted in a cover letter that "the attached is not correct. I am being fired."

On August 9, Lundwall called Cyrus again, ostensibly to make sure that his fax had arrived. Then he added, "Look, Cyrus, I have something you should hear."

Cyrus almost dropped the phone. If he wants me to hear something, not just look at something, he must have tapes, he realized suddenly. Oh my God, he's got tapes!

He put the question to Lundwall directly.

"You've got tapes?"

"Yeah, I've got tapes."

What's on them, Cyrus wondered. "If there are any conversations between you and Texaco's counsel, I don't want to come near them." he told Lundwall. "I can't listen to them."

"No, there are no lawyers, just managers," said Lundwall. "One of them is a former treasurer of Texaco."

Cyrus figured that meant Ulrich, who had recently retired.

Lundwall went on to explain that he had been responsible for the minutes of certain meetings in the finance department. To ensure the accuracy of his reports he had secretly taped the sessions on a tiny microcassette recorder. He still had the tapes. He had spent hours listening to them over and over during a recent stay in the hospital. He seemed to hint, without saying it, that they concerned tampering with evidence.

Cyrus's heart pounded. This was a crisis, replete with threats. Lundwall might be lying about what was on them. If, despite his assurances, the tapes really contained conversations with Texaco's counsel and Cyrus listened to them, Cohen, Milstein would be in very deep trouble, and Cyrus's career would be over. If, on the other hand, the tapes actually contained incendiary proof of evidence tampering, Lundwall might change his mind about sharing them—or even destroy them. He had to convince Lundwall to get the tapes into the hands of a trustworthy lawyer right away.

"Have you got a lawyer to take my case yet?" Lundwall asked again.

"No," said Cyrus, "we're still working on it. I'll be in Danbury, Connecticut, on August 12 to visit my parents. Let's get together at a place I know. Bring the tapes."

He was taking an enormous risk.

Cyrus felt like a secret agent when Robin Anne dropped him off at the Marcus Dairy restaurant in Danbury. He arrived twenty minutes ahead of schedule to give himself time to case the joint before selecting a table as far away from the other diners as possible. Lundwall, dressed in a baseball cap, denim jacket, jeans, and wearing a cocky grin, arrived right on time, at 3 P.M.

"These are the two you're interested in." Lundwall teased, taking two microcassettes from his shirt pocket and waving them seductively at Cyrus. "This stuff is at the very crux of your case." In addition to proof of Texaco executives "cleaning up" documents, "there's highly offensive language not acceptable in the civilized world that reflects a company-wide attitude of discrimination.

"Look, Cyrus," Lundwall went on. "My motives are not as pure as snow. I don't want to give these to you until you help me find a lawyer to handle my case against Texaco."

"We're still working on that," said Cyrus. "But, meanwhile, it's urgent to get the tapes into the hands of an officer of the court. Give them to me and I will put them in escrow until you can get your own counsel. I won't listen to them. Once you get your own lawyer we can speak to you about substantive issues because you'll have your own representation. Then we'll give the tapes back to you and your lawyer."

"Don't worry, Cyrus," said Lundwall, waggling the tapes at Cyrus again before stuffing them back into his shirt pocket. "These tapes aren't going anywhere. They're safe with me."

The meeting had come to an end. Cyrus looked down at his hands and saw that they were trembling.

By now, Michael Hausfeld was going berserk on a daily basis. "Get me those fucking tapes," he screamed at Cyrus whenever he saw him. "I want those fucking tapes." In Cyrus's view, Hausfeld was being reckless. But as a young lawyer and not yet a partner, Cyrus did not have the stature to fight a legal legend like Hausfeld alone. In desperation, he appealed to Cohen, Milstein's senior partner, Herb Milstein, to weigh in on the side of caution in dealing with Lundwall. The very thought of going slow made Hausfeld furious. "Caution? Fuck that," he shouted at Cyrus. "If you don't get me those fucking tapes, this case is going to go on for another ten years! The delay will be all on your head!"

Milstein advised Hausfeld to seek the opinion of an outside expert on legal ethics about whether our team could legally obtain the tapes and interview Lundwall.

"I want those damn tapes, too, Cyrus," Dan Berger shouted during a telephone conference call.

Sil, I, and the other plaintiffs were blissfully unaware of the warfare that was raging among the lawyers. If we'd known about the infighting, we would have been severely alarmed. "We never told you guys about it because it was too radioactive," Cyrus told me, "but the fact is that we were near to a meltdown."

Finally, in late August, Lundwall rendered the argument moot by getting an attorney on his own. With legal representation, he was free to cooperate with our legal team.

Lundwall's attorney was Peter Gass, of White Plains, New York. He had been referred to Gass by Katherine Malarkey, on whose behalf Gass had brought a sex discrimination case against Texaco. Cyrus and Gass spoke by telephone on September 5, four days after Lundwall's three-decade-long career at Texaco had come to an end.

"Lundwall told me there are two kinds of things on these tapes, offensive language and some kind of evidence tampering," said Cyrus. "Can you tell me if he's even in the ballpark or is he crazy?"

According to Cyrus, Gass replied that he had listened to portions of the tapes with Lundwall and they sounded like a Ku Klux Klan rally. They were filled with racist remarks, including the N-word. Even more alarming, Gass continued, there were extensive recordings of Texaco executives destroying or altering documents that had been sought in the case.

"If there's evidence of obstruction of justice on those tapes, the U.S. Attorney might be interested in them," Cyrus responded.

"Frankly," said Gass, "Mr. Lundwall is more worried about Texaco than he is about the federal prosecutor. Before this goes any further, we need some assurances, Mr. Mehri. We need to know that you can protect Mr. Lundwall against retaliation from Texaco if he provides you with this material. Without that we cannot go forward."

Cyrus promised Gass that the plaintiffs' legal team would do its best to protect Lundwall, as it would any witness, from any attempt at intimidation by bringing the matter before Judge Brieant.

With that guarantee in hand, Gass agreed to proceed.

His first look at the partial transcript of Lundwall's recordings that Gass faxed to Cohen, Milstein's office in Washington sent Mike Hausfeld into a giggling fit. "Listen to this," he cackled, " 'I'm still having trouble with Hanukkah, and now I have Kwanzaa.' Now they're picking on Jews up there. They've broadened the scope!"

This was explosive! Steve Singer sped to Gass's office to retrieve copies of Lundwall's transcript and cassettes. The lawyers needed their own transcripts because they did not trust

Lundwall enough to rely solely on his version of what had been said. It took until October 4 for Dan Berger's office staff to transcribe the tapes, with the assistance of an audio expert.

Just as Gass had said, the resulting transcript contained snatches of dialogue between Texaco executives about withholding and destroying of key evidence—not the TIPPS database, as the lawyers had surmised, but the notorious master books that Texaco and Andrea Christensen had repeatedly claimed did not even exist. One meeting had taken place on August 14, 1994, a few days after the plaintiffs' lawyers had first learned of the master books' existence during Lundwall's deposition. A Texaco executive could be heard boasting that since he didn't want to become his "own Watergate," he was "gonna purge the shit out of these books."

The next step was to question Lundwall directly and get him to attach names to the voices that could be heard on the tapes. Without such authentication, the transcripts would have far less credibility as evidence. But when they asked Lundwall's attorney to set up a meeting, Gass unexpectedly balked.

"Mr. Lundwall is trying to get back into Texaco," Gass explained to Cyrus. "He has applied for jobs that are being posted. He's trying to contact a very high-ranking person there to see if he can get his job back."

This was a devastating revelation; the timing could not have been worse. Our lawyers were due back in court on October 25, just three weeks away, to file our crucial class certification papers. They needed to nail down the explosive evidence on the tapes before that deadline. If Texaco offered Lundwall a job, he was certain to withdraw his offer of cooperation. The single most compelling piece of evidence that we had obtained would slip from our hands. Over the next several days Cyrus made one frantic call after another to Gass to find out if Texaco had put Lundwall back on the payroll.

Fortunately for us, Texaco did not make Lundwall an offer. On October 22, Gass informed Cyrus that Lundwall had abandoned his efforts to get back on Texaco's payroll. He would meet with the lawyers three days later at a hotel in Danbury.

The review of the transcripts with Lundwall must have been a remarkable occasion. I wish I could have been there.

As my lawyers perched on the edge of their chairs, Lundwall patiently examined the transcript that Dan's staff had prepared with the help of an audio expert, correcting mistakes and identifying the speakers. Remarkably, Gass was not present, though he said he would be available by phone if Lundwall needed to consult with him. Cyrus reminded Lundwall that he could call Gass whenever he wished to, but Lundwall did not call him. He was all on his own.

Under questioning from the lawyers, Lundwall acknowledged that high-ranking Texaco officials had conspired to hide evidence from the plaintiffs. Portions of the master books had been shredded. Managers who had kept copies of the documents had been instructed to say that they had not retained them. Handwritten marginal comments had been expunged. It amounted to a huge cover-up. Among those who had taken part in the meetings were Lundwall, Ulrich, and Dave Keough. He said that Ulrich was the man heard on the tape saying that he was going to "purge the shit out of these books." He was also the source of the vile comment about Hanukkah and Kwanzaa. Lundwall said he had "no independent recollection" of Ulrich actually using the N-word. Ulrich often slurred his words and they were not clear. He thought Ulrich might have said "nigglas." No one in the room had ever heard that word before. It wasn't even a word. The audio expert whom Dan had hired agreed that the word was "niggers." When they wrote on the transcript that Ulrich had said, "niggers," Lundwall did not agree or disagree.

Suddenly the lawyers were faced another dilemma. Their encounter with Lundwall was taking place on the very same day when the supplemental papers supporting our motion for class certification were due to be filed. They were so enthralled with Lundwall's presentation that they had lost track of the time. The deadline, at four o'clock, was fast approaching, and there was no way they could make it. They needed at least a one day extension, but that would take Kaye, Scholer's consent.

They did not want to put the request for a postponement to Andrea Christensen, for fear that she would reject the request or sense that something was up. Instead, Dan Berger phoned her young associate, John Howley. "Mind if we take another day before filing our papers?" Dan asked, trying to keep any hint of tension or urgency out of his voice. "No problem," said Howley. Everyone breathed a long sigh of relief.

On the following Monday, Hausfeld and Cyrus reached me at my Texaco office and told me to go to a secure telephone. I left the building immediately and drove to a nearby restaurant that had a telephone booth.

"You must not share this with anyone, even Sil or Waldo," Hausfeld told me. "It's too explosive. It could break this case wide open. We can't let it get out."

After I agreed, Hausfeld read the transcript of a conversation between Ulrich and Lundwall about destroying copies of the master books and minutes of meetings:

Ulrich: Boy, I'll tell you, that one, you would put that and you would have the only copy. Nobody else ought to have copies of that.

Lundwall: Okay.

Ulrich: You have that someplace and it doesn't exist.

Lundwall: Yeah, okay.

Ulrich: I just don't want anybody to have a copy of that.

Lundwall: Good. No problem.

Ulrich: You know, there is no point in even keeping the restricted version anymore. All it could do is get us in trouble. That's the way I feel, I would not keep anything.

Lundwall: Let me shred this thing and any other restricted version like it.

Ulrich: Why do we have to keep the minutes of the meeting anymore?

Lundwall: You don't. You don't.

Ulrich: We don't.

Lundwall: Because we don't, no we don't because it comes back to haunt us like right now.

And this insulting chat between Ulrich and Lundwall about blacks' attempts to gain a foothold in the workforce:

Ulrich: This diversity thing. You know how all the jelly beans agree.

Lundwall: That's funny. All the black jelly beans seemed to be glued to the bottom of the bag.

Ulrich: You can't have just we and them. You can't just have black jelly beans and other jelly beans. It doesn't work.

Lundwall: Yeah, but they're perpetuating the black jelly beans.

Needless to say, I was disgusted by what I was hearing, but I wasn't surprised at all. This was the true voice of Texaco, the language of bigotry that the good old boys had been hurling at me since my first day on the job. Black Panther. Militant. Uppity. Little colored girl. Now black jelly bean. What in the world would they come up with next? The words had been used so often that they had lost their power to shock or wound me. I was beyond being offended. I was thinking strategically about the impact these revelations would have on our case. I wanted to exploit them.

"How are you planning to use this stuff, Mike?" I asked through tightly clenched teeth.

"Give it to the judge and leak it to the *New York Times,*" he replied.

CHAPTER EIGHTEEN

SIMPLE JUSTICE

The date was Friday, November 1, 1996, the place was Magistrate Fox's courtroom, the occasion was the advent of justice. The dramatic proof of bigotry and the destruction of evidence in Texaco's executive suite that were recorded on the Lundwall tapes had turned the tide of *Roberts v. Texaco* decisively in our favor. Sil and I were enjoying the spectacle of watching Texaco sweat. This was the moment I had been waiting to savor for more than two harrowing years.

"Sil, see how the mighty have fallen," I whispered as I pointed at Andrea Christensen. She was sitting less than twenty feet away, the picture of abject defeat. Her eyes were hollow, her complexion was ashen, and her hands were shaking. There was a distinct tremor in Christensen's voice as she rose to address the judge. Texaco was shocked and dismayed by the words on the tapes, which clearly violated company policy. The magistrate heard her out and then issued his ruling: a full-scale hearing at which Texaco would have to show why it should not be sanctioned for tampering with evidence would be conducted three weeks later. When he banged his gavel and left the bench, I almost stood up and cheered.

A few minutes later, outside on the steps of the courthouse, our lawyers were in an equally jubilant mood. Cyrus exchanged high fives with Sil and gave me an enormous bear hug. He, Mike Hausfeld, Sil, and I spent the next hour or two at a celebratory lunch, then walked back to the lawyers' hotel. There was a message waiting for Hausfeld. "It's from Dan Berger," he announced. "Andrea called to say that Texaco wants to talk with us. I think they might want to settle." We all stood still for a moment or two and then hugged each other again. I hadn't felt so confident in a long, long time.

I was probably still on my way home when the tensions on our legal team flared into the open. Dan's eagerness to accept Andrea's invitation infuriated Hausfeld. Sensing that a huge victory was in our grasp, he was in no mood to debate legal strategy with Dan or anyone else.

"I'm not sitting down in a room with that woman and discussing anything, period," Hausfeld declared during a conference call. "We spent weeks negotiating with her during the mediation and we never got anywhere. She's totally evil."

"Mike, I think that's unreasonable," Dan said impatiently. "If you won't meet with her, I will."

"If you go, you're going yourself because I'm not showing up," Hausfeld shot back. "There's only one person at Kaye, Scholer who can settle this case and it's not Andrea Christensen. It's Milt Shubin. He's the guy who settled the case I brought against Texaco for leaking oil in my neighbors' backyards. He's their crisis control man. If Milt's not taking the lead in this, they aren't serious about settling anything. If they want to drag this out, I'm prepared to drag them through it. I'm going to call Milt."

By the normal standards of his profession, Hausfeld's attempt to dictate Texaco's choice of its lawyer would be considered unorthodox or outrageous. Even he admits it was "a little bit flaky." By my standards, it was his finest hour. At worst, we'd be stuck with the status quo—Texaco would leave Christensen on the case and try to ride out the storm. At best, Shubin would take over as Texaco's bargaining chief, increasing the odds for a quick settlement. But getting rid of Christensen was not the only tough precondition for negotiations on Hausfeld's list. He insisted that before the talks could begin, Texaco had to commit itself to settle the case on a class-wide basis, and that the first order of business would be a discussion of the amount of pay that black Texaco employees had been cheated out of by Texaco's discriminatory practices.

As he explained it to the plaintiffs, he wanted the company to put up the total amount of compensation that it finally agreed to in a lump sum that would be paid out immediately, instead of making the class members wait for years as they had in some other cases. Such a strategy was almost unheard of, particularly in employment discrimination suits. Hausfeld had delivered an unmistakable message to Texaco's managers and attorneys: There was not going to be any compromise on those issues. This settlement was going to cost them. As Cyrus described it to me and Sil, "Mike is throwing the long ball."

It took only a few hours for Hausfeld's audacity to pay off. Christensen telephoned Hausfeld to inform him that although she would remain on Texaco's team, Milt Shubin would become its leader. Hausfeld's first condition had been met. Could we get together on the following Tuesday, election day, Christensen asked?

That was fine with Hausfeld. It played into our hands. Our lawyers knew that a hard-hitting account of the racial slurs and evidence tampering at Texaco would appear in the *New York Times* on Monday, November 4, igniting a media frenzy and a firestorm of unfavorable publicity. The pressure on the company would escalate. Texaco might not be able to withstand it.

When Hausfeld explained the strategy to me, all I could say was "I love it, I love it."

I wish that I could have seen Peter I. Bijur's face when he picked up the *Times* that Monday morning. He had been Texaco's chairman and chief executive officer for less than six months, replacing the combative Al DeCrane. My guess is that his minions in the legal department had told him that Texaco was winning our case, if they'd mentioned it to him at all. I can imagine Bijur sputtering and spitting coffee all over the breakfast table as he raced through reporter Kurt Eichenwald's sensational article:

> *Senior executives with Texaco, Inc., bantered comfortably among themselves in August 1994, planning the destruction of documents demanded in a Federal discrimination lawsuit and belittling the company's minority employees with racial epithets. Unknown to almost everyone in the room, one executive was carrying a tape recorder. . . . The recordings . . . appear to have captured senior Texaco officers conspiring to illegally destroy documents subject to discovery requests in the lawsuit. The tapes, in which the executives are heard referring to black employees as "black jelly beans" and "niggers," raises the stakes in the discrimination suit brought against Texaco by six company employees on behalf of as many as 1,500 other minority employees. . . .*

By the time he reached the end of the story, Bijur must have realized that Texaco was headed for a legal and public relations disaster. He had to cut the company's losses. Within hours, he issued a statement expressing Texaco's dismay at the words on the tapes, which clearly violated Texaco policy. A prominent criminal lawyer named Michael Armstrong would be brought on board to investigate the allegations of bigotry and obstruction of justice. Texaco would take "immediate disciplinary action" against any employee who had taken part in any of it.

Meanwhile, Sil and I had flown down to Washington in order to make ourselves available to the media. We spent some time with Cyrus, rehearsing our answers to the questions we expected the reporters to ask. But none of us were really prepared for the storm of controversy that erupted around the country after Eichenwald's story broke. The phones were ringing off the hook in Cohen, Milstein's offices. Our lawyers, Sil, and I received more than two hundred requests for interviews from newspapers and TV stations.

We accommodated as many as we could, which turned out to be an ordeal almost as trying as being deposed by Andrea Christensen. The vast majority of reporters knew absolutely nothing about our case beyond what they had read in the *Times.* All day, one after another of them put the same obvious questions to us as cameras poked into our faces and spotlights shone into our eyes. Had we ever heard anyone at Texaco use the word *nigger*? How did it make us feel? Were we angry about it? We repeated the same answers over and over again until my throat ached. It was intense and monotonous. By the time the last camera crew had picked up its equipment and left the office late that afternoon, I was completely exhausted. I flew to New York and Waldo picked me up at the airport. I don't think I've ever been as happy to see anyone in my life. I collapsed into his arms and cried like a child.

By the time Hausfeld and his team sat down with Texaco's lawyers at Kaye, Scholer's office in New York on Tuesday morning, the story of the Lundwall tapes had exploded into the headlines and the airwaves. A surge of revulsion against Texaco was spreading all over the world. Staci called from the college to say that the tapes were the talk of the campus. We heard that even at Kaye, Scholer people were pounding their fists on their desks, disgusted that their firm was connected in any way to a company like Texaco. Milt Shubin had telephoned Hausfeld to tell him that Texaco was ready to discuss the "class-wide, nationwide monetary relief" that we were demanding. When our legal team arrived at the meeting, Shubin was sitting in the power position at the head of Texaco's end of the table, flanked by Christensen and a Texaco lawyer. The line-up indicated that Texaco was finally ready to deal.

So why was Andrea Christensen doing all the talking? She seemed to have recovered all the bile that had been so conspicuously absent at the hearing in Judge Brieant's courtroom the previous week.

"You guys did so much media yesterday, you probably didn't have time to think about our meeting this morning," she began in an insinuating tone.

"To the contrary," Hausfeld replied, tossing out copies of a twenty-page booklet listing our demands that Cyrus had completed the night before.

As Christensen rifled through the pages, her lip began to curl. She tossed the papers down with a thunk.

"Let's make sure we're all on the same page with regard to this settlement. Texaco is not going to throw a bunch of money at a bunch of blacks."

Our lawyers were horrified. These were the very same words that Christensen had used to turn the mediation into a fiasco. Where in the heck was Milt Shubin?

The angrier Mike Hausfeld gets, the more softly he speaks. Now he was almost whispering.

"Andrea, we're not on the same page. We're not even in the same book. We're not even in the same library. There is no point in getting together today, tomorrow, or any other day unless you can get over this problem you have with paying money to blacks, because we are not going to settle this case without substantial monetary relief for the class."

"Mike, if we give money to all the blacks in the company the white employees will never stand for it," Christensen replied in a patronizing tone. "The blacks will become isolated from everyone else. The whites will be furious. It will just increase everybody's alienation."

At this point, Max Berger, Dan's senior partner, spoke up. An imposing man with a mane of dark hair, he had joined our bargaining team to lend it additional weight.

"I'm moved by your tender concern for the welfare of Texaco's black employees, Miss Christensen," Berger intoned sarcastically. "But I want you to know that I agree a hundred and ten percent with everything Mike just said. You know that we have an obligation to the class of black employees at Texaco. Don't pretend otherwise. If we don't get a substantial monetary settlement, we are prepared to go to trial."

Meanwhile, Hausfeld was silently shoving his papers back into his briefcase. He stood up and cocked his head at the team. "Let's go. We're leaving."

Milt Shubin had sat throughout the exchange without uttering a single word. It looked like Texaco and Christensen were going to try to stonewall us again. Despite the company's public air of contrition, in the secrecy of the bargaining room it was up to the same old tricks.

Totally unaware of the tense drama that was playing out in Kaye, Scholer's offices I reported to work at Texaco on Tuesday morning. The atmosphere in the building had undergone a complete reversal. I was greeted like a conquering hero. One after one, my black coworkers, including many who had shied away from Sil and me throughout our long ordeal, ran up to offer congratulations; some had grateful tears in their eyes. Even some of the good old boys clapped our shoulders in approval and smiled at me as I made my way from the elevator to my office in the finance department. The telephone was already ringing when I reached my desk, and my in-box was filled with a stack of messages. Blacks from Texaco branches all over the world were calling to express their thanks. Some from other companies wanted to know how to contact my lawyer so that they could bring lawsuits of their own.

I only answered a few of the calls right away because I had urgent personal business to attend to. I wanted to confront my boss, Shelby Faber, and watch him squirm.

He was sitting behind his desk, trying to look non-committal.

"So, Shelby," I asked, "What do *you* make out of all this?"

"Bari, I'm shocked."

"I'm sure you are."

"My eighty-five-year-old mother called me last night and asked me if I had anything to do with this."

"So what did you tell her?"

"I told her I didn't." He paused, and an imploring look came into his eyes. "Bari, is there anything else on those tapes?"

"Well, Shelby," I said, "what's been in the paper is only snippets."

"Am I on any of them?" he asked.

"Well, Shelby, you tell me," I said, twisting the knife. "Do you think you could be?"

He lowered his head into his hands and spoke in an agonized voice so low I could barely hear him. "I don't know. I don't know."

I got up and left him to deal with his misery. We were even. I almost let myself feel sorry for him—but not quite.

The feeling of vindication that I had been enjoying since my encounter with Shelby gave way to gloomy alarm that night when Cyrus delivered the bad news about the breakdown of the bargaining session.

"What are we going to do now?" someone asked.

Said Cyrus, "Mike says we're going to sit tight. In a fluid situation like this, chaos is our strongest weapon."

Indeed, the tension was rising. H. Carl McCall, the comptroller of New York State, one of the nation's highest black elected officials, sent a letter to Bijur demanding a full accounting of the issues raised by the Lundwall tapes. The clear implication was that if McCall wasn't satisfied with the answers he got, he would sell off millions of shares of state-owned Texaco stock at fire sale prices. It might be the first step in a widespread divestiture campaign like the one against South African apartheid that would drive the value of Texaco shares even deeper into the tank. A federal grand jury in White Plains began an investigation of whether the Texaco executives captured on the tapes had committed the felonious act of obstruction of justice; it eventually returned criminal indictments against Ulrich and Lundwall. A coalition of civil rights leaders in Washington demanded that the Government throw its weight behind the plaintiffs in *Roberts v. Texaco*. As word of these developments raced like a bonfire through Wall Street, the price of Texaco stock fell by more than three dollars a share, knocking more than a billion dollars off the overall value of the company.

For the first time since *Roberts v. Texaco* had been filed, Bijur and his top assistants seemed to realize that our case was a serious threat to the company's financial stability. They stopped listening to the glib lawyers who had assured them that our lawsuit was no cause for concern and took their first personal look at the powerful evidence of discrimination that our legal team had assembled—the compelling testimony from our witnesses, Charles Mann's analysis of how much money black workers had been cheated out of by Texaco's biased employment policies, the Lundwall tapes. It had to be obvious even to the arrogant men of Texaco that their company was in the most serious crisis it had faced since the dark days of the Pennzoil case. They needed to control the damage. Bijur called a press conference to proclaim that "the statements on the tapes arouse a deep sense of shock and anger among all the members of the Texaco family and decent people everywhere . . . They are statements that represent a profound contempt not only for the law, not only for Texaco's explicitly clear values and policies, but even more importantly, for the most fundamental standards of fairness, of mutual respect, and of human dignity." He was clearly trying to distance the company from the nefarious deeds that the Lundwall tapes had revealed.

Hausfeld let the tension rise until Wednesday afternoon, and then telephoned Shubin. "Let's be practical, Milt. I will not enter a negotiating room with Andrea. She is not to conduct the negotiations. Let's you and me handle this. I will not deal with her. If the company's position is that they are really not going to pay any money or they are going to pay only a minimal amount of money, forget it, there's nothing to discuss."

"I'll get back to you," Shubin replied.

Meanwhile media interest in the story had soared to an even higher pitch. Tom Brokaw of NBC News and Ted Koppel of ABC's Nightline were vying furiously to be the first to broadcast an interview with Bijur. Koppel pulled out all the stops to get the scoop. He promised that he would dump his scheduled guest, Newt Gingrich, and devote his entire show to the Lundwall tapes if my lawyers would give him a copy. Cyrus quickly agreed. Koppel and his researchers then spent hours on the phone with Cyrus and Hausfeld getting background about the case. "How much would you settle for?" one of Koppel's assistants asked Hausfeld. His reply: one hundred million dollars.

That night Koppel posed a series of pointed queries to Bijur.

"I realize this is the kind of question that is probably going to make your lawyers cringe, but you know one way to put the old chapter behind you and to clearly signal the beginning of a new chapter, is to say, 'clearly injustices were done, let's settle the damn lawsuit, get it out of the way and move on.' "

Considering how much the price of Texaco stock had gone down, Koppel added, while "a lawsuit for one hundred million dollars is not exactly chump change, wouldn't it be better just to pay it, get it out of the way and move on?"

Bijur looked ruffled. "Clearly, Ted, injustices were done and we are exploring every possible opportunity to put this behind us and begin the healing process within our company," he replied.

Koppel bore in again. "Well, if you're exploring every opportunity, one easy way to do it is to have your lawyers call their lawyers and say, 'let's make a deal.' "

"That's certainly one of the opportunities that we're looking at," said Bijur, who seemed to be getting even more uncomfortable.

Koppel kept up his probe. "And since you're the man at the top and you're the man who wants to put this behind you as quickly as possible, is that something you'd like to see happen?"

"It is something that we are considering," said Bijur.

Yet again, Koppel pressed him. "You're not being directly responsive to my question. What I'm asking you is whether you'd like to see it happen."

"Yes," Bijur finally conceded, "I would like to see it happen."

He had committed himself, on live TV before an audience of millions, to settling *Roberts v. Texaco.*

Even so Texaco tried to buy us off cheaply. The next day, Shubin called back with a ridiculous offer: $15 million.

Hausfeld just said no. And hung up.

Cyrus and the New York lawyers totally lost it.

"You just said no?" Cyrus demanded.

"Yes," Hausfeld replied.

"That's all you said?"

"No is no," Hausfeld reiterated.

A day later Shubin called back again. How about $35 million?

"Milt, the value of Texaco stock just went down by a billion dollars because of the flak you're catching. It's gonna get worse. Get real."

Hausfeld kept up the routine until Shubin reached $75 million, divided between a compensation pool for the black employees and a separate amount for attorney's fees. Hausfeld smelled a rat. The amount that Texaco was proposing to give our legal team—it may have been more than $20 million, Hausfeld never told me exactly—was far more than they were likely to get if they followed customary legal procedure and let Judge Brieant determine their compensation. To Hausfeld it looked like a bribe in exchange for wrapping up the settlement quickly and probably for a whole lot less than the company's real bottom line. Again he said no.

By now, most of the other lawyers were ready to cry uncle. Early in the case, our lawyers had estimated that *Roberts v. Texaco* could be settled for $15 million. During mediation, the figure had risen to $30 million. Now Texaco was offering to pay more than twice that amount, with a colossal lawyer's fee tossed into the bargain. Had Hausfeld lost his mind? What was he aiming for?

When Texaco upped the ante to $95 million, and Hausfeld turned it down, most of his colleagues almost went apoplectic. I'm glad I didn't know about it, because I might have joined them in questioning his judgment, if not his sanity. Like almost everyone on our side, both lawyers and plaintiffs, I wondered if Hausfeld was not overplaying our hand. But he was like Buddha. He actually started working on other cases while he waited for Shubin's response. His serenity was almost unnerving.

Finally, at the end of the week, Hausfeld and Shubin finally agreed on a figure: $115 million in damages with another $26.1 million thrown in to give all of Texaco's black employees an eleven percent raise to make up for the lost wages they had suffered because of discrimination.

When Cyrus called to tell me the size of the bargain, I was so shocked I could hardly breathe. "Hang on, Bari," he cautioned me. "There's more in the pipeline."

The major financial issues had been resolved, but Hausfeld had another demand that in some ways overshadowed the fortune he had managed to extract from Texaco. He did not just want to make money, he wanted to make history. During lulls in the bargaining, he had sat with Charles Mann blue-skying about the best way to transform Texaco from a bastion of bigotry into a model of racial fairness and equal opportunity. He wanted to create an agency that could permanently change the stifling climate within the company and set an example for the rest of corporate America.

The idea they finally came up with was so bold and imaginative that I predicted Texaco would never accept it. Essentially, it called for Texaco to create an independent task force that would monitor the company's treatment of minorities for a five-year period, with unrestricted access to company records. If the task force found fresh evidence of discrimination, it could make binding recommendations on how to correct it. If Texaco then refused to implement those suggestions, the plaintiffs' lawyers could haul Texaco into court—at the company's expense. It could force the company to make changes in the PMP process. No corporation had ever ceded so much authority over its operations to an outside group like the one Hausfeld was proposing. Most of Hausfeld's colleagues thought he was nuts to risk the lucrative financial settlement he had achieved by even bringing it up.

*   *   *

Meanwhile, the media coverage began to play ping-pong with our hopes and fears. One day it lifted our spirits, the next day it drove them into the ground.

For example, on that Sunday, November 10, another story by Kurt Eichenwald appeared in the *New York Times*. It vividly recounted Jimmy Porter's riveting tale of black workers being called "porch monkeys" and "orangutans" by Texaco supervisors and Michael Moccio's outraged account of being instructed to "fire the nigger" who had complained about racial discrimination. It also added an especially poignant story that Eichenwald had dug up with Cyrus's help.

In 1988, Sheryl Joseph, a secretary at Texaco's office in Harvey, Louisiana, had learned on the day before her birthday that she was pregnant with her second child. After she shared the good news with her colleagues, they planned a small celebration in the office. But the next day, when her boss stepped forward with a birthday cake, Joseph was stunned and appalled. On top of the cake was a figure of a black woman with dark skin and an Afro, obviously far along in pregnancy. Beneath it, an inscription written in icing read, "Happy Birthday, Sheryl. It must have been those watermelon seeds." A big picture of the cake ran alongside the article on the front page of the *Times'* business section.

Eichenwald's story provided the general public with its first detailed glimpse of the poisonous racial atmosphere that had enveloped Texaco for decades. It showed that there was still so much, much more to *Roberts v. Texaco* than the sensational Lundwall tapes. I was sure it would put even more pressure on the company to respond favorably to Hausfeld's unprecedented proposal to create the task force, which he planned to bring up the next day. Florence called me with congratulations. "I think you've got them going now, girlfriend," she said. "They'll have to stop playing with you all now. This is serious."

"I hope so," I said.

But on Monday morning, the case took another dizzying twist, again courtesy of Eichenwald. Michael Armstrong, the criminal lawyer whom Texaco had hired to make an independent investigation of the tapes, issued a preliminary report that I feared could knock the props from beneath our agreement with the company. According to Eichenwald's latest bombshell, enhanced versions of the tapes revealed that Ulrich had not used the word "nigger" in the recorded conversation. What he'd actually said, according to Armstrong, was "Poor St. Nicholas. They shitted all over his beard."

My heart was racing as I sped through the story. Would Texaco use this revelation to back away from the deal? Would the public outrage that had helped us keep the heat on during the bargaining now dissipate? Would our legal team be falsely accused of doctoring the transcript to stampede Texaco into a more lucrative settlement? All I could do was wait.

Publicly, Bijur reaffirmed his commitment to reaching a settlement. In a statement released along with Armstrong's preliminary report, he forcefully insisted that the change in the language did not change "the categorically unacceptable context and tone of these conversations." That made it sound like we still had a deal.

But that night Cyrus told the plaintiffs that Texaco had flatly rejected the idea for the task force along with a host of other more modest proposals we had made for changes in employment policy. Texaco had apparently concluded that the news that the N-word was not on the Lundwall tapes would allow the price of its stock to rebound and ease the pressure on the company to concede any more to us than it already had. As Shubin told Hausfeld when he outlined the idea, "You must be crazy. Texaco's never going to go for anything like that."

But on Tuesday, November 12, the calvary arrived. Cyrus had told Sil and me on the previous night that Jesse Jackson was organizing a large group of civil rights leaders to meet with Bijur. He wanted us to join him for breakfast in New York in the morning. Could we be there?

I didn't want to see him. I remembered all the unanswered appeals for support we had made to Jackson's Rainbow Coalition, the NAACP, and other black organizations during the case's darkest hours. They had totally ignored us. Even after the case had exploded into the headlines, none of them had even called us to say in effect, you all have fought a good fight, we're ready to back you up.

Sil was so eager to meet with Jackson that I decided to go along. But when we arrived at the Plaza Hotel, there were so many people at the table there was no place for us to sit down. I nearly walked out.

"Sil, you better handle this by yourself," I said. "This is just not me."

Sil nudged me to the table. It took some rearranging of the furniture before we could sit down. Jackson asked Sil and me a few questions about the case, but didn't give us time to reply. His goal in meeting Bijur, he said, was to extract some concessions for "the community." I assumed he meant his own organization and supporters. I think I fidgeted throughout the entire meeting. I was glad when it finally ended so I could go home.

That night on the news I saw Jackson and his supporters standing in front of the Texaco building after their meeting with Bijur. They threatened to launch a nationwide boycott of Texaco by Saturday if the company didn't settle our lawsuit and agree to a plan for vastly expanding Texaco's purchases from black businesses. Jackson and company may have been AWOL during the early phases of our struggle, but when they arrived, they arrived with a vengeance. "Better late than never," I said to Jackson's image on the TV set, and gave him a little salute.

The story about Jackson's threat was all over the papers on Wednesday. The heat was back on.

On Thursday, November 14, it was time for Hausfeld to play his last and most powerful card. He telephoned Shubin and reminded him about the court hearing on document destruction that was set for November 22, a mere eight days away. "If you don't settle this case by tomorrow, we're going to take depositions and prepare for that hearing. We're going for full disclosure. All the evidence Texaco has been trying to hide will be discussed in open court and blasted all over the media. If you think things are bad for the company right now, just wait for all that to happen."

Hausfeld's threat was more than Texaco could stand. The company was under assault from every direction. Jackson and the other civil rights leaders were planning to launch a boycott on Saturday, November 16, guaranteeing a new bout of damaging headlines. The price of the Texaco stock was still gyrating wildly. The last thing Bijur wanted was a full-scale public airing of the sensational proof of evidence tampering in the Texaco executive suite. If creating Hausfeld's task force was the price of peace, Bijur was willing to pay it. He instructed his lawyers to capitulate to Hausfeld's demands.

On Friday morning, Shubin called Hausfeld to relay Texaco's agreement to creating the task force. It would cost $35 million over the course of five years. Added to the $115 million in compensation and $26.1 million in pay increases that would be granted to Texaco's fourteen hundred black employees, it brought the value of the settlement of *Roberts v. Texaco* to $176.1 million, the largest amount that had ever been won in a class action racial discrimination suit. He also agreed to set up a company-wide program of diversity training, step up recruiting minorities, and revise the hateful PMP system to make it more fair and equitable. We had achieved everything we had asked for. Texaco had caved in.

When Sil, Florence, and I had made similar suggestions only three years before, a Texaco vice president had spitefully called us Black Panthers. How far we had come.

I was at home in Stamford when Cyrus reached me. "You and Sil have got to get down here right away," he panted. "We've got a settlement that includes the task force. Texaco insists that we announce it today to head off the boycott from the civil rights leaders." As I listened to him, an extraordinary feeling of exultation spread over my body, so powerful that it seemed to lift me right out of my chair. I could not contain it. I threw my fists into the air, tilted back my head and hollered, at the top of my lungs, "Yes! Yes! Yes!" Then I boogied all over the house until I collapsed into a chair and just started laughing out loud.

After I calmed down, I called Brooke and Staci to share the good news. They were both delirious with joy. "See, I told you to fight back Mom," whooped Staci. "Justice always prevails!"

As it turned out, Sil and I couldn't make it in time for the hastily arranged press conference in Washington. Instead we went to Dan Berger's office for a press conference of our own. Waldo was there, beaming proudly. So was Sil's beautiful wife, Sharon. Even the reporters broke into applause when Sil and I walked into the room. The sense of victory in the room was so intense I felt like I could reach out and touch it.

As soon as the press conference was over, I slipped away to an empty room in Dan's office. There were two phone calls I had to make.

The first was to "Dora."

"I already heard about it," she said. I could hear the joy in her voice.

"Without you, it would never have happened," I told her. "You made it all possible. There's no way I can ever thank you."

"Don't worry about it," said "Dora." "You already have."

And then I called Daddy.

"We won, we won," I told him.

I could see him smile.

"Well, Cootsie," he said, with a chuckle, "I guess that means you won't have to come home."

The triumphant moment on November 15 was not the end of my struggle with Texaco. As part of the overall settlement of the case, Hausfeld and Texaco had agreed on individual relief for Sil and me. Sil would become a Texaco executive-on-loan; the company would pay his salary for a year while he worked as the financial manager of his beloved church in Harlem. In my case, the arrangement was unbelievably sweet: Texaco would pay my full salary for two years while I studied for an executive MBA at the business school of my choice. I could start school in September. When I returned to Texaco, I would be given an immediate promotion to grade eighteen and be placed in charge of the 401k division of P&B as an assistant manager. I could not have asked for anything more.

Meanwhile, I reported back to work, ready to resume my duties in the finance department. It was impossible. The huge monetary award in *Roberts v. Texaco* had started an avalanche. Black people, women, Hispanics, gays—all day long they were calling, asking for advice, for referrals to my lawyers, encouragement, even, in a few cases, a loan. People thought that the six name plaintiffs would be splitting up all that loot among ourselves and that I was an instant millionaire! Little did they know. It would take months before the award was actually paid, and my share would be determined by the very same formula that would be used with every class member. Based on my salary and years of service, I received approximately $70,000 as a member of the class and an additional incentive award of $85,000 for being a class representative. The average award to a class member was $67,000. Quite a few others—including some who had shunned our case and badmouthed us as the case slogged through the courts—would receive substantially more. Even Ed Gasden got a share.

I realized that something was really wrong after a strange encounter with Peter Bijur in the Texaco cafeteria a few days after the settlement. I was in line at the sandwich counter when I noticed that he was standing right in front of me. He turned and our eyes met. We looked at each other for perhaps half a minute. I am sure he recognized me. Neither of us said anything. Then he turned back to the counter, picked up his sandwich, and walked away. To this day, I don't know why I didn't greet him or just nod my head. Perhaps I thought it was up to him to make the first move. He probably felt the same way.

I was still pondering the incident a few days later when Sil rushed into my office. "Bari," he said, "they want us out of the building right away." A short while later I got a call from Ed Gasden. We met that afternoon. He didn't shake hands. He got right down to business.

"I suppose you know why you're here," he began.

I felt prickly. "No, Ed. Why don't you tell me?"

"Management wants you out of the building right now."

"Why, Ed?"

"You know why."

I did know why. The good old boys could not stand looking at me. My mere presence was a thorn in their side. It reminded them of the humiliating defeat they had suffered. It reminded them of the lies they had been caught in. It compelled them to look at themselves and the things they had done, and they could not stand it.

And neither could I.

I agreed to start my leave right away. I was tired of being at Texaco. I could use the time to prepare for taking the difficult GMAT test I needed to apply for business school, and to just let my head clear. I'd have enough leave to complete three semesters on my MBA before I came back to work. I could finish up when I returned. There was not much more that I needed to do as a class representative. We had not yet signed the final settlement papers and were still considering our nominees for the diversity task force, but the lawyers did not expect any huge problems. Texaco had already transferred $115 million to a special account to cover the damage awards to its black employees.

It was around that time that I first got the idea of writing this book. I contacted an editor I had met in a writing class six months prior, who made me an offer within a few days. The more I thought about it, the more intriguing the prospect became. I decided to sign on with a literary agent named Faith Childs who ended up negotiating a deal with the editor, who was at Avon Books. Needless to say, I was elated.

But when Texaco learned that I had signed a book contract from an announcement in the *New York Times*, Peter Bijur exploded. Hausfeld called me and said, in a voice as heavy as lead, "Texaco doesn't want you to write a book. They say that if you go ahead, they're going to hold up the entire settlement. They're afraid you're going to reveal things about the case that no one knows and make them look bad."

"Mike," I responded, "my book is about what I went through. I don't have to try to make Texaco look bad because they're doing a pretty good job of making themselves look bad. I'm not going to make up any tales out of school or anything like that."

Hausfeld asked me to send him a letter about the book I wanted to write so that he could relay it to Texaco's lawyers. How many people are there on this planet who could write about what it is like to go through a whirlwind like *Roberts v. Texaco*—the ups and downs, the personal toll, and best of all, the ultimate victory? Apart from me and the other name plaintiffs, I could not think of anyone. Hausfeld faxed it to Milt Shubin, the Kaye, Scholer lawyer.

Later that day Hausfeld told me that Shubin had said it sounded like a book that he would enjoy reading. But Shubin was sure that Bijur would not approve of me writing anything. Bijur was taking a lot of heat from other CEOs who feared that the settlement in our case would make them more vulnerable to discrimination suits brought by their own employees. Shubin said he was going ballistic. In the words of the special master who reviewed the matter on Judge Brieant's behalf, Texaco confronted me with a "Hobsonian choice."

Bijur insisted that Texaco would not sign the final settlement papers unless I agreed to either resign from the company or remain silent. Mine was a story that Texaco never wanted to be told. I had to tell it. After a brief negotiation over severance pay, I turned in my resignation. It was dated January 22, 1997. The final settlement papers were signed. My soujourn at Texaco had ended. Since I was no longer a Texaco employee, so did my role as a class representative in the case that still bears my name.

In November 1997, almost exactly a year to the day after the settlement was announced, I listened to the entire Lundwall tapes for the first time. Some parts were so marred by static that the dialogue was barely discernible. Others were crystal clear. They knocked me back on my heels.

"I drive her crazy. I play mind games with her," boasted

Bob Ulrich to Rich Lundwall in a voice filled with rage and resentment.

"I can't punch her in her face, so I play mind games with her," Ulrich continued. "I eyeball her, eyeball to eyeball.

"I have little ways of getting even.

"She's lost more ground than him," Ulrich went on, in an apparent reference to Sil. "Now she's got herself cast as a fucking liar."

To which Lundwall replied, "I just nod [when I see her]. I would crush her hand. I can't shake her hand."

They were, of course, talking about me. Listening to them made me sick to my stomach.

Those words made me wonder what the outcome would have been if *Roberts v. Texaco* had gone to trial. What would a jury have thought of those remarks that never made it into the newspapers? What would it have made of the powerful stories of Jimmy Porter and Mike Moccio and Cheryl Joseph and our other witnesses—the tales that got lost in the controversy about the tapes and whether the N-word was on them? Would the company's defense have been any different from the line that Peter Bijur spouted on the anniversary of the settlement—that Texaco's racial problems were no worse than any other corporation's? He claimed that the bigoted acts that led to our suit were aberrations, not the product of a corporate climate of racisim. I believe the evidence we gathered in our suit proved otherwise. Texaco prides itself on being a leader within the petroleum industry. It wants to be way ahead of the pack. But when it comes to racial fairness and decency, Bijur's comments suggest that the company is still content to be judged by the lowest common denominator. If so, then Texaco is still in a state of denial about its racial problems and so is much of America.

As we are catapulted toward the twenty-first century, our country is embroiled in a war of words and attitudes about equal opportunity. The air is filled with simplistic attacks on the principle that everyone, regardless of color, should be treated equally. The quest for equal opportunity has been redefined by its opponents as "racial preferences," "quotas," and "reverse discrimination." They claim that they want a "colorblind" society in which race is irrelevant, but they are unwilling to take even the tiniest steps toward making that wonderful dream a reality. It they really meant what they said, they would face up to the truth. I think it is more than coincidence that the story of the Lundwall tapes broke just one day before California voters endorsed Proposition 209, which forbids affirmative action. Divine Providence may have played a hand. We needed a reminder that bigotry of the ugliest kind still stands in the way of the "level playing field" that Ward Connerly, the black leader of the anti-affirmative action crusade, and people who think like him claim has already arrived.

America—and much of corporate America—has made enormous strides toward leveling the playing field for all of its people, but there is still so much to be done. We must not declare victory and walk away from the battle for equal opportunity before the fight has really been won. I hope my story will encourage anyone who has been discriminated against because of race or age or religion or gender to realize that they do not have to sit there and take it. They, too, can fight back and win.

I am enormously proud of what Sil, Marsha, Beatrice, Veronica, Janet, and I accomplished with the help of our courageous lawyers. The most important part of our legacy is the Texaco equal opportunity task force that was sworn in by Judge Brieant in June 1997. Its chairman is Deval Patrick, formerly head of the U.S. Justice Department's civil rights division. Its other members are John Gibbons, a retired judge; Mari Matsuda, a Georgetown University law professor; Thomas Williamson, a prominent lawyer in Washington; Jeffalyn Johnson, president of a consulting firm; Louis Nogales, a Los Angeles businessman; and Allen Krowe, Texaco's retired vice chairman, who once raised my hopes by telling me that I was on Texaco's high-potential list. Its goal is to eradicate the corporate culture of bigotry that made *Roberts v. Texaco* necessary and replace it with an environment in which all employees have an equal chance to contribute and rise as high as their talent and hard work allow. The task force faces a monumental and frustrating struggle. But if it can accomplish even a part of its mission it could become a role model for corporate America. I pray with all my heart that it succeeds—for Brooke, for Staci, and everyone who shares my belief in the American Dream.